# The Sound of Many Waters

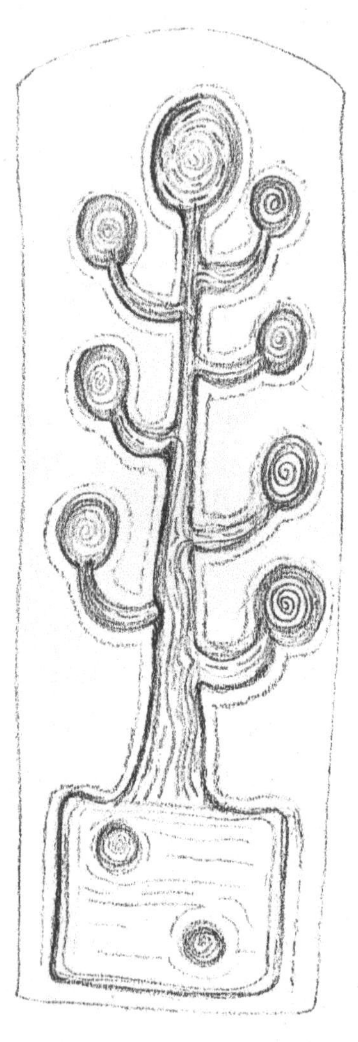

# The Sound of Many Waters

## A Journey Along the River Tay

Robin A. Crawford

This edition first published in Great Britain in 2025 by
Birlinn Ltd
West Newington House
10 Newington Road
Edinburgh
EH9 1QS
*www.birlinn.co.uk*



ISBN: 978 1 78027 911 4

Extracts from 'The Cailleach' and 'What the Pool Said, on a
Midsummer Day', published in *A Handsel: New & Collected Poems*
(Polygon, 2023), were printed with permission from the publisher.

The publisher acknowledges support from the National Lottery
through Creative Scotland towards the publication of this title.

Typeset by Initial Typesetting Services, Edinburgh

Papers used by Birlinn Ltd are from well-managed
forests and other responsible sources

Printed and bound by Clays Elcograf S.p.A.

*To brothers,
the drowned and the saved*

# Contents

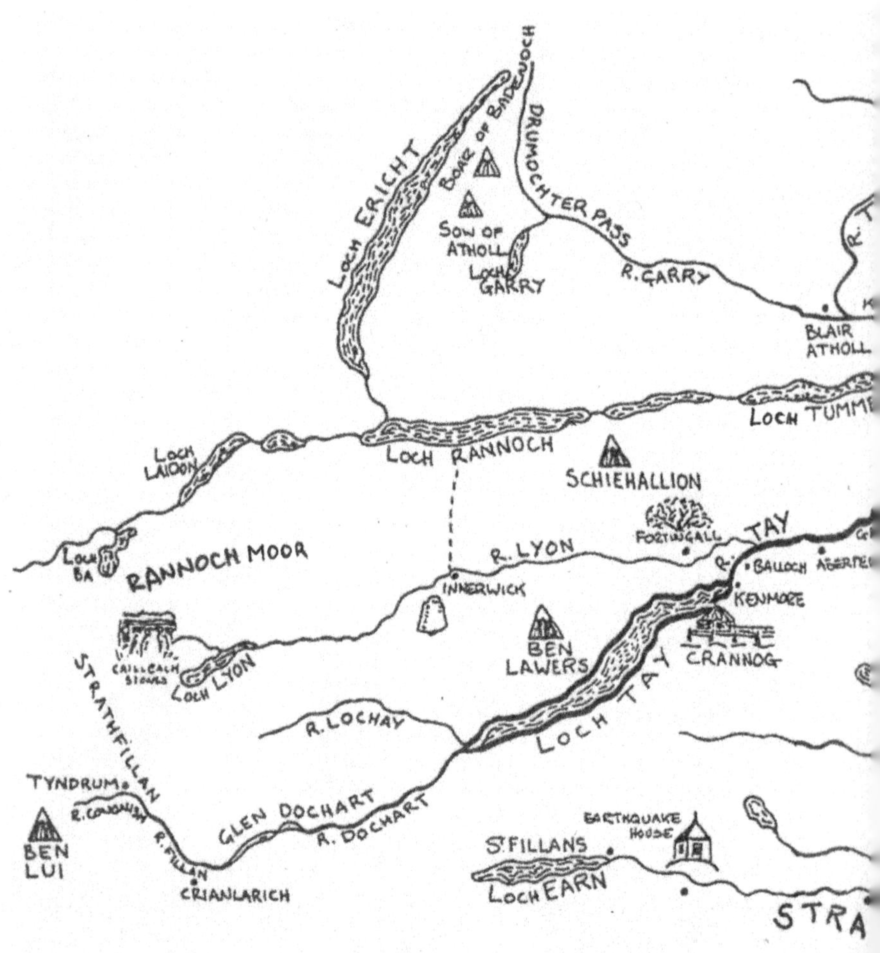

Loch ERICHT
BOAR of BADENOCH
DRUMOCHTER PASS
Sow of ATHOLL
Loch GARRY
R. GARRY
R. T
BLAIR ATHOLL
K
Loch TUMME
Loch LAIDON
Loch RANNOCH
SCHIEHALLION
TAY
FORTINGALL
R. LYON
Loch BA
RANNOCH MOOR
INNERWICK
R.
BALLOCH
ABERTE
Gr
KENMORE
CAILLEACH STONES
BEN LAWERS
CRANNOG
Loch LYON
STRATHFILLAN
R. LOCHAY
Loch TAY
TYNDRUM
GLEN DOCHART
EARTHQUAKE HOUSE
R. CONONISH
R. DOCHART
S. FILLANS
BEN LUI
R. FILLAN
Loch EARN
CRIANLARICH
STRA

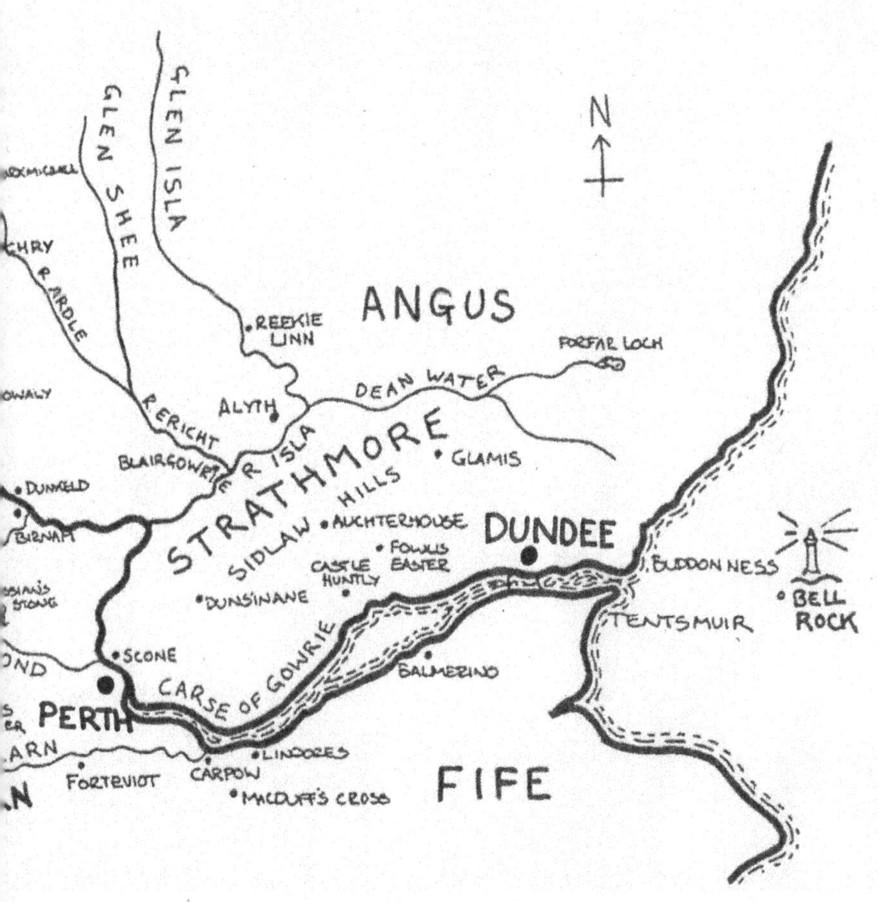

N
GLEN SHEE
GLEN ISLA
ARKMICHAEL
CHRY
R ARDLE
OWALY
DUNKELD
BIRNAM
OSSIAN'S
STONE
OND
ER
PERTH
ARN
N
FORTEVIOT
ANGUS
REEKIE
LINN
FORFAR LOCH
DEAN WATER
ALYTH
R ERICHT
BLAIRGOWRIE
R ISLA
STRATHMORE
SIDLAW HILLS
GLAMIS
AUCHTERHOUSE
DUNDEE
CASTLE
HUNTLY
FOWLIS
EASTER
BUDDON NESS
DUNSINANE
BELL
ROCK
TENTSMUIR
SCONE
BALMERINO
CARSE OF GOWRIE
LINDORES
CARPOW
MACDUFF'S CROSS
FIFE

# Tributary

Drip. Drip. Drip. High above Loch Tay, the rain drops from the sleeve of my waterproof jacket on to my hand. The fingers are spread, like a delta. From the tips, the water drips on to my waterproof trousers. It forms tiny streams, conjoining with others – like the blood in my veins under my waterproof skin – until a micro river system of water is flowing off me and on to the summit of Ben Lawers beneath my feet.

In Turner-esque clouds, each drop is refracted by heavenly light into its constituent rainbow colours. The river has many sources, but all begin in clouds like these, blown in from far out on the ocean, sometimes deposited as snow on mountaintop or in sheets of rain on bleak moors, then filtered through tiny mosses, or, having seeped beneath our earth, welling up from deep underground caverns.

I watch as a gust of wind blows a drop into a rivulet. At this altitude a matter of centimetres dictates its flow eastwards, westwards, north or south. Such vagaries shape the lives of those who live and die by the river – the creatures, the plants, the people. A twist of fate, an act, small or big, changes histories.

*

## GALLANT DEED

Three sons of Mr Mitchell . . . went into the water hand-in-hand, and by some means one little boy . . . sank into a deep hole out of sight. His older brother, James (14), seeing the little fellow thus likely to be drowned, plunged down to the bottom, though he could not swim, and with a heroism worthy of the stake at issue, crept on his hands on the bottom of the pool, seized hold of his brother, gave him a vigorous push out of the place towards the shore, which had the desired effect in saving him, but most unfortunately James, the gallant hero of the noble deed, sank himself, and was drowned . . . The younger Mitchell, who for some time appeared in a critical position, recovered. Numbers soon appeared at the water's edge, and by the aid of creepers pulled out the body.

At the end of a long life the youngest Mitchell brother commissioned a stained-glass window to be installed in the local church at Alyth, Perthshire. In the heavenly rainbow light, Christ walks on water before his own sacrifice:

And Jesus, walking by the sea of Galilee, saw two brethren, Simon called Peter, and Andrew his brother, casting a net into the sea: for they were fishers. And he saith unto them, Follow me, and I will make you fishers of men.

– Matthew 4: 18–19

*

Standing on the bridge over the river Isla, I watch two boys fishing, casting and recasting. On the opposite bank, a funereal heron is immobile but misses nothing. The river, like time, slips by. The peaty mountain stream glints over the golden gravel shallows in the August sun before it flows into shadow and unknowable depths and currents. As I stand, firmly anchored on the solid stone bridge, it is disconcerting to watch the cooling liquid, flickering under the momentary flames of evening sunlight, moving under your feet. I think of James, who thrashed from life to death in moments in this very water, from the earthly paradise of youth. And – with tears welling up, dripping down my cheeks into the water below – of his brother, my great-grandfather, emerging, spluttering, gasping, reborn back into life from this river.

*

The Isla is one of the Tay's largest tributaries. It has many. With the widest catchment area of any river in these islands, at 3,000 square miles, the Tay drains much of the lower Highlands of Scotland. It draws its waters from many sources – as far west as Argyll and the Rannoch Moor, as far north as the Drumochter Pass, as far east as the Firth, where it discharges into the North Sea. Hold up your left hand, palm facing away, and spread your fingers: if the Tay is the index finger, then imagine your thumb as the Isla, flowing in from the east, your middle finger the rivers Garry and Tummel from the north, and from the west the ring finger represents the Braan and the Almond, your pinkie the Earn. Behind these rivers lie a network of lochs that gather the rainwaters dumped by Atlantic clouds on the Highland massif. Loch Ericht, Loch Rannoch, Loch Lyon, Loch Tay, Loch Tummel and Loch Earn are the largest, but many, many more bodies of water feed into the main river.

The river flows from source to sea, as does my journey in this book, but it does not end there. Twice every day the tide pushes the waters of the Tay back up the Firth. And while the structure of my writing flows geographically from Ben Lui to the North Sea, over time I have followed the Tay as it pushed its way inland, only to return to the sea once again. My journey along the Tay took place over many years – the writing of it began one midsummer's day in June six years ago as I dipped my bare feet in a peaty pool in Rannoch Moor, but the story started decades, indeed centuries, before. It arcs from my family, who for generations have lived by the Tay, to my childhood visits to them, dips into my adolescence as a student on the banks of the Tay, then flows back with my adult years, working by this same river, and so then onto the next generation, with my son, born in Dundee.

The themes that ripple through the book are expected: the river's natural and human history, and our interdependence with it. There's swimming (elegantly by frogs, more wildly by humans) and fishing (by humans, for salmon, of course, and whales, and by herons), and bridges (built elegantly but also disastrously). Poetry, art and sculptured stones all illuminate this river.

But there are also some unexpected themes which surface: brotherhood, the sound of ringing bells, the lowing of cattle, and again and again I am drawn to the small acts that change lives.

This journey took many years and, like the Tay, takes many forms: it is never the same twice.

# Breadalbane

*From the source at Ben Lui to Crianlarich*

Bràghaid Albann, Breadalbane – Upper Alba – is one of the old Scottish provinces. It includes most of the Tay's Highland sources, and within these catchments are Ben Lui, Strathfillan in the west, and the Rannoch Moor and its lochs in the north. Its eastern border is the A9 and the River Tummel, and in the south it is Strathearn. Once part of the neighbouring lands of the Earls of Atholl, it was removed from their possession and awarded to the Campbells of Glenorchy (who we shall meet later) by James II for the apprehending of his father's Atholl assassins. It is mountainous and wet.

On 1 January, I set off in darkness from my home on the south bank of the Tay to find the source of that river. There are barely a dozen cars on the sixty-mile route to Ben Lui. On the journey, dawn has smudged barely noticed into day. It creeps up on me as stealthily as Hogmanay, when you go to bed early and wake unwittingly to a new year (if you haven't been disturbed during the night by the neighbour's forced jock-ularity).

A new year. For well over half a century I've been experiencing it, and into this one comes a constant and welcome presence. In the car park at Dalrigh my brother Mark draws up as I wash down a piece of Christmas cake for breakfast with already tepid coffee from my flask. We don't really do the festive thing – I'm usually working and he has recently taken to spending the holidays on cycling tours in the Middle East. He's just back from Jordan. Mountain biking along dry wadis, floating in the Dead Sea – it's a bit different to the West Highlands in the first week of January. We hug and exchange gifts. For me, a CamelBak water bottle; for him, thick hand-knitted socks from the Hebrides.

We've met up to climb Ben Lui and find the source of the Tay. At 3,710 feet, Ben Lui, or Beinn Laoigh ('the Mountain of the Calf'), is one of the thirty highest Munros in Scotland.

As we slip on our waterproofs, we discuss the Tay. We both first encountered the river when crossing the then new road bridge by bus as children.

'I was scared,' I confess.

The bridge seemed to go on and on. Of course, there

are shorter ferry crossings – it really was like travelling to an island, to a different world.

We were going to visit our great aunt and uncle at their house on the Blackness Road. There were terrific views from their conservatory south over the river, and we sat in there eating pink jelly, entranced, watching the trains snaking over the railway bridge. It was like a step back in time, as visits to elderly relatives can seem to young children, especially if like Tot and Mac they didn't have grandchildren of their own.

They told us of the old wooden battleship that used to be moored across the river that was a home for orphans and bad boys, pointed out the piers of the old bridge that collapsed into the river, taking a train and all the passengers with it one new year. Everything in their house seemed old-fashioned: dark wooden furniture; sepia photographs – a man wearing a pith helmet on a camel by the Nile, a grave in India, an old soldier in the kilt. Their own clothes were different from ours, woven from tweed, not the least bit as beautiful and modern as our dad's belted safari suit and mum's polyester orange-and-brown mini-dress.

I wish now that I could go back in time to listen to their stories and family gossip, but we were more interested with the old Anderson shelter in their garden, an underground playhouse full of Second World War treasures.

On leaving, Uncle Mac gave us a big hardback book entitled *The Wonderful World of Nature*, which was new and full of brilliant colour photographs of plants, animals and fish, and on its dust jacket a plunging waterfall cascaded into tropical forest from an Andean mountain. In retrospect that visit seems to have had a significant effect on the future course of my life.

It's a bit of a hike in before the ascent starts, so we've brought our bikes to speed up our journey. With short daylight hours, we want to maximise our time on the hill. Almost immediately we are free-wheeling through water, the Crom Allt, which flows crookedly out from Tyndrum and joins the river Cononish just below the car park. Our route takes us up this convergence of streams flowing off the mountain at the foot of Ben Lui. Our aim is to climb straight to the summit, then follow the ridge down to the bealach between Bens Lui and Oss. This route allows us to pass through the snowfall above Coire an t-Sneachda, the highest point that the Tay flows from on the mountain (2,600 feet), and then along to the watery, boggy pools that are its actual source at about 2,275 feet.

The river's waters may have their source here, but what of its name? It is only after being Allt Coire Laoigh ('the Stream of the Corrie of the Calf'), the Cononish, the river Fillan, Loch Dochart, Loch Iuibhair, the river Dochart and Loch Tay that finally the river Tay proper begins at Kenmore, 40 miles north-east from the source. And these are only the direct water courses. In the less than two miles it takes Allt Coire Laoigh to merge with the Cononish, it is joined as it flows through the glen by at least twelve other streams, many themselves formed of multiple lesser burns.

Throughout my journey, I find myself wondering what is the Tay? Where does it begin and end?

Thanks to a team of surveyors from the Tay Western Catchments Partnership this exact source on the mountain was only confirmed as recently as 2011. In this liminal zone, the tiny nuances of geography are illustrated. On the boundary between two mountains and two corries the water in one boggy pool flows north-east and becomes the Tay; it is then carried to the North Sea a hundred miles away. In an adjacent boggy pool, the water flows south-west, and through Loch Lomond it enters the Clyde and eventually joins the Atlantic Ocean.

The road that runs parallel to the Cononish here is wide and grey-gritted. Heavy lorries servicing the latest attempt to mine gold commercially from under the mountain rumble down it. Cononish Farm — lean, functional, weather-defiant — sits between road and mounds of glacial deposits on the narrowest of valley floors along which the river twists. Over on the other bank it's only a few metres before the steep mountainsides rise again, discharging more scurrying waters into it.

Beyond the mine the road narrows to a track, constructed of small stones and grit dug out from surrounding glacial deposits, fenced by barbed wire to the right, dropping sharply down to the river on the left, a river that now gurgles throatily as it hurries past you. I envy its vigour.

Glad to dismount, we chain up our bikes by a rusting iron-barred sheep fank and stomp off upward, sticky with sweat, through a toffee-coloured landscape. I take time to look closer at the colours of withered brackens, the heathers and mosses of these, the foothills: rusted reds, burnt umber, oranges, pale yellows, dead fawns, muted golds.

In them this place has a bleak beauty; in this vegetation thinly laid over raw geology and cut through by water whose only imperative is gravity, there is beauty but of a strange kind.

Geology and glaciers have sculpted Ben Lui with a shape that appeals to our idea of what a mountain should look like, its alpine and supposedly feminine form garnering it the epithet 'Queen of Scottish Mountains', or sometimes just 'Queen of the Southern Highlands'. As the Cononish and Allt Coire Laoigh meet, thick cloud is veiling the mountain's beauty. As we start to climb steeply, my thighs are cramping; the shock of cycling up the track has flooded my leg muscles with poisons. Starved of oxygen, they feel like bags of stones.

We are following the Allt Coire Ghaothaich straight to the north-eastern corrie. As the waters gambol and scamper I drag myself upwards.

Ahead it seems pockets of snow have formed regularly by the route, but as we get closer we see that they are white builders' bags. Full of rocks and boulders to repair the path, they have been helicoptered onto the mountain. By the time I step up to the last of them, puddles on the crumbling path are turning to slush under our boots; soon, they solidify to ice. Water lies between hummocks of fawn bog grass and exposed brown peat. The allt is plunging down a black gorge carved by glacial ice or molten liquid rock, a series of spillages from a tumbling white paint pot. Looking back, the path we have come up is a series of watery zigzags of cracked and flaked rock among textured dots of beige moor grass. It also becomes clear that visibility is deteriorating: the cloud has closed off the surrounding world. As the waters freeze and the hill around us closes in, I start to slow, each step becoming thicker, the toes of my boots catching a recumbent rock or sunken boulder, panting my breath. I take more frequent breaks as the water flows faster. Like my lungs, the allt constricts but – opposite to me – it speeds up as the going gets steeper. It takes fewer breaks in ponds and pools. Below a thatch of reedy grass it bubbles and gurgles, frothing and burbling where it falls down upon itself. In the act of falling the splashing droplets have, on or soon after impact, started to freeze – from animation to suspended animation. The cryogenics of the mountain will hold them until spring – unless a heavenly shaft of random sunlight should discover the drop and resurrect it for the resumption of its journey.

We keep climbing. Up, rest, resume. The icicles forming in the bog grasses and mosses fringing the burn are refreshing to sook until our fingers go numb. Waterproofs keep us dry and warm even as, despite wicking, underneath our sweat is pouring as we overheat. But stop and instantly we start to get cold.

'Keep moving up,' we tell ourselves, though our legs are wanting to rest, aching to turn around and flow with the water back downhill. We are climbing with our heads and will as much as with our bodies.

We reach the bowl of the corrie under the ridge and rest. Here it is relatively flat, a respite before the steepest ascent. The waters are slower here, forming pools, the allt widening in places, pulsing rather than rapid like our breathing as more oxygen pumps into our blood. Slowness exposes the water to the cold hand of winter and around the glacier-deposited boulders it has turned to sheets of ice. While I stand and cool, Mark is never still. He's off in search of a route up the ridge. I look back, still pechin', but beyond the cliff-like edge of the corrie 30 feet away all I can see is grey hanging cloud. Above the bowl of the corrie it swirls on the updrafts, and a sudden patch of blue sky reveals the dark ridge above – crags lined white with snow, and under the scree fading in from grey a monotone of dull olive grassland. Across it, shallow scars where the very beginnings of water 'flows' – not yet able to be called streams – have come together to form a common path. Just as suddenly the gap disappears and our cloud-enclosed world returns.

A shout from Mark and we are off again. It is hard going. Water runs down rocks and the crags of my grimacing face. It has stopped forming any kind of river now. It is a series of wetnesses, individual drops with a shared imperative. We too withdraw within ourselves; our chatter slows as we draw on our desire to reach the top, to push on to our goal as the physical effort becomes harder. We focus on the next step. We search out the handhold above us. Fingers numb as the thinning, slowing water becomes prey to the cold. We push against the rock with boots slipping as much as through exhaustion as because of ice.

Although our ascent has been up the steepest side of the mountain it has been sheltered from the south-west wind. On reaching the ridge to the summit the prevailing wind blasts us. It is cold – so cold that the sparse vegetation has been frozen in a northeasterly direction. Rain water, melted snow, dew, cloud mist – all have been blown by the wind along the length of the grass stalks and on reaching the tips have frozen in an ice lozenge. These shatter underfoot between boot and ice-glazed rock like Fox's Glacier Mints. The bitter winds have frozen the same waters to the bare, exposed rock, flecking the black canvas white with frenzied strokes of a paintbrush and forming a thicker rim of white at the edges. It has solidified the moisture inside the exposed peat, cracking it like a dried riverbed in drought. It has cemented together the gravel of the mountain, turning each step into a delicate test – it's as if we are walking on a frozen lochan's brim. As we edge up the ridge, the frozen grasses get shorter and shorter until all is iced rock. The wild wind is forcing us to bend, unable to stand upright in its cauld blast. The cloud is now completely enveloping us, visibility down to a few metres.

We are at 3,500 feet on a narrow ridge, sheer drops on both sides. Underfoot we are walking on ice. We cannot stand up, so instead crawl on our hands and knees, one behind the other. Even travelling like this we are slipping. For a moment I imagine the young Mitchell brothers edging in a line out into the River Isla.

Our brotherhood means that we take the right decision and stop. We look out for each other, no egos involved. We have climbed plenty of hills together; we can always come back. We turn and in small, controlled slithers start to flow back down the mountain.

From an icy world wrapped in cloud we emerge into a dun upland. Back down at 2,300 feet the cloud thins and a vista opens up along the glen to Dalrigh. It is an umber world, a ginger world save for some faded dark green rectangles of conifer plantations, a damp world, a world of wisping cloud. Through the middle of it runs a stream, the Cononish. We are looking into the future, looking to where the waters now at our feet will soon be, and also where these feet will be on this journey from source to sea. It feels that we are now in sympathy with the river, following its direction of flow rather than struggling against it, that our futures are now running in parallel.

Here on this mountain is the misty world of the Tay's creation. Among dewy pearls on bog grasses is the purling sound of water rising up. From a pool no bigger than my hand it bubbles, gurgling like a baby. This nature's child is cocooned in a green mossy blanket. Without forming any kind of rivulet or channel, it runs downwards, nurturing two lines of green sphagnum: thriving, vital, luminous among the waning brown of soil-based vegetation. Cupping my hands, I slake my thirst. Slipping through my fingers, dripping from my chin, it rejoins the flow and with a breathless gush disappears over a rocky precipice. I am slower to follow – going downhill is never as easy as you imagine it to be when you are struggling upwards.

The waters start to form a recognisable stream, the Allt Coire Ghaothaich. The flanking areas of moss widen, the flow starts to speed up. Green weeds like those growing at the seaside cover the black rocks here at the source. White pebbles veined red shine, polished by the now fast-flowing burn, turning itself left and right like a child's marble run.

The black water forms white bubbles as it swerves either side past rocks or flows over the ones it can't avoid. The sound is of bath taps running but the plug pulled out. Unrestrained, it careers on downhill into its chosen path. It is powerful enough to wash away any soil from a section of mountainside, stripping it all the way back to the rock. Over this bedrock and these boulder beds it sends watery fingers spraying, like pipes that have burst in a hard frost. A cascade. As it reaches the base of the mountain it straightens and is joined by its twin, the Allt an Rund, flowing round from the mountain's west face. They run together until they are joined by the Allt Coire Laoigh. With the three Ben Lui streams now joined, they form the river Cononish and celebrate with a short but dramatic dive over the Hole in the Wall waterfall. This marks the upper limit of the Tay's many fish spawning grounds. This feels like a significant place. The natural limit of the world of fish and people ends, and a temporary world inhabited by hillwalkers and seasonally grazing sheep begins.

*

Under the mountain something twinkles, enchants. Deep below the foothills of Ben Lui is gold! Strewn through the Dalradian metamorphic complex rock are thin galaxies of precious metals in this deep space. The mountain has been tempting and frustrating prospectors for years. The profitability of excavating its running streams of both gold and silver have fluctuated as their prices vary on the ever-changing world markets – when gold supply dries up and prices rise, the £25 million capital and £75 million operating costs become viable, but when it sinks, those costs-to-profit ratios are just too high to make mining worthwhile. Even when successfully excavated, the more gold extracted, the less unique it becomes, and so the price drops again. Deep underground in Hades, Tantalus stands thirsty in his ever-receding pool of water, ever stretching for lush fruit in the tree's out-of-reach branches.

On the surface, the pale daylight glints on the small-time but no less avaricious panners in the river Cononish. Even when the sun is at its nadir these prospectors are drawn to the bright solar gleam of gold. They have the patience of marksmen lying for hours flat in the freezing stream. I guess that makes sense of their nickname – 'snipers'. In drysuits with sieves and trowel they search, scouring for that elusive gleam out of the darkness of the stream bed, a nugget of hope. They stir and probe the nooks and crannies among the rocks where a tiny fragment of gold may have been washed. The gold, being heavier than the grit and sand, falls to the riverbed fastest. Any tiny flake that glimmers in the water is sucked up into a waiting squeeze bottle. They dig and sift, dig and sift, and all the while the river flows past and beyond them. Like words written and read down a page, minutes become hours and suddenly the day has passed and the long night of winter has set in.

Time, its elasticity and its passage, flows with the river. The geological forces that formed the Dalradian metamorphic rock at Ben Lui operated in a time whose scale is beyond seasons, human lifespans, the existence of life on this planet. The land that is now cut through by the Tay and its tributaries was formed by the smashing together of tectonic plates that had been in flux for such a vast period of time that they had travelled north from the other side of the equator. The hard Precambrian and Cambrian rock of what is now the Highland massif crashed up against the softer sandstone of the southern plate, forming the fissure known as the Highland Boundary Fault, which cuts diagonally across Scotland. When water flows over that line it forms waterfalls, cataracts. Along the fault at Comrie in Perthshire, halfway between the Tay's source and firth, is the Deil's Cauldron waterfall, which is spectacular, especially after heavy rain.

At Comrie not only do the waters move but the earth also. It is said to be the most seismically active area in Scotland. An Earthquake House was built there in 1874 to monitor geological activity. This was done by means of a 'Mallet seismometer', a basic but effective method of recording the strength of any tremors using a series of wooden cylinders balanced on a wooden cross set into the rocky floor. Different cylinders would tumble depending on the strength of any quaking. Today a modern seismograph has replaced this basic but effective science, though you can peek in a window and see the original nineteenth-century wooden 'X' marking the spot.

Despite the odd tremor, Tayside is now an area of geological stability. In contrast, the formation of this landscape began with the folding, flowing and crumpling of molten lavas in the Highlands 490–425 million years ago. From about 320–290 million years ago, the softer Devonian and Carboniferous rocks of Midland Valley formed, sedimentary and volcanic. All were compressed, buckled, twisted, flowing into and out of each other in eddies and whirlpools and liquefactions.

When I went for a walk beside the Deil's Cauldron I'd not long returned from a trip to Iceland. I was struck by that volcanic landscape just north of us, its newness and its molten fluidity. Throughout my life that north-east Atlantic island landscape has been in a state of flux – the Heimaey eruption in the early seventies; Eyjafjallajökull in 2010 that brought air travel around Europe to a halt for several days; and in the past year on the Reykjanes Peninsula. In the calm of the pool below the bubbling 'Cauldron', layers of water-borne proteins are churned by their passage through the waterfall into foams. Subtle creamy tones ranging from pale white to fawn define each layer, which form strata at the end of the pool furthest from the falls. Their textures also vary: those most recently added were airy with big bubbles, between them the black malt stout colour of the pool's peaty water. As more foam joins, these are compressed, popping, deflating, becoming denser until pressed against the moss green rocks of the chasm's edge. They cover the surface of the water with a foam blanket, its texture like grained wood. It also reminded me of an exhibit in the National Museum in Reykjavik, a cross section cut through the Icelandic earth that was similarly stratified but this time each dark horizontal line was the fallen ash from a volcano that had covered the land, its thickness dependent on the power of each eruption. Today in Iceland, 'the land of fire and ice', the danger to living creatures like us is not only from the exploding volcano but that the heat released will melt the ice and cause flooding. Melting ice, and the consequent grinding movement of glaciers carving into Tayside's ancient rocks, has sculpted the landscape of the river catchment we know today. Underneath, traces of its ancient formation can be discovered within the rock itself and the claybeds left behind by retreating glaciers.

Downstream of the Hole in the Wall waterfall I look into the waters of the Cononish, searching for fish. I spot a smolt languidly holding position in the icy current. Victorian fossil hunters excavated the carcasses of fish that once swum in the waters of an ancient world and had sunk to its seabed and petrified. Four hundred and ten million years later, they were hewn out of the Devonian sandstone at Balruddery Den, near Invergowrie in the Tay's firth. In Perth museum today you can look upon the plates of one of these armoured prehistoric fish, or gaze at the Pleistocene invertebrate and vertebrate fossils from the Errol Clay Formation through the reflective glass and imagine – for a moment – you are witnessing them swimming under the dappling surface of the primordial river.

Back in the Cononish I watch as scales slide and interlock, the smolt's young body rippling muscle, and imagine tectonic plates sliding, molten rock buckling, boiling lavas flowing. In the blink of an eye, it is gone. Three hundred and eighty million years ago some fish began the long transition where fins started morphing into limbs, swim bladders to lungs.

Dart forward from the primordial and the river we recognise as the Tay was winding east following the last Ice

Age, but the sea it flowed into was radically different from the North Sea of today. Ten thousand years ago a land-bridge connected the south-east mainland of these islands to continental Europe, and the Rhine and Thames formed a river delta flowing south-east into what is now the Channel. Doggerland occupied much of the area between what we now call Denmark and East Anglia, making a smaller North Sea look like a large estuary fed by a myriad of north European rivers, not least among them the Tay. Its firth, though, discharging its waters northwards rather than to the east.

*

The Tay begins on Ben Lui. But it is also beginning to the north. Hold up your left hand again, palm facing away from you. If the Tay is your index finger, your middle finger is the rivers Tummel and, towards the tip, the Garry.

Pulsing like an upland river, the early morning traffic on the A9 flows from single to dual carriageway and back again irregularly throughout its 270-mile length. The road joins Lowland and Highland Scotland, following the Earn, Tay, Tummel and Garry as they cut through that central massif of the country's mountains. It is joined along its route by many tributary roads and for decades it has been notorious for the number of lives lost – impatient locals, tourists driving on the wrong side, people falling asleep at the wheel. The entire route, during the writing of this book, is in the process of being dualled.

Today, sunshine and showers break out intermittently all the way up the road. It's that kind of transitional day when winter has ended but spring doesn't really seem to have begun. I think of Noah on his ark: the rains have stopped but the flood waters haven't started receding. Over the sign to the Noah's Ark soft play centre, just outside Perth, a fragment of a rainbow – 'watergaw' in Scots – forms an arc. Fragments of the river's story are glimpsed as I pass Beatrix Potter's holiday home at Dalguise, peer down into the gorge as I fly over the Pass of Killiecrankie, catch sight of the waded anglers in the Tummel at Pitlochry, and, occasionally, the shadow of the current road's predecessor, the old A9, runs beside this modern route.

An hour out of Perth I stop at the Drumochter Pass, just shy of its 1,500-foot summit. Routes for road, rail, cycle and electric pylons all squeeze in here, between the gap in the mountains, the watershed between rivers Garry and Truim, tributaries of the Tay and the Spey. Snow frequently lies in the pass and in the corries of the hills above well into spring, and often into summer, but mainly it is a wet place. The annual rainfall here is four feet. The hills are barren of trees or bushes. They are mottled with years of patchy muirburnt heather, varying in colour and tone depending on when they were last burnt or the season; grey scree landslides offer a contrast of texture, and today withering bog grasses are a wan sepia on a tiny strip of the flat valley floor along which a stream meanders. Some call these human-degraded Highland landscapes 'wet desert'. Climb down from the current road to the old one below and you enter another world. Tarmac is nibbled by the chittering frost; it has cracks where the ice has melted and refrozen and melted and refrozen over this and many winters (and at this altitude, in spring, summer and autumn too). Mosses colonise the damp slits; lichens grow in the pure air; wind-blown seeds fall into the cracks, watered by all that rain. Though in the heart of the wet desert at the extremity of the Tay, there is a gradual, inexorable reclamation of the human-built environment by nature, tiny seed after tiny seed swelling under the old A9. This is how the human age will end. It is not the only ghost road. Just above hovers the spectre of General Wade's eighteenth-century military road, unseen but, throughout these high lands, ever present.

The water flowing off the old road settles in the flat ground at the foot of the pass. It forms boggy pools that feed sphagnum and bog grass, or seeps, eventually, into the stream – the Allt Dubhaig – that slowly snakes its way round ziggurat mounds of glacial deposits. A soggy, wet half-land forms at the southern end of the pass, its surface dappled silver by a shaft of sunlight breaking through from the low cloud. Snowmelt, fog drip, evapotranspiration – the clouds are in a state of constant exchange with this water world that rises high to meet them. The waters from the surrounding hills – Meall an Dobharchain ('the Sow of Atholl'), An Torc ('the Boar of Badenoch') – choose their paths to the sea, north to the Moray Firth, south to the Firth of Tay, snorting and snuffling their way through a moraine landscape more like Iceland than the flat fertility of the Flemish fields at the Firths; this is one of only two sites in Scotland that the subarctic Norwegian blue heather (Phyllodoce caerulea) grows. Here the Ice Age is still present.

The water flows down tracks cut out of the hillside to allow access by grouse shooters and deerstalkers, big business across Highland Tayside. There are growing calls among environmentalists to regulate such roadbuilding, which seems to be accelerating, one reason being that they speed up the flow of water off the land. Today the only cries are of invisible grouse, the males warming up for the spring mating with echoing 'tuck, tucks' sounding hollow in the mist. It is not only the birds that are keeping ready for the season ahead. Above the stream, suspended between two staves, a half-inch-thick steel plate swings suspended on a shiny metal chain – a forlornly bling decoration for a medallion man of the mountain. Beside it a disintegrating sheet of hardboard decorated with white circles like a giant nine-spotted domino. Both steel plate and white circles are peppered with bullet holes.

At each end of the pass north and south are huge vistas westwards. Your view is channelled down the steep mountainsides flanking Lochs Ericht and Garry, two of that series of long lochs stretching deep into the west that act as storage basins, filling the Tay, signature features of the catchment here in the Highlands. At the end of the Drumochter Pass, you pass under the Inverness to Perth railway line and come to a small dam, neither high nor long, that runs behind the village of Dalwhinnie. Bags of salt are stacked ready to melt ice on the walkway to briny liquid. On the lip of the dyke a tiny ringed plover – usually more at home on the beach than here in the centre of the Highlands – patrols with urgent steps. Either side of the dam are turbulent in-flows, so wild they are caged behind steel fences: the first cascades down the mountain behind, then is channelled down six concrete steps out into the loch; the second is collected from underground, run-off from the pass that is redirected into the loch in a constant foaming, bubbling cauldron of brown, cream and white water, snuffling and blowing like a trapped, harpooned whale. On the fence beside this boiling pot of ice-cold water, the first of many signs along the Tay's catchment claiming ownership and informing you of what is and is not permitted: 'Scottish Hydro/Danger No Bathing'.

The majority of the Tay's catchment lies to the west. To the east, it runs close to the feet of high mountains that top it up from their short, steep streams until joined by the Tilt at Blair Atholl and, further south, the Isla.

At the southern end of the pass, the river Garry picks up speed, flowing out of its loch. Collecting the slow, ambling waters of the pass, it rushes with them into Glen Garry just as the slow, speed-limited road widens to a new stretch of dual carriageway and the traffic hurtles full throttle towards its ever diminishing future.

But winter here can slow even the fastest-flowing. Snow poles mark the route to keep the road safe, but snow gates testify that even the constant passage of gritters and snowploughs is sometimes not enough to keep the traffic moving. Look north and Inverness is a city that can be cut off, but change your perspective and it's the southerners who are isolated. Life in the north is different, even in the digital age. It is still controlled by weather. In the upper catchments of the Tay, sometimes you just have to thole it until the thaw comes.

Beside the snow gates at Dalnaspidal, the Allt Coire Mhic-sith comes down from A' Bhuidheanach Bheag. Below the hillsides of charred heather and exposed and deteriorating peat, the narrow floor of the deep, gouged corrie is strewn with small rocks, gravel silt and sand. At the end of the last Ice Age, about 12,000 years ago, an ice dam restrained the waters of a mountain loch here. When the proglacial lake melted, the moraine debris scoured parallel roads along the glen – dual carriageways. The stones continue to flow. An earth science study in the British Geological Survey archive describes how grit and pebbles from the riverbed of the Allt Dubhaig ranging in size from a tiny 15mm to 25cm move and disperse along the glens here, continuing a journey started long before humans ever travelled this landscape.

*

Moving along the glen at the foot of Ben Lui, with legs heavy as stones, Mark and I reclaim our bikes. As we cycled downhill to the car park at Dalrigh it was our own prehistory we were discussing. Passing behind the Tyndrum Hotel, we talk of our father Joe, who worked there in his student summer holidays. Glancing over at the cascading Cononish on our right, the small pools of white water transform in our blethering into dinner plates stacked on our father's arm, serving tables sixty years ago.

This area, called Strathfillan, is another transitional place. Travellers by road and railway from Oban and the west curve round the side of Ben Lui to Tyndrum. There they meet those making the journey from Fort William,

Glen Coe and Rannoch Moor in the north. Passing Dalrigh together along the rivers Cononish and Fillan, they come to Crianlarich and diverge again, south to Glen Falloch, Loch Lomond and Glasgow, or eastwards along Glen Dochart to Killin and Loch Tay. Along these routes, countless travellers have passed for millennia. They have been looked after in croft and byre, priory and castle, inn and hotel. The names of a very few stand out from the anonymous flow. At the car park the information board explains that Dalrigh means 'the field of the king' in Gaelic, the king in question being Robert the Bruce. But this was not a field of glorious victory but the site of a brutal massacre of his small band of supporters long before he ascended the Scottish throne. In the literally cut-throat struggle for kingship, Bruce and his troops were defeated by Clan MacDougall here in 1306. Axes were used against men and horses, brandished steel ripped flesh, swords slit, kerns and gallowglasses were unseamed from nave to chaps, blood flowed. The future king barely escaped this boggy field with his life.

Beneath the battlefield the Cononish is joined by the river flowing north out of the glen between two mountains, Ben Dubhchraig and Fiarach, and together they become the Fillan, which gives its name to the whole area around here.

In winter this far north, daylight is a commodity as valuable as silver. On many of our hillwalks my brother, myself and our Munro-bagging friends have stayed overnight in Strathfillan to give us as early a start on the northern hills as possible. On the banks of the Fillan at Ewich, between

Dalrigh and Crianlarich, the wooden 'wigwams' have provided the perfect overnight shelter for six to eight middle-aged men and large amounts of liquid refreshment. The Fillan, along with road, rail and West Highland Way, cuts through a narrow green valley floor hummocked by glacial mounds that give the landscape here a strange, otherworldly feel. The wet mossy environment absorbs and softens sounds. Mists can cocoon this glen, yet when the sun comes out and the clouds lift, the panorama of the high mountains to the south is one of the most stunning in Scotland. Ben More, Stob Binnein, Cruach Àrdrain – all hills we climbed – and at their feet Crianlarich.

At its elevated station, the four-coached trains from the south split in two and those from the north and west reconnect. While this is engineered, take a break in the station tearoom. Walkers are welcome. In summer, under the Victorian canopy, a pair of housemartins – travellers from the far south – have constructed a pot of a nest. In blue livery that matches the trains, they never rest, constantly swooping in and out to fill their insatiable chicks' open beaks. The cream-and-green-painted iron rail bridge over the Fillan just beyond the station is one of the most beautiful on the West Highland Line. Under the viaduct, inches over the water, the housemartins' sandy-coloured cousins swoop. Fish rise for the same flies rippling the smooth tawny surface. White clouds, and clouds of white riverside meadowsweet, are reflected in its surface. Pale purple hairbells, green willow and silver birch line its banks. A fallow deer bounds like a hare at the sound of squelching footsteps. Over a burn that feeds the river a fallen silver birch is a living bridge painted cream and green by lichens and mosses that thrive here in the pure West Highland air. High up in its vertical neighbour a heronry booms to the big bird's call. Higher still, above the green tubes of newly planted tree protectors in the clear felled hillside, a buzzard circles. A sheet of rain clouds the lower slopes of the massive Ben More yet the undulating ridges of its neighbour, Cruach Àrdrain, are clearly etched against the sky.

I think back to previous seasons by this water, some of them crystal clear, etched on my memory, others cloudy, indistinct. Fishing on a hot June evening, the only things we pulled from the water being our cooled tins of beer. Seven of us crammed into one of the wooden huts at Ewich, the night before a hillwalk. Gazing up at a river of stars over Cruach Àrdrain at 2 a.m. on a January night, clouds of steam rising as I piss out a stream of the evening's beer in the minus-five night, then waking in the morning to find the weather so atrocious we have to abandon the idea of climbing and go for a walk along the river instead.

The Fillan takes its name from an evangelising holy man who brought Christianity from the west around the year AD 700. There was a priory named after him here, and a handbell and crozier said to have been his are in the National Museum of Scotland in Edinburgh. There is also a pool in the river associated with him. Baptism is one of the seven sacraments of the Church. Christ himself was baptised in the river Jordan, so those converted by St Fillan mimic this physical manifestation of a spiritual cleansing. But the pool also retains some of its pre-Christian use – a use that is physical rather than spiritual. It is said to have healing qualities, though ritual must be followed:

> . . . in order that the cure should be effective, the afflicted were taken to the riverside towards the end of the moon's first quarter. Where a rocky point projects into the river, men were plunged into the water on one side and women on the other. The patients were then required to gather nine stones from the river-bed and on coming out to go to the top of the rock, 20 feet in height, and to walk three times round three heaps of stones, the accumulations of countless dippings. It was necessary after each turn to deposit on each heap one of the stones from the river-bed. After this ceremony, the devotees proceeded to the ruins of St Fillan's Chapel, about a mile away to the east of their immersion. Here they were tied to a great stone with a large hole it in, and the ancient bronze bell of St Fillan was placed for an instant upon their heads. The patient was left in the ruins all night long, and if in the morning he was found to be free from his bonds, a cure was deemed to have taken place.

Six iron links of the chain by which the afflicted were attached to the stone survive in the Stirling Smith Art Gallery and Museum. Kill or cure? Robert Heron, travelling through Scotland in 1792, notes that if 'the patient . . . is still bound, his cure remains doubtful. It sometimes happens that death relieves him during his confinement from the troubles of life.'

St Fillan's Priory was destroyed by iconoclasts during the Reformation, but still people held on to elements of pre-Reformation – or in this case probably even pre-Christian – practices. The belief in curative properties of water and the clearing of evil spirits by the ringing of bells survives on the fringes of society into the modern era. While cures were gradually discovered for physical ailments, treatments for mental illness were less forthcoming. This led to traditional methods like those described above being practised and recorded.

These beliefs extend beyond the Tay and Western culture. Reading *Dandelions* by Japanese novelist Yasunari Kawabata recently, I came across a passage describing a temple converted to an asylum that allows the patients turns at ringing the daily bell. The doctor explains that the deep resonance of the bell 'carries beyond the clinic . . . reminding the world that they're here – they exist'.

*

Across the Tay's catchment the bones of animals now extinct have been found – elk, wild ox, brown bear, lynx and wolf. These creatures were driven from this landscape by us over the 9,000 years since we began to colonise the banks of the river. Just as St Fillan and his evangelists drove out all but a tiny fragment of our knowledge of pre-Christian religion, so too do we know very little of the first 3,000 years of people living here. Foragers, gatherers, hunters, trappers, fishers: we left few traces of our existence except the charcoal remains of campfires, the flakes of our stone-blade chipping.

Some historians' current thinking is that 50–60 per cent of the post-glacial land was by the late Mesolithic period covered in woodland, perhaps permanent closed forest in some places and in others grazed cyclically at the edges by large herbivores. For thousands of years, they believe, humans had little impact on this dynamic woodland, taking only seasonal fruits, animals in the hunt and wood for fuel. Even as humans began to herd livestock they still only used the Tayside forests for shelter for themselves and their beasts, its plants for dying wool, bark for tanning leather. Other historians argue that early humans had a distinct impact on this forest: using fire to clear grassy spaces among the trees, making spaces attractive to grazing herbivores, providing clear lines of sight for a spear thrower or predictable spots to hide traps. These clearings later became the model for places to graze their own semi-domesticated beasts. A strong awareness of seasonality and how to subsist using only naturally available resources sustained these Stone Age peoples. We must assume that they used the rivers and lochs in the same way as they did the forest: by taking gratefully what the waters naturally provided. Perhaps building as well various forms of fishing platforms, setting traps and nets for fish returning to shallow waters to spawn, netting seabirds nesting off the cliffs at the Firth, positioning hiding places along the banks where animals crossed, beside waterfowl landing lines among its reedbeds. Ancient fishing weirs were constructed using stones to build underwater walls or by planting wooden stakes in the riverbed and weaving poles or branches horizontally to trap fish, techniques that carried down to recent historical times. In Scots, 'garth' is an enclosure, usually fenced but also a shingle bank on a river, a fishing weir. A 1609 Act of the Scottish Parliament noted 'All & haill the salmond fischeing . . . comprehending the garthis and pullis vnder-writtin'. Evidence of fishing weirs exist now only in place-names, such as Inchgarth ('fish weir island').

A Mesolithic harpoon head with two barbs in the National Museum of Scotland has been fashioned from an animal's rib. Closeness to the natural world, a vital dependence on understanding its movements, moods and seasons, allowed our hunter-gatherer ancestors to survive either part or the whole of the year here. What they knew of living off this land, how they interacted with it, and what they believed remains a mystery. As tempting as it is to align our present-day concerns of climate emergency and the breakdown of humanity's relationship with nature to some sort of imagined ethical 'one-ness' with nature of the earliest humans to inhabit Tayside, to wish that there once existed a golden age in our relationship with the natural world is unrealistic. As historian T. C. Smout writes, we 'cannot make assumptions . . . however tempting, about the ideology of those who lived too long ago and with too ephemeral a material culture to leave any trace of their belief systems'.

What we can say is that Taysiders then killed beasts, birds and fish, herded animals and managed these lands and waters for their own benefit as we still do today.

*

The mountain is the source of the river. Melting ice transports its stones. The river polishes them. High in the glens, deep in the west Central Highlands, they are collected by human hands and revered.

I am looking through my old hillwalking journal and come across a blurry photograph: my brother against a scattering of drenched grey rocks and a vague sense of looking into a corrie through mist to a tawny moorland below. This was Spidean Coire nan Clach ('Corrie of the Stones'). At least some of the considerable amount of water that dripped off us that day would have poured eastward into Gleann Cailliche ('Cailleach's Glen') and into its stream, Allt na Cailliche, thence into Allt Meurain and thus into Loch Lyon. From there it would have flowed into the river Lyon and, eventually, into the Tay itself.

Even if it had been a clear day, we would not have seen the 'stones' that give their name to the corrie, glen and burn. They are the Cailleach, translated from the Gaelic as 'old woman' or 'old hag', and her family. Human-like in shape, these water-sculpted sandstones are small – the Cailleach is only 18 inches high – yet they have endured.

Having spent the summer in the open Highland air, the Cailleach, the Bodach (her husband) and their 'family' of ten smaller stones are returned to their winter shelter inside the Tigh na Cailleach ('the Old Woman's House'), a small drystane-built shrine with turfed roof, re-thatched biennially. From Samhain (Halloween) to Beltane (May Day), they hibernate. The pre-Christian practice of moving the stones into shelter is said to be the oldest continuous pagan ritual in Scotland. It is founded on the belief that the Cailleach is also the creator goddess, and in her role as Queen of Winter she moves from the exterior world of light during the growing months to the dark interior as the sun wanes.

On nearby Ben Cruachan it was once said there was a sacred well on the summit which would send out fountains of water each day. To prevent too much escaping, a massive boulder was used to cap its flow each night. This was removed in the morning by the Cailleach Bheur ('the Old Hag of the Ridges'), a shepherdess sometimes known as Cailleach Mhor nam Fiadh ('the Old Woman of the Deer'), who would travel all over the mountainsides to find pasture.

One day, as evening drew close, she had wandered so far and was so exhausted that she lay down to rest before returning to the stone but fell fast asleep. Uncapped, the well and the fountain continued to spill down the side of the mountain. So great was the flood that it formed Loch Awe and, breaching the surrounding hillside, cut a passage through to the sea in the west, now the river Awe. For her negligence she was turned into stone and can be seen to this day still as the Creag na Cailleach above the Pass of Brander.

Winter queen, moon queen, witch queen – she reigns from Samhain to Beltane and is unloved. In her poem 'The Cailleach' Liz Lochhead describes her as 'old Mama Iron Heel', ready to grind us through winter's mill. 'She's all set to put us through it . . . she'll make us rue it.' Unlike Bride, the spring queen of the Gaelic tradition, the Cailleach has not been incorporated into the calendar of Christian saints. Revisiting her glen in late May, it is lit by watery spring sunshine, warming the ancient stones.

What is it like to be in this place? It is quiet. It is a space that requires time and physical effort to reach, a place of beauty, but it is not a wilderness, not a landscape from an ancient past. No stone-worshipping hunter-gatherers would be able to recognise this wet wasteland or entice wild herds into an ancient forest clearing, for there are no trees. The watery footprints of deer are seen, but in the puddles on the quad-bike track; if golden eagles fly over this glen, then so do transatlantic airliners. Nonetheless there is that sensation of connection to the past that is felt in ancient places, in historic landscapes: the feeling that there is a connection with people stretching far into the past who have been here before you and have felt the warmth of the same sun.

From the burn, I scoop a palmful of water and anoint the Cailleach. Most of the water runs down her earth mother form but a little evaporates into mist from her radiant warmth.

At the head of the glen I encounter two groups of teen-agers on an outdoor activity week. They have come over from the Rannoch Moor and are heading for the dam at the end of Loch Lyon to meet their minibus, boys in one group, girls in another, 50 yards apart. The boys have a ghetto blaster pumping out 'Get Lucky' by Daft Punk.

The hunter, for all their skill and knowledge, relies on luck. The squelch of a gently placed foot on waterlogged moss alerts the stag. The drip of a raindrop into a pool as a harpoon head brushes a wet reed and under the ripples the salmon darts away. Humans learnt to minimise risk by clearing spaces to make hunting more successful, using natural features to channel prey towards them. The control of herbivores, their corralling and domestication, created a need for pasture to feed them. To prevent overgrazing, new clearings had to be created, grass in them given time to replenish. Wild boar could be hunted and eaten, but also funnelled into areas of forest floor, turning over the ground and gradually becoming domestic pigs. With little or no evidence of field enclosures, fencing or stalls, it seems probable that beyond natural hedging, most cattle – predominantly sheep and cows – were closely supervised rather than corralled in one place. The herds who shepherded the cattle, sheep, deer and goats, who tamed and trained dogs, lived a semi-nomadic life with the animals, on the move to fresh pasture with each season, the natural music of birdsong and burbling burn joined by the simple reed pipe, a cow herd tooting their horn, hunkering down in one place for winter, hoping that there is enough fodder for the beasts to survive to spring.

Those who lived in the upper glens of the Tay catchment until the last century and a half would move with the seasons. In an ancient transhumance culture, mainly women, youths and children would come out to the upper glens, spending the brief summertime in the high pasture with cattle and sheep at the airigh or shielings. These were small annual dwellings with walls of dry-stone construction, the roof of turfs cut from the moor over a wooden beam transported up from the winter home and returned at the end of the summer, a heather-woven door ('cailleach-fhraoich') constructed on site, a seat made out of stone with a cut turf for a cushion (also 'cailleach'). In recorded history the men would be away in service owed to their clan chief, working his land, labouring for him, waging war or raiding cattle. Or maybe they would be working hard to earn hard currency: salmon-netting at the Firth or fishing out at sea. For those adolescents too young to fight but old enough for love, then, as today, thoughts of romance would swirl in the long, light summer days and twilight midnights, hoping to get lucky. In the high moorland it is a time of birth and of rebirth: the cailleach reappears, among the bog grasses tiny flowers start to bloom, the waters in the burns flow gentler and are warmed by the sun, lambs and calves are born. The calf suckles from its mother, feminine hands then coax warm milk from its udders, her voice soothing the cow.

> Give the milk, my treasure,
> Give quietly, with steady flow,
> Give milk, my treasure,
> With steady flow and calmly.

Then the butter-making.

> Thou who put beam in moon and sun,
> Thou who put food in ear and herd,
> Thou who put fish in stream and sea,
> Send the butter up betimes!

> Come, ye rich lumps, come!
> Come, ye rich lumps, come!
> Come, ye rich lumps, masses large,
> Come, ye rich lumps, come!

For many of the women churning the butter, life was forming in the amniotic fluid of their wombs. Between tending the beasts, milking them, churning butter and pressing cheeses they would collect berries and fruits, lichens for dyeing, flavoursome herbs, mosses for sanitary pads and dressing wounds, and medicinal plants, all while the cattle fattened before being bartered, eaten or over-wintered back down in the glen.

Knowledge of which plants grew where and how they could be best utilised was essential for survival. Roid (bog myrtle, Myrica gale), flourishing in the wetness of these Highland glens, would be used as a balm for sweats and fevers, and as a yellow or brown colourant for wool and cloth. It continues to be used today as a midge repellent, a sprig decorating the jacket of many a Tay angler or placed in a clothes drawer to dissuade moths. Leamhnach (Tormentil, Potentilla erecta) was used to prevent diarrhoea and for clotting wounds. Leaves of mòthan (bog violet, Pinguicula vulgaris) were sliced, wrapped in cloth and added to milk to counteract the work of fairy folk, evil spirits and witches, who were frequently blamed when things went wrong during butter- and cheese-making, hence its other name, bodan measgan, the butter mixer (in English, butterwort). Its leaves produce an enzyme which acts as a rennet. In *Flora Celtica* the authors note a similar use by the Sami people as described by the botanist Carl Linnaeus in his eighteenth-century travels in Lapland.

Belief allied to adaptability has kept the seasonal ritual of the Cailleach going, even if the culture that initiated it, and those who followed a similar relationship with this landscape, have long gone. Flow with the Allt na Cailliche to the Allt Meurain and thus into Loch Lyon, then down the river Lyon, down to the far end of the glen, and this is also manifest by an ancient tree. In what is now Fortingall Kirkyard, a yew had already been growing for at least a thousand years before Christ and is still alive 2,000 years later. It is a tree unlike any other. The whole of the central trunk has disappeared over the ages of its long life so that there is now a negative space where once it flourished, but on either side a gnarled collection of side-shoots and branches have continued to grow. Pale green tips of this year's leaves fringe its multitudinous boughs. It is akin to the Tay drying up but all its tributary lochs remaining. We know that wood from the core of the tree was burnt as part of Beltane in spring, so this ancient tree was also a sacred tree, but much beyond that remains a mystery. We are in awe of its longevity, aware of its relevance to our ancestors, but, lacking their way of life, their level of belief, meaning has flowed out of it.

The same could be said of the Cailleach stones. In the heart of this mountain landscape, faint echoes of the themes of birth, life and death are still close to the centre of one's experience, handfast as it is to stark, northern, seasonal nature. To the west, on the Outer Hebrides, there are still a few communities sharing ancient experience, but here on the mainland the people are mostly gone and the few individuals living here service commercial interests that cater for tourists, that breed lamb to become mutton, manage deer herds to be shot, preserve fish for the hook, maintain lochs for hydro-electric power. The empty ritual of the stones retreating to their shelter for winter and re-emerging in spring continues, but what, I wonder, is the point? A solitary ghillie, his godlike hand dealing out life and death, regulated by seasonal killings for pleasure – grouse, trout, salmon, stag – has become the last keeper of this once communal female shrine.

# Loch Tay

*From Glen Dochart to Kenmore*

The mountain is the source of the river. Humans transport its stones, polish them, venerate them.

Monte Viso in the far-off Italian Alps was the source of a polished stone axe found near Rattray, ceremonially buried in the banks of the river Ericht, an eastern tributary of the Tay. The carving of the long flake of jadeite, splintered from a boulder that had been heated and burnt into an axehead, could take more than a thousand hours of chipping, flaking and polishing. It was careful, laborious human work. Time spent making tools was rewarded in time and energy saved in utilising them. With stone axes, humans began felling forest and clearing land to grow crops, yet this axehead was never used to cut down primeval forest for farmland by its Neolithic makers; it was purely ceremonial. We cannot know why it was revered beyond its sculptured beauty. It was hewn from the mountain − perhaps seen as the misty residence of the gods and so retaining something of their spirit, their power? Maybe this stone was associated with a particular deity, like the Cailleach. It and others similar to it were passed or traded across Europe in the years after 4000 BC, travelling through France to Scotland, often ending up, like this one, in watery places.

The significance of water is perhaps linked to its transience: these liquid places in a solid world could be entrances to another world. Archaeologists think that the glassy surfaces of some of these axes could have been achieved by polishing with a paste made of ash from burnt waterside bullrushes, but we will never know how ancient Taysiders viewed them.

For practical use, axeheads could be crafted from many stones, but some rocks were better than others. They were easier to bring to a blade, stayed sharper for longer and didn't shatter. One such outcrop occurred above Killin on Loch Tay, where axe production was intense and the tools manufactured there were of such quality that they too were traded far and wide.

Killin lies fifteen miles from Crianlarich along a glen that runs west to east. The River Fillan flows for a couple of miles or so along this glen before it enters Loch

Dochart. Where the Fillan flows delta-like into the loch, the ruins of an old building sit on a small island. It was not, as some guidebooks say, a refuge for Bruce after the slaughter at Dalrigh, or 'Rob Roy McGregor's Castle', but a house built by one of the McGregors' arch-enemies, Sir Duncan Campbell of Glenorchy – 'Black Duncan' – sometime between 1583 and 1631. It did not stand for long. Despite its defensive position in a turbulent country during a turbulent century, it was burnt down in 1646. The loch itself is short-lived, a mere two-thirds of a mile in length, but it nonetheless gives its name to both the glen and the river that flows out from it.

The River Dochart has barely got going before it widens into another short loch, Loch Iubhair ('Loch of the Yew'). This small body of water is compressed between the foot of the huge mass of Ben More and the Breadalbane mountains. The waters pouring off these hills need to be channelled and controlled if the traffic along the A85 through Glen Dochart is to be kept flowing. Depending on the season, water drips or spurts from the array of white plastic pipes that protrude from the embankment along the route, collecting into gravel traps that cover drains by the roadside. As the Allt Coire Chaorach, which collects the waters flowing from Ben More and Stob Binnein, snakes into the river Dochart, bridges carry the modern road and the dismantled Oban to Callander railway line. On the hillside above, a tiny lochan with an unusual feature caught the eye of Thomas Pennant travelling the glen in 1769:

opposite to the farm of Achessan (sic), is a lake, noted for a floating island, fifty-one feet long, and twenty-nine broad, that shifts its quarters with the wind. It has strength sufficient to carry an involuntary voyage, the cattle that might be surprised feeding on this mobile solum, deceived with the appearance of its being firm land . . . [it] may be launched from the sides of the lake with poles, and can show plenty of coarse grass, some small willows, and a little birch tree.

The thickness of the island on Lochan Saorach (sometimes Lochan Dun Saorach), he says, was 'twenty-five inches. Perhaps . . . this might have originated from the twisted roots of the Schoenus mariscus (a bog-rush), and Scirpus caespitosus (deer grass), converted into a more firm mass by the addition of the Carex caespitosus (a sedge).' This island has long sunk into the waters of time.

Using a pole to punt a mat of rushes around a Highland lochan sounds a wonderfully peaceful recreation, your own miniature free-floating castle. Its opposite is using a pole or spear to vault over the moat of your enemy's castle and engage in hand-to-hand combat. Long before Pennant Celtic bards would travel this glen, telling tales from Scotland and Ireland passed down orally for generations. Heroes like Cú Chulainn, whose 'salmon leap' set him apart from other men. This appeared to be a kind of vault, using his spear as a pole, allowing him to cross the defences of his enemies' forts. Another tradition tells of the blind bard Ossian's father, Fionn (or Fingal), leaping onto an island of Loch Iubhair in Glen Dochart:

There lived a man named Taileachd whose sweetheart was one of the Sidhe [fairies]. Fionn too fell in love with her. In a stormy meeting between Taileachd and Fionn the fairy woman spoke as follows: 'He of you who gains the victory in a leap will I follow with pleasure.' Taileachd leaped from the isle to the mainland shore, and Fionn had no difficulty in making the same jump. Taileachd then said that they must carry out the leap backwards, and this he did successfully, but when it came to Fionn's turn he just failed to reach the mainland shore and sank into the mud as high as his neck. Taileachd, before Fionn could move, struck off his head with his sword.

An island in a loch in such a legend usually suggests a crannog, an iron-age house built on stilts out from the shore for defensive purposes. Many of the small islands that dot Scotland's lochs today are collapsed crannogs rewilded. No such crannog exists on the loch now, perhaps having sunk under the weight of its years. The bards tell of Fionn's headless corpse floating and being washed out of the loch and along the river Dochart, as it meanders the ten miles across the flat valley floor to Killin.

By the time the river reaches there, it needs to drop 150 feet to reach Loch Tay. It does this by plunging down the Falls of Dochart, spectacular after heavy rainfall and conveniently close to tourist coach parking for social media opportunities.

Fionn's body was found at the foot of the Falls, his burial place supposedly marked by a monolith in the village that bears his name. Midstream, an island in the Falls has been the traditional burial place of Clan McNab, whose crest bears a wildman's head, not representing Fionn's but the founder of the clan who was a relation of St Fillan. The McNabs had joined their neighbours in attacking Bruce at Dalrigh. Just as the Dochart flows into the western end of Loch Tay, it is joined by the river Lochay flowing from the glen of the same name. On the ithmus of land is the village of Killin.

Snaking north-east from Killin, Loch Tay is fourteen or so miles long and averages a depth of 200 feet. It has seven islands, none large, some probably former crannogs that have been colonised over the centuries by nature, or, like Priory Island, the largest, by humans. Others have, over time, sunk.

Very slowly walking out into the waters of Loch Tay, I feel the current of the Dochart behind me and the waves from the loch rippling against my ankles, then my knees, then I take the plunge and *splash*, I'm in! The water is cold, very cold. Chattering, brrrrrr-ing, I swallow some by accident, then inhale more up my nose. Panicking, I stand up instantly, blowing, spouting, snorting, forefinger and thumb on my nose snottering it back into the loch. My reaction to the water disturbs the peace of the day. Two reproving mallards go quacking off in disgust at my human antics. My skin is goosebumped. I start to walk again. My lower legs are tanned by the peaty waters, by the flecks of sediment I stir up. My feet slither over slimy rocks and stones. Green water weeds slip between my toes, exfoliating. Ouch, I've stood on something sharp. Lifting my foot out of the water, I see a trickle of blood, red where the cut is, diluting and flowing delta-like over the wrinkled skin of my sole. That's it. I'm getting out. I need to pee. In the space of a minute, I have ingested some of the loch's water, but it has also flushed out of me some of my liquid DNA.

High above the loch's north shore looms Ben Lawers. I have climbed it in summer and winter. It is impressive at nearly 4,000 feet high. But then it does have the advantage of a car park for its nature reserve at 1,500 feet. That nature reserve is an eye-opener, more revealing than standing atop the mountain. Instead of the massive vista, it is the micro-world at your feet that draws you in. By fencing off part of the mountainside along the Burn of Edramucky from sheep and deer-grazing, the native flowers have been given the time and space to regenerate. At first it is the plants of the wetlands that flourish, ones that need little soil – bog cotton and asphodel, marsh willow and arrowgrass, butterworts and sundews, mosses, heather (as we have seen in the heavily grazed Cailleach's glen). As time has passed and the sheep and deer have continued to be excluded, small, low-growing alpine plants such as purple and yellow mountain saxifrages and moss campion have become re-established. They flourish in soil enriched by the burn flowing over and eroding the mineral rich bedrock – a process called 'flushing'. Among the burn's rocks, mountain willow has been planted, broad-leaved plants – once driven out to isolated cliff faces high on the hillside out of grazing beasts' reach – are regenerating:

water avens, wild angelica, purple-flowered wood cranes-bill. Cocooned within the nature reserve, caterpillars of moth and butterfly feast. Under the water of the burn are the larvae of caddis and mayfly. Dippers dip in for them, skaters glide over its surface. Skimming above, the shimmering wings of dragonflies reflect the silvery mica on the riverbed rocks. Trees, too, have started to flourish. Montane scrub species – aspen, birch, hazel and downy willow. Wheatears and ring ouzels – blackbirds with a white chest – can be found here. But it is a short summer at this height. The tadpoles will take two winters to grow into frogs. As the land around the burn thaws after a deep winter, the meltwaters will drain from the upper levels, causing the soil to collapse into terraces. Low-growing plants thrive on this 'solifluction': species like the stag's horn clubmoss with its vibrant green antlers.

Two red deer and a smattering of sheep look enviously in from the other side of the fence. Paths either side of the burn climb to the old shielings at 2,100 feet. In summer people from Loch Tay-side would come up here to cut peats from the boggy moss for fuel. To dry it before transporting it back down the mountain, they would stack it on platforms constructed of boulders known as stances. The remains of these can still be seen.

Following the burn back down to the lochside, a cuckoo is flitting from fencepost to fencepost above the remains of a homestead, the old school house, the sheep buchts, the grouse butts, the inevitable Sitka spruce plantation, the cattle grid, the luxury lodges and glamping pods, the cup-marked rocks . . .

There are many of them here on the north shore. Between Loch Tay and the confluence of the rivers Tay and Tummel twenty miles away at Ballinluig, at least seventy cup-marked rocks have been recorded by the Breadalbane Heritage Society. They have a small circular indentation carved into them by a neolithic hand. Some rocks have many – most under a dozen, but a few as many as twenty-five or more. Some are circled by an outer ring, sometimes as many as five, giving the effect when the sun is low in the sky of ripples from a stone plopped into the loch below, or a sacred, polished axehead offered to a river goddess. Perhaps the sculptor used an axe quarried locally at Killin. The rocks themselves are not sculpted and are of various shapes and sizes – triangular, monoliths, natural outcrops. A few have a gutter running from the cup to the rock's edge, suggesting liquid flowing. They are prolific around Fearnan. As winter comes, snow begins to fall, filling the cups first, dappling the grey rocks white.

Snow in February is winter at its most beautiful. Even at night its faint glow gives out a chill reflective beauty. All is still, quietened and softened under a Highland sky awash with stars and the glow of rivers of galaxies. The gentle wind seems to be an echo of this astral tide washing across the ocean of space. It is well past midnight on a Friday in the late 1970s. At the outdoor centre at Fearnan at the eastern end of Loch Tay a hallway light spills yellow out onto the undisturbed snow. The muffled sound of warfare comes next. Inside, I am in one of two opposing troops of Scouts battling for possession of the stairway just for the sake of it, with no other objective than to have raucous, semi-violent teenage fun. After the fourth and final, final warning from our exasperated leaders, the two clans eventually retreat for good into their rooms. Even back in the hushed dorm the high spirits continue. The dangling fingers of Campbell Duncan's sleeping hand are being dipped alternately into cups of hot and cold water while in a falsetto imitation of his mother's voice Gregor Robertson repeatedly whispers 'Time to go to the toilet, dear' in an attempt to get him to wet the bed.

The next day, tired and weary Scouts are breaking fingers of icicles off the side of the burn as they slog uphill on our winter weekend adventure break. The snow is too deep to attempt the planned ascent of Ben Lawers, but we still manage some expeditions skirting around the foothills. Following the Lawers Burn up from Loch Tay, we reach a hydro-electric dam. This particularly sticks in my mind: the gap where the frozen water had shrunk away from the brutalist concrete engineered to withhold its flow, and the fantastical cracks and crevasses formed as the temperature dropped and the surface water froze, whilst underneath it must have still run, were unlike anything I'd seen before. As the cold period extended, the waters had frozen to a greater depth, contracting to produce the ten-foot-deep zigzagging hacks across its surface, a river's surface that was two feet deep in unmelted snow. All the time we were on it, we pretty much knew we were safe, but we also were thrilled by the possibility of the surface giving way. I can still recall thinking of a serialisation of *Little Women* that I had recently watched and the horror of Amy trapped under the ice.

Strong in my memory is the bleakness of Lochan nan Cat in the bowl of the mountains and realising that in pure winter whiteness could also be gloom. As we came back down the Lawers Burn the landscape opened up before us. A melancholy mood descended, snow starting to purple in the early sunset mixed with tiredness as the exertions of the previous night caught up with us, the adrenalin draining away. The cold on our cheeks, legs weary like the despondent 'Hunters in the Snow' in Bruegel's famous painting, trudging downhill after an unsuccessful, dissatisfying short-lit day curtailed by snow on the Tay's mountains.

A break in the Lawers massif at Fearnan allows the road to cut through a gap in the hills to lower Glen Lyon and Fortingall. This is not the only route to Glen Lyon. As well as water, a small road – impassible in winter – flows down to the glen from the north side of Ben Lawers. Two ways meet, Christian and pagan, at Innerwick. A metre-high stone is angled into the ground between the road and the river Lyon. A rough cross is carved into its grooved, lichened surface, a poor relation to the sophisticated interlacing knotwork of the Pictish crosses downstream. Legend has it that this is the cross of Adomnán, Abbot of Iona from 679 to 704, biographer of St Columba. To the sound of the handbells of Adomnán and his Irish evangelists, ringing out between these Highland hills, the people became Christians.

Tigh na Cailleach, too, became Christian. The ritual lustrations in honour of the goddess in her native mountain stream became instead christenings mirroring Christ's baptism in the far-off river Jordan.

Her priestesses were replaced by male priests; the goddess herself transitioned from female to male – now St Meuran and his eleven disciples, her temple Tigh nam Bodach ('House of the Old Man'). In Gaelic the word cailleach has gradually become associated with old women and given a negative slant – infertile, single, witchlike even; a definition in Dwelly's Dictionary has it as 'a supernatural or malign influence dwelling in dark caves . . . and corries'. The ancient tree at Fortingall had its heart cut out, the place – of obvious native religious significance – falsely associated by the incoming Irish Christian missionaries with the Roman governor of Judea, Pontius Pilot, who washed his hands of all responsibility and sent Jesus to his crucifixion. They said that he was born there. A church was built on the site where the ancient tree grew.

A hole was excavated from a rock, water filled it, it was blessed, a holy man's cupped hand scooped a handful in baptism. A still-standing ancient stone known as Clach Mo-Luchaig has variously claimed to be named after one of these male Christian saints – Moluag of Lismore, Lochein, Luchta or Luchar – but Luch (Mouse) was a woman's name. It is said that witch-ish women or scolds were chained to it as punishment.

Time flows like water, its currents swirl and eddy, mixing in its ever bubbling cauldron. In the fields between the Clach Mo-Luchaig and the river Lyon a standing stone has been transplanted to the top of the Cairn of the Dead, a medieval communal burial which has come to be named Clach a' Phlaigh and has a modern plaque attached, reading:

Here lie the victims of the Great Plague of the 14th Century, taken here on a sledge drawn by a white horse led by an old woman.

Having collected the waters from the Allt Cailliche and the myriad other bodies of water along its glen, the river Lyon does not have long to flow now before it merges with the Tay a couple of miles past the end of Loch Tay at Styx.

The stone circles at Carse Farm, where the river Lyon feeds the Tay, have been immobile since constructed in the early Bronze Age, yet they continue to exude an undefinable, wyrd power – a kind of supernatural sense. The recent construction of the Beauly to Denny overhead power line afforded an opportunity to excavate the site, but after a fruitless search archaeologists concluded that any deposits that may have existed have been destroyed by the intensive ploughing of the field over millennium upon millennium of agricultural activity. The Highland power lines that pass through Drumochter cross the Tay here. On the south side of the river, Croft Moraig is the site of a previous engineering project. The archaeology of another stone circle here gives a little more insight. The most complete of its type in Scotland, post-holes suggest an initial circular construction of wooden upright staves with a break for an entranceway into the centre. This and the second phase – an oval of eight stones – seem to be focused on a large recumbent stone bearing cup marks. The site was further augmented with stone banking to make a raised platform. Towards the turn of the third and second millennium BC a final phase saw twelve more stones added and two massive outliers flanking the entranceway. Adjacent to these were two graves where the bodies of the dead were buried, not cremated.

Who were these people? What are they to us? What do these ancient stones mean to twenty-first-century people? I'm walking around this site with my two boys. Yes, it is possible that we could live meaningful lives and yet be ignorant of our past, but it seems to me, standing among these circles of stones, that both ancient stones and Taysiders today are linked. Each is a ripple from a progenitor's action, like a glacial pebble lobbed into the waters of the Tay many generations ago; the undulating waves from a common centre, part of a continuous undercurrent fizzing like eels with a now hidden energy. Who are these two people interred in these ancient graves? Anonymous. You could say they were nobody, nothing to do with us, but what if one was your mother and the other your grandfather, or imagine into the future and your grandchild, older than you are now, is standing here in the centre of this circle. The moon that transits the sky above, the river that flows beyond this circle are the same as when our forebearers first constructed this place, so special that they continued to build on it over long periods of time. It stands at a junction that is still important to us thousands of years later. Here lines of power ferry their electricity over the river of time to us – only connect.

Head back to Kenmore and Loch Tay appears before you. At its eastern end projecting out into the loch is a reconstruction of another ancient circular structure.

Here, where the Tay proper begins, embedded and preserved in the deep sediment of the loch, the points of sharpened timbers which once supported houses built over the water were discovered. One of these circular Iron Age structures – a crannog – has been reimagined, originally as an experiment by the Scottish Trust for Underwater Archaeology to understand how these 5,000-year-old structures functioned. The Rev. J. B. MacKenzie, minister of Kenmore at the end of the nineteenth century, photographed the remains of one of these crannogs west of the village pier before it was destroyed by the wash from the loch's steamships. Using experimental archaeology techniques, the defensive family homestead that once housed about twenty people has now been brought to life.

Reached by a wooden bridge that walks 30 feet out from the foreshore, the roundhouse is constructed on dressed tree trunks 10 feet above the surface of the loch. On a platform of logs a wooden structured house with basket-woven walls insulated with mud and wool is capped with a cone-shaped roof thatched with heather. A hole in the centre acts as a chimney, funnelling out smoke from the hearth below. The interior is centred on this hearth, with communal areas, sleeping quarters, storage areas and pens for animals all radiating out from the centre.

Objects that slipped between the floor timbers of the Oakbank crannog and splashed into Loch Tay have been preserved in its mud and describe ancient domestic life: hazelnut shells and cherry stones; loom weights and a swan neck cloak pin; a butter dish still containing butter; a wooden whistle. Hear by the loch today the piping shepherd as their collie rounds up a hillside flock. The legacy of these crannogs can be seen in many Scottish lochs, where a small island populated by Scots pine marks where one of these houses once stood. In June 2021 a chance ember set the reconstructed crannog ablaze and within six minutes it was completely destroyed. A new crannog has since arisen in the loch.

Skills that endured from prehistoric times have only recently been going out of use and an element of the reconstructed crannog's mission is to explain, demonstrate and let visitors try their hands at them. Skills such as using a handwoven basket to separate the chaff from the grain before grinding meal on a quern stone; using the tension of a bent loch-side willow branch as a lathe, or using horse-hoof fungus (*cailleach-spuinge*) as tinder; animal skin trouser- and jacket-making; hand-twisting rope to make into nets to catch fish, hares or birds.

Fishing skills, too: spearing a salmon at night with a seven-pronged leister and hooking underneath it with a gaff to pull it out of the river; taking trout with a dubrach, a kind of sideways trident; using a dart-headed harpoon in shallow water; or the most basic of skills – guddling for trout. With your hand held in the water, slightly swirling to attract and fascinate the fish, the fingers then mesmerise it by tickling its belly until, with a whip of the hand, the fish is in the air and frantically writhing on the riverbank, drowning in air. Today's anglers can buy all their equipment online, or purchase from the few remaining angling shops in Tayside. A visit to Malloch's on Perth High Street was a vital place of research when I started writing this book. A handwritten yellow Post-It note on the door notified customers, 'Worms and Maggots now in stock. We also stock DEADBAIT'.

People like us fished in the streams that feed the loch or from the shore, from the crannog itself, or out on the water in boats hewn out of tree trunks or in coracles. Log canoes that could easily carry eight paddlers, ferry people or transport goods and cattle more efficiently, safely and quickly than by land, have been discovered along the length of the Tay. Their use stretches back beyond the time of the crannog, the canny archaeologists asking themselves, 'Is it a log boat or a cattle trough?' The log boat discovered in the inter-tidal mud at Carpow, where the Earn joins the Tay, is of late Bronze Age. The mud, like the sediment of the loch, has preserved details – the gouges made in its wood during construction by socketed bronze axe or adze; traces of mosses used for caulking; even the transom board in the stern has survived. A mere harpoon's throw from the Tay, it is now in Perth Museum.

The coracle or curragh has been in use since at least the early Bronze Age and is constructed by attaching semi–spherical basketwork to a circular frame with rope made of animal hair and then waterproofing with animal hide, usually that of cattle, hence the alternative name of 'bull boat'. They were light enough to be carried on your back but also immensely sturdy. It is said that one such small craft brought Columba and the big idea of Celtic Christianity from Ireland to these loch shores and riverbanks.

# Atholl

*From Strathtay to Dunkeld*

Atholl is a district that sits in the centre of the southern Highlands, connecting to all points of the compass. Current thinking is that the name 'Atholl' derives from these transitionary, connecting channels: ath, meaning 'ford, way through', and fochla, 'north', northern crossings. It is here that the majority of the catchments of the Tay flow from the lochs and glens of the Grampian

Mountains. To the north opens the Drumochter Pass. To the east the Spittal of Glenshee leads to the catchments of the Dee and Aberdeenshire. At the Linn of Campsie, on its southern boundary, the Tay tips over the Highland Boundary Fault into the Lowlands. But it is at Kenmore, on its western border, where the Tay proper begins.

If its prehistory is swathed in West Highland mists and a series of constant changes of name, then the word 'Tay' is similarly obfuscated. Where does its name originate? In Gaelic, it is Tatha. Or Tausa in Brythonic, conjectured to be a language associated to that spoken by the Picts – 'the flowing one, the strong one, the silent one'. Does that name refer to the river or the goddess of the river, or both? Was the river that the Roman historian Tacitus refers to as Taus in his description of Agricola's campaigning in Scotland around AD 79 the Tay? No one knows.

The beginning of the named river marks the beginning of the transition from Highland to Lowland. Before journeying down the river, as it widens and becomes prodigious, it is worth mapping this liminal landscape a little more. To the north is Glen Lyon, source of the Tay's first major tributary; to the south, mountain passes lead to Loch Earn, source of the Tay's last major tributary and to Glen Almond, whose river joins the Tay at Perth. If river, stones, cup marks and floating islands are enigmatic, then here the waters begin to become a little clearer.

James MacGregor (*c.* 1480–1551), Dean of Lismore, was a notary in Fortingall. He collected many of the stories, songs, epic verses and prayers he heard, told by bards at firesides around the area, and, importantly for us, he wrote them down. The *Book of the Dean of Lismore* is a treasure trove of Gaelic verse — one that preserves the work of many Celtic poets, whose art only exists by being told and retold down through the generations. He also preserves for us the names of these bards, introducing each with a line of biography:

A houdir Ossan M'Finna [The author of this is Ossian, the son of Fionn] . . . of this here is Fergus the Bard . . . the author of this is Gormlay, daughter of Flann, the good wife . . . of this the Blind O'Cloan . . . Isabella Ni vic Cailien . . . Finlay, the red-haired bard, said this:

To Mac Gregor the brave . . .
. . . To praise him is our duty.
To whom courage is a right;
When summer time comes round,
Peace he never knows,
He's in the throat of all his fellows.
When men of him do speak,
As Gregor of the blows,
'Tis his delight to drive,
Flocks and herds before him.
Of that flock John's the head,
The king at lifting cattle,
I myself will sing,
Mouth with mouth at daybreak.
When his sharp-armed men see,

Mac Gregor at the Bealach,*
His way so gently soft,
No weight to them their burdens.

The verses cover a range of subjects and the language of
the 'strolling bards', transcribed not in classical Gaelic but
with MacGregor's fifteenth-century Perthshire Gaelic,
writing in a Lowland secretary script, making interpretation extremely nuanced. For example, is Gilchrist Taylor's
verse a diatribe against the Stewarts of Atholl, the assassins
of James I?

Curse them that 'gainst thee fierce contend.
There is a pack of cruel hounds,
Who the king's children sorely grieve;
I hear the baying of these dogs,
Every glen is full of it . . .

Or are they lines on the hunting down of the wolves
which ravage flocks along the Tay?

Many the dogs to Tummel's stream,
Who know to hunt along its side,
The eye of Christ is on them all . . .

. . . Destroy all surly cruel hounds.
Smoke every den in Schiehallion,

------------

*Bealach, the modern Taymouth, was, with the territory
around, in possession of the M'Gregors down to about 1490,
when it passed by royal charter into the possession of the
Knights of Glenurchy.

John Stewart of the bounding steeds,
Ere I must call a sweet-voiced pack
This litter of ugly, snarling curs.
By Garry of John Stewart of the white steed,
No antlers are seen without the head,
While 'mongst the rocky rugged woods,
Are seen the grey-skinned pack of hounds.

The translator of the nineteenth-century edition, the Rev. Thomas M'Lauchlan, in his notes on the texts comments on the need to keep the verses 'smooth and flowing'. He also notes that patronage by clan chief and victory in poetic contests were vital to the bards' livelihoods, 'the large prizes usually conferred by the wealthy on successful poets'. Thus verses praising the genealogy of the MacGregors, naturally, are included; 'kings' they were of Breadalbane: 'Three there were north and three to the south' (meaning the north and south sides of Loch Tay; in Gaelic, *Tuaruith* and *Deasnuith*):

After the time of Malcom Kenmore.
Ten of the race did wear the crown,
From the time of Malcom up to Alpin.

The great bard Ossian is the subject as well as the author/ teller of epics:

Long are the clouds this night above me,
The last man of the Feine am I,
The great Ossian, the son of Fionn,

Listening to the sound of bells.
Long are the clouds this night above me.

Ossian is celebrated in Glen Almond by a mighty stone said at one time to have covered his grave. We will visit it later in our journey.

Twenty years after the Dean of Lismore's death, a new generation of bards was recording the all-too-brutal realities of life at the eastern end of Loch Tay. These lines from 'Griogal Cridhe' were written by Marion Campbell, Mrs MacGregor of Glenstrae (fl. 1570):

Ochain, ochain, ochain uiridh

Ochone, ochone my little one,

Is goirt mo chridhe, laoigh,

My heart is deathly sore,

Ochain, ochain, ochain uiridh

Ochone, ochone my little one,

Cha chluinn t'athair ar caoidh.

Your father cannot hear.

They put his head on an oaken block
and spilled his blood on the ground,
If I had had a cup there,
I'd have drunk my fill of it.

Marion Campbell uses *ochone* (alas), the Highland expression of regret. Alas, indeed. Her beloved husband, the child's father, Gregor Roy ('Red Gregor'), could not hear because his head was no longer attached to his body, executed by her own kinsman, 'Grey Colin' Campbell of Glenlyon.

Inter-clan warfare operated on the same principles as international warfare: dispute resolution with intermarriage after resolution, only for border warfare to open up again, this time with added familial bitterness.

By the mid to late sixteenth century the barbarity remained, but the power of the law, written proof of landownership against oral kinship tradition, tipped the balance of power towards the Campbells of Glenlyon and against the Clan MacGregor in the upper Tay. 'Grey Colin', by his avaricious coveting of neighbouring lands, was the most active agent in the feud that drew in huge numbers of actors across the Highlands for generations and so can justly be represented by his personal decapitation of Gregor Roy.

Though barbaric, it was just one of the weapons he deployed on the MacGregors. He used the law to assert his claim to lands north and south of Loch Tay and placed his own stewards on them to gather rents and manage tenants; he supported the Reformation to acquire former church lands and to appoint Protestant ministers, thus gaining influence; he weaponised language, with Scots and English gradually becoming the lingua franca of his administration against the Gaelic MacGregors; he built bridges over Highland torrents to improve communication and access to inaccessible glens; and for himself he established a powerful and strategic base at the bealach of the MacGregors, Balloch Castle at the head of Loch Tay, what is now Taymouth Castle.

Across the upper catchments of the river he ensured that kin-based lineages experienced a loss of power. He acquired the rights to Glenstrae, the heartland of the MacGregors, but did not administer it through Gregor Roy; instead, he gave its running to his own Campbell son, 'Black Duncan'.

The MacGregors, unlike other clans suffering similar incursions into their traditional heartlands, reacted violently to his attacks and rebelled. In 1562 they raided Campbell lands along Loch Tay and so the first decade of bitter feuding began until Gregor Roy's execution. What is remarkable about the feud is that it had a ripple effect, drawing in clans and testing alliances and allegiances across a huge area of the Perthshire Highlands – Breadalbane, Atholl and Strathearn – but also further afield – Argyll, Lennox and Menteith. Also, remarkably, though it covered such a vast area and drew into its vortex at different times national actors, using it as part of their wider political manoeuvrings – Mary, Queen of Scots; Regent Morton; King James VI – it remained a Highland dispute.

Into the seventeenth century it developed different phases, flowing silently for a few years, then suddenly resurfacing in a torrent of violence, the weapons of both sides the weapons of war still used today: murder, rape, theft, destruction. The personalities changed, but the bitterness, the cruelty, carried on down the years – even the MacGregor name became outlawed, so fragmentary, so elusive, they became 'the Children of the Mist'. Elusiveness is associated with the MacGregors, with Highlanders, with Griogal Cridhe, with his ancestor Rob Roy. Campbell and later Wade built bridges and roads, castles and forts, but the Highlander evades them in the mist. Like the salmon, they leap.

At the eastern end of Glen Lyon, where the Highland river is about to be subsumed by the Tay, it enters its death throes with thunderous rage through a narrow gorge in a spot now known as MacGregor's Leap. Gregor Roy is that MacGregor.

MacGregor's Leap may have been a jump, a vault like Cú Chulainn's, an act of extreme physical suppleness and strength borne of lifestyle and age, added to the fact he was running for his life. Another kind of leap is described in Highland stories and traditions collected orally in the nineteenth century. In Gaelic society, there was a test of strength where a man should lie face down on the ground with his arms tight by his sides so that he resembled a fish. He then flexed his chest muscles to raise himself up and propelled himself forward like a salmon up a waterfall. Perhaps Gregor Roy's wife had given him a sprig of bog violet to safeguard him on his journey. If a man makes a remarkable escape, it is said of him '*Dh'òl e bà a dh'ith am mòthan*' ('He drank the milk of the guileless cow that ate the bog violet').

He escaped, but within a year of his awesome feat he was dead. We recoil at the horror, admire the physical prowess, but perhaps the greatest accomplishment is the ability of the grieving Marion to project her voice down the years to us and for her grief and humanity to resonate still. She mourns her husband, describing herself sitting on the edge of his gravestone beating her hands with grief while other wives sleep sweetly in their marriage beds. She dreams of the life they led or could still be leading together, despite any privations: 'Although there would be storm and snowdrift,/a day of seven gales,/Gregor would find me a little nook where/we would sleep in shelter.' She pours scorn on the patriarchy of Grey Colin and Black Duncan, her kinsmen who, having murdered her husband, now forced remarriage upon her with 'the Baron of the Watermeadow' who, despite the outward trappings of property and wealth, is old and mean and dry:

| | |
|---|---|
| 'S mor a b' annsa bhi aig Griogair, | I'd much prefer to be with Gregor, |
| Cuir a chruidh do 'n ghleann | driving his cattle to the glen, |
| Na bhi aig Baran crion na dalach, | Than with the dry old Baron-of-the-river meadow, |
| 'G ol air fion 's air leann. | drinking wine and ale. |

This indirect form of rape is added to her sufferings, yet her voice is strong.

Today, white water canoeists plunge down the gorge in safety helmets and life-vests, salmon leap up it, and the river, echoing in the narrow cleft like a widow's fingers drumming on her husband's coffin, flows on.

Twelve miles along the outflow from Loch Tay in western Atholl, the river passes Grandtully, more a scattering of houses than a village. On the hillside above is a difficult-to-find and tiny church. If you didn't know it was there, you'd miss it, and if you did stumble across it you'd think it was an old, single-storey barn. It was consecrated 500 years ago, whitewashed and completely devoid of decoration on the outside. It is reached through a field strewn with fresh daisies, grazing sheep and springing white lambs.

On a beautiful early summer's morning warm sunshine fills the strath, highlighting the green spring growth fringing the river, even budding high on the mountainsides across Tayside. The air is warm and still. The sounds of the day are the trilling of a blackbird fledgling in a hawthorn-blossomed hedgerow, the bleating of lambs. Yet in the lush kirkyard lies the corpse of a kestrel. On an old gravestone a father raises his knife to sacrifice his son; an angel with kestrel wings hovers. Inscribed on the stone:

Abraha/Mofferi/ngIsaac/Stay/ed/BY AN/ANGEL
[No angel stayed Grey Colin's hand]

Opening the wooden door and stepping over the threshold of the kirk, the contrast to the bright sunshine outside is stark – all is dark, dank, silent. I press the light switch and suddenly in my blinking vision an intricate pattern of colour and decoration starts to come into focus overhead. The wooden barrel-vaulted ceiling is a mass of late Renaissance ornament, heraldic escutcheons and scenes from the Bible. Painted over half the ceiling on wooden panels are a cornucopia of early seventeenth-century motifs, swags of lush fruit, naked angels with fat bottoms and puffed out cheeks tooting trumpets, vases of beautiful flowers, birds of all kinds – there's a heron . . . is that a capercaillie or a bubblyjock? They fit within a scheme of decorative panels dedicated to the Evangelists writing the gospels: St Luke dips his pen in an ink well; St John has his book open on his lap; a winged angel points out a line of text to St Matthew. Part of verse 11:29 of his gospel is written above a trompe l'oeil painting of a noblewoman before two open books on an altar or table:

of.me.for.I.am.lovlie.and.humbl

Another line – 'Hope.in.the.Lord.' – beseeches an allegorical figure with an anchor.

Some of the imagery is difficult to interpret – none more so than that of Christ, who in the act of ascending to heaven appears to pour water or wine or blood on a flaming, sacred heart. That an image so strongly associated with the Catholic Church should survive from this date is almost entirely down to it being a private chapel, and suggests that the family who commissioned it were powerful and sympathetic to King Charles I and his desire for anglicisation of the church in Scotland. It was a move that would ultimately see civil and religious war come to the Tay and the king beheaded.

Other elements of the decorative scheme are heraldic, relating to that local ruling family, 'W.S.' (William Stewart), 'The.Laird.of.Graintuilie' and of Murthly, further downstream, whose coat of arms contains two rather splendid three-masted, twelve-oared ships. Other noble houses remembered include the 'Duik.of.Lennox' and the 'Earle. of.Athoil', both fellow Stewarts – Atholl's forebearer committing the regicide of James I at Perth mentioned in the Dean of Lismore's book. The central panel at the apex of the ceiling is a scene of resurrection, where out of his canopied bed the laird, harpooned by a skeleton Death, is recalled to life by the blasts of two trumpeting angels. Outside, his ancestors rise from their tombs.

Someone who would not have approved of such decoration in a church was the Covenanter Donald Cargill. Cargill, born at Rattray, was the holder of such extremist Protestant views that even moderate Covenanters such as the Rev. James Ure of Shargarton baulked at supporting him: 'I told Mr Cargill that he rendered himself odious by his naughty principles. He was very much offended with me.'

A century after MacGregor's leap, Cargill – cast in the role of rebel, hunted and pursued under sentence of death – is said to have performed a similar jump at the spot on the river Ericht just outside Blairgowrie that bears his name. Given that he was fifty-five years old when first outlawed in 1674, and thus over sixty when executed in 1681, his supposed leap is all the more remarkable. By 1960 so many people had attempted to emulate his exploit and either injured or killed themselves in the attempt that the council used explosives to widen the gorge at Cargill's Leap to dissuade future jumping.

The leap leitmotif jumps from the action of rebel to that of brave government soldier at the Battle of Killiecrankie a decade later in July 1689. Following his side's defeat it is told that a redcoat was pursued down the pass by Jacobite troops of John Graham of Claverhouse, 'Bonnie Dundee'. Trapped between capture and the raging torrent of the river Garry he leapt more than twenty feet across the gorge and so to safety. To put this into context, a leap of a similar length would have won him the first long jump competition of the modern Olympic era. Why didn't they just shoot him? It may be that the pursuit took place in the dark. Claverhouse had held off engaging the Government troops until near sunset, so once over the water the red-coat would have been protected by night in the narrow pass. It would also explain this version of the story:

> At the Battle of Killiecrankie, a soldier who was running for his life, leaped across the pass and when he had got to the other side he shouted to his pursuers, '*Is gort a lean thu mi*' ('You have followed me closely'), to which the other, who turned out to be a Highlander, replied, '*Nan robh fios agam gu robh a' Ghàidhlig agad, cha do lean mi thu cho teann.*' ('If I had known that you spoke Gaelic, I would have not have pursued you so hotly.')

Highlander against Highlander, Lowlander against Lowlander, Campbell against MacGregor, Presbyterian against Episcopalian, brother against brother. A policy in the landed classes of one brother supporting the Hanoverians and another the Stuarts was a prudent hedging of bets throughout the Jacobite period.

A young man serving in the Jacobite army at Killiecrankie was Robert MacGregor. He was a descendent of Gregor Roy, Griogal Cridhe, and after being immortalised by Sir Walter Scott, in his novel *Rob Roy*, is Scotland's most famous outlaw. He was a watcher.

'Watch yer cattle fur yuz, mister?'

'Shame if thae wild Heilan' keelies stole them.'

'Me and the boys can take care o' them fur youze. Verrry reasonable rates, by the way.'

I am minded of my last trip to Tannadice to watch the Tayside derby – Dundee United v. St Johnstone. Parking in a residential road nearby, I wasn't even out of the door before three wee laddies are standing over me.

'Watch yir car, mister?' says the first.

'Five quid,' adds the second. 'Each.'

The third, under a mop of ginger hair, says, slowly running a hand over the bonnet, 'Nice paintwork.'

I am reminded of Rob Roy.

The patter's the same and the intent's the same. Watch money, or blackmail, is explained by Pennant while taking his eighteenth-century tour of Scotland: 'A contribution called the black meal, was raised by several of these plundering chieftains, over a vast extent of country: whoever payed it had their cattle ensured, but those who dared to refuse were sure to suffer.'

Blackmail was 'black' (wicked, evil or illegal) 'meal' (rent), as opposed to legal payment in white or silver coin. As Walter Scott writes in *Rob Roy*: 'They take pride in it, and reckon driving a spreagh (whilk is, in plain Scotch, stealing a herd of nowte) a gallant, manly action.'

It was Scott's novel that immortalised Rob Roy and his writing that made popular so many of the stories we now tell ourselves about the Highlands.

To the east of the Tay, a walking route follows the passageways north and south taken by these cattle rustlers. The Cateran Trail is a modern 64-mile circular walking route through the river's tributaries in Glen Shee, Glen Isla and Strathardle. 'Beware Adders' says a sign on a gate. If people are still defensive of their property here in this border country, then the caterans are, perhaps, one of the reasons why.

*Ceathairne* is the Gaelic name for men fit to bear arms in service of the clan, but as well as being defensive it can also signify men who will act at the behest of the chief; stout men, men who would form a raiding party. These raiding parties or spreaths descended on to the rich farming land of the Lowlands to steal cattle.

From the medieval to early modern period when cattle were currency, these caterans would come out of the Highlands plundering and killing men likely to pursue them, then disappear back into their intractable mountain homelands with their booty. While some incursions could be small scale, others were highly organised, with as many as 500 men from different clans cooperating on the bigger raids. Along the borderlands of Highland and Lowland Tayside strong defences were necessary. Pursuers were liable to be ambushed in the close and steep-sided glens, and thwarted by the extremely effective guerrilla tactics of the Highlanders before they got any chance to recover their beasts.

But why raid? Balances between survival and death were extremely precarious in these centuries. From state level down, stable and consistent governance was sporadic outside the main towns and burghs; in the Highlands local clan rule kept alive ancient practices, both good and bad. The geology and geography that separated north from south also meant that poorer soils, and less of them, led to subsistence farming. Being more prone to the vagaries of weather led to a vicious cycle of more frequent poor harvests to illness to famine to need. If your neighbour has plenty and you are in need, they may offer you sustenance, but if you continue to suffer the same shortages year after year that sympathy grows thin and a sense of injustice on both sides arises. The normal rules are set aside and thus it spirals downwards – chance and opportunity lead to scheming. The fox may occasionally steal the golden eagle's kill but the two crows flanking the buzzard on the fence post is a learned behaviour; for generations, they have relieved its forbearers of their catch. The eventual settling of the border warfare between Scotland and the adjacent kingdom of England in the mid seventeenth century saw the gradual ending of bloody internal disputes. It was to counteract the caterans and Jacobites and to keep order in the Highlands that the Independent Companies were first raised in the reign of Charles II and later recommissioned by General Wade in the 1720s, Perthshire's Black Watch, the 42nd Regiment of Foot, being raised in 1739.

Un-harassed ploughing and legitimate cattle dealing from Highland to Lowland along drove roads expanded, reaching a peak in the early nineteenth century. This intricate network of routes through and from the north to the main cattle markets at Crieff and Falkirk connect intimately to the Tay and its tributaries. Passing Barry Hill, the drovers would gather their cattle at Alyth before heading westwards to Blairgowrie and Dunkeld. In the next glen west from Glen Isla, drovers would transact business at Sillerburn on the Ardle by Kirkmichael, the name itself demonstrating the transition to a money-based culture. Transactions would be done with vendor and purchaser standing on opposite banks, sealing the deal over flowing water, making it indissoluble, oft-times settled with a dram.

In cars, planes, coaches and trains, in cabins aboard cruise ships docked at Dundee and freighters leaving Perth harbour returning to the Baltic, even in kayaks, whisky flows up and down the river. From airport duty-frees, distillery visitor centres, up the A9 from Cadenhead's shop in Glasgow or down from Gordon & MacPhail, Elgin, it pours. It travels inside 'special edition' bottles, tweed-lined boxes, handcrafted cases, single casks, supermarket malts, in drams glowing inside contented partakers. But it also travels in industrial bulk. In green 'Mundell' tankers, pilgrims from the west bearing peat-smoked Islay magic. From the north-east trundle 'MacPherson, Aberlour' and 'Chivas Brothers, Speyside'. They blend with aged 'Bell's' from the Tummel-side distillery at Pitlochry, on its way to bottling in Glasgow.

The Edradour distillery just south of Pitlochry, by comparison, is just a nipper. Situated on the eastern hillside above the Tummel, the now independent Edradour was, until recently, the smallest distillery in Scotland. It produces the same volume of whisky in a year that a Speyside distillery produces in a week. Legend has it that it was once controlled by the Costello mafia brotherhood through its purchase in 1938 by American bootlegger Irving Haim. In its long history, whisky has often found itself in that liminal world between the legal and illicit. As well as cattle, the Highland drovers heading for the southern markets would be carrying whisky distilled in a 'poit dhubh' (black pot) to sell. Edradour (in Gaelic, Eadar Dhà Dhobhar – 'between two rivers') has its source springs on the misty Moulin Moor and uses some of that water to cool the wort from the mash tun in a unique way. The wort is the warm liquid created when malted barley and spring water are mashed together in a large vat. With a temperature of about 70°C, it needs to be cooled before entering the washbacks, where the yeast is added to turn the sugars into alcohol. As a good baker knows, too hot a yeast will froth, bubble and die. At Edradour this cooling is done using a modern copy of a Morton Refrigerator, an old-fashioned method which uses cold water drawn from the burn to cool the wort as it gently flows down a series of weirs on a slatted metal table. This is the last of its kind still working in the whisky industry. The wort flows slowly over the slats like a river down a long series of gentle cataracts, taking two hours to cover six feet and lose 50 degrees of heat. A calendar hangs by the refrigerator, advertising its makers – Forsyths of Rothes – and this month's picture? A cascading Highland burn – human enterprise inspired by nature.

Inside the distillery's warehouse are stacked row upon row of barrels of whisky created from the local water: Edradour 2011 no. 043, 044, 045 . . .; Ballechin, the distillery's other main brand; and barrels already bought by customers like Mr Sakamoto's 2019, slumbering in the Tayside atmospherics. Whisky created from other waters, in other distilleries, some a long time ago, are also maturing here, drinking in the Perthshire air to add a unique flavour for the distillery's 'Signatory' brand: Islay Laphroaig 1998, Highland Tomatin 1993, Orkney Highland Park 2019. Some no longer in existence: the Speyside Dallas Dhu 1979 and Lowland Linlithgow 1982.

Over at Aberfeldy, the Tayside distillery of Dewar's is thriving, busy with seasonal visitors from the holiday chalets at Kenmore, the Taymouth Castle estate, the Breadalbane Arms, the caravan site across the road. Using the bespoke app or enjoying a dram in the tasting lounge, the living heritage of whisky-making is explained with clarity and passion. The name 'Dewar' comes from the Gaelic deòradh, a hereditary keeper of relics. The Dewars are said to originate in Glen Dochart, near the source of the Tay, and the relics are those of St Fillan, particularly a crozier and bell.

One of the duties associated with the 'Coigerach', the bearer of the crozier, was that of a clan shepherd or herdsman who had the authority to restore stolen cattle to their rightful owners, who could cure cattle diseases with the relic.

Now in the National Museum of Scotland, in 1819 it emigrated with the then hereditary keeper, Archibald Dewar, to Ontario. Even on the other side of the pond it retained its power, blessing the drinking water of the Canadian cattle of those who crossed over the sea. The quadrangular handbell was carried in ceremonial procession and rung at the coronation of the Scottish monarch at Scone, the last recorded instance being James IV's crowning in 1488.

Time flows, but at the Firth the tide turns and the waters – and other liquids – return. The Tay's newest distillery is by the ruins of Lindores Abbey. In its prospectus it makes much of the record in the Exchequer Rolls for Scotland for 1 June 1494 that refers to one of the Lindores monks: 'To Friar John Cor, 8 bolls of Malt, wherewith to make aqua vitae for King James . . .' This the earliest record of whisky making in Scotland.

Four miles south of the confluence of Tay and Tummel lies Dalguise, and opposite it Dowally, which gives its name to an island that is really no more than a large shingle bank, one of three or four which dot this section of the Tay. Here the wide river eases through the valley floor of Strathtay, which, though Highland, has a feel of the Lowlands, its wide lea meadows currently being excavated by mechanical diggers laying lines of ditches with black ribbed plastic drainage pipes. These meadows separate the river from the main A9 road on the east, which is further protected behind the embankment of the Inverness–Perth railway line. Signs shout 'PRIVATE. KEEP OUT'. The river is present, but difficult to access.

Wandering in the Dowally kirkyard, browsing the gravestones for familial names, I feel excluded, though I have deep connection to this place. My ancestor James Borrie was baptised here in 1730, as was his daughter Isobel in 1764, but when she married David Hume thirty years later, she moved a dozen miles downstream to set up their family home in Spittalfield in the parish of Caputh.

The year before their marriage the *Old Statistical Account* for the Parish of Caputh of 1793 records the birds on the Tay:

Migratory Birds − Of these, the cuckoo, the swallow, lapwing, sandy-lark, plover, rail or corncraik, seagull, sea-magpie, pictarny [black-headed gull] or kittiwake, curlew or whaup, and clocharet [wheatear], are summer birds. The fieldfare, woodcock, and wild geese are winter birds. The swallow appears about the 14th of April; the earliest time of the cuckoo's being heard, is the 25th of April, but usually not before the 2d or 3d of May. It is heard till the 10th of June, and last year, as late as the 3d of July.

The cuckoo has been a long-time visitor.

A frog hops into lush vegetation. Cuckoos have spat on this morning's fresh stems. Perched on an erect pine, thyrus-like, at the entrance of the ravine, a male bird creates an echo each time it calls. 'Cuckoo − oo, cuckoo − oo.' Without eliciting a response from a female, however, its singing pleasures only itself.

In the perfect blue sky a buzzard is being harassed by a shabby crow, flipping from top to side to underbelly, annoying the raptor off its patch before returning to its treetop nest at the very top of an amputee oak tree. A robin is sounding off (nothing new there). Chaffinches call to each other across the scar of the gorge, which is healing the winter's sharp assaults with rounded oak leaves, soft green cones and orange flower clusters of the

Norway spruce, the sweet-scented rowan blossom, the pussy willow catkins fluffing to seed. Lower down in the understory I find the identification of the small tree birds confusing, with their avian havers, never still. The 'weeeet' bird – pale fawn, buff, a black dash of pirate mascara – has one of the stream's mayflies in its beak but still keeps singing, keeps on hunting. How does it grab another without dropping the first? A darker brown bird hopping from branch to branch in the next birch seems to be making the same call. All the while the curlews on the hill pasture above have been periodically raising their voices, piping in 'whirrrr, whirrrr, whroooooo'-ing complaint.

A throaty grumbling joins their chorus of discontent from a channelled burn forced into the unnatural confines of a ribbed black plastic pipe. A flock of crow-like flies takes off from a footprint-squashed shit while more feast on the squeezed oozing innards of the pipe-like body of a black ribbed slug, its silver flow of life crusting and drying in the hot early June sun. Green-veined whites and small copper butterflies join feather fluff teasel seeds of the willow in animate and inanimate cavorts, both, to my eye, utterly irrational in their apparently mindless hoverings, flitterings, yet both brim full of life. A honey-brown bee is investigating blue/purple flowers of creeping bugle plants, but as to naming the type of bee, again I am flittering – bumble, honey, mason, mining? The second wasp – or is it the very similar cuckoo bee? – of the morning investigates me. I stay stock still, not letting it mob me. Over the rasping hum I hear the crow, having seen off the buzzard, now squabbling with its family.

The drooping flowers of water avens hang their heads mournfully in the damp ground splashed by the gorge's stream, waiting to snare a passerby with the hooks on their seed heads. Prickly thistles – spear, creeping, marsh, melancholy – are starting to thrust up; burnt gorse has charcoal sticks of branches still waving stegosaurus tails of spikes. Nettles brandish stinging antlers. The bark is deer-stripped from a willow trunk. New spines on a young conifer jag out from the plastic netting of the guard mesh protector, bursting with life but around it plenty of the cages are empty where the saplings have failed to grow. On the bleached trunk of a felled tree the black diamonds of an adder lie as lifeless as its twin carved on a Pictish stone. It soaks up the returning sun's heat, rejuvenating, last year's skin cast aside. The same sun bleaches the discarded plastic wrapper of a PowerBar with '35% more protein, fruits of the forest', snared in the thorns of a patch of white flowering brambles and wild raspberries that are spreading black, spiked stems round, over and through the moss-tumbled drystane dyke. Follow the wall along and on a part-rusted six-bar metal gate there again is the cuckoo.

The cuckoo, or gowk in Scots, is a harbinger of spring. It fools other birds into rearing its young and thus is both clever and cunning. On the first of April the children along the river would play Huntigowk, or 'Hunt the Gowk', a game where people were sent on fools' errands. Perth poet William Soutar uses the bird's reputation for trickery in his 1933 poem:

'The Gowk'

Half doun the hill, whaur fa's the linn
Far frae the flaught o' fowk,
I saw upon a lanely whin
A lanely singin' gowk:
Cuckoo, cuckoo;
And at my back
The howie hill stüde up and spak:
Cuckoo, cuckoo.

There was nae soun': the loupin' linn
Was frostit in its fa':
Nae bird was on the lanely whin
Sae white wi' fleurs o' snaw:
Cuckoo, cuckoo;
I stüde stane still;
And saftly spak the howie hill:
Cuckoo, cuckoo.

Over the mirror surface of the Loch of the Lowes in Caputh parish, I am looking at two other spring visitors from Africa 60 feet up in lochside trees. Travelling all the way from the Gambia, ospreys are recorded here in Dunkeld parish in the *New Statistical Account* of 1845 as one of its migratory birds.

LM12 has found a mate and is perched calmly at the very top of a silver birch. His mate, LF15, is sitting on the brim of their nest in the century-old Scots pine overlooking the Loch of the Lowes. Underneath her, two hungry chicks peek out. I stare back from the two-storied hide across the water at their nest, artificially constructed out of branches and twigs on an old potato basket, their every move monitored on live-streaming cameras, strategically sited after fifty years of egg thieving, human nest destruction, bad weather and inept ospreys. The female is agitated; her mate has not supplied her and her chicks with fish.

All down the river, other birds have fish in their mouths. On the loch below, grebes feed them to their young, then, after preening, give them some feathers to eat to help the chicks digest the bones. At Loch Tay a piscivorous red-breasted merganser swallows a grayling. Perched on a blue door in Newburgh, a shining brass kingfisher knocker, fish in beak. On Lindores Loch the roles are reversed and a pike swallows a duckling.

Hunger steals childhood. What do you do when you can no longer feed your children, when you see the sources of income drying up and the tide of household costs and debts rising, each day a perilous balancing act between surviving and going under?

Though aged forty, David Hume, one of 130 weavers in Caputh parish on the Tay, reached the tipping point in the summer of 1803. Ten years earlier the *Old Statistical Account* had noted:

> . . . weavers earn from 1s. 4d. to 2s. a-day: when trade is brisk, an active workman will gain much more; for as he usually buys the yarn which he manufactures, his profits from the sale of his cloth are, in this case, very great. It is to be observed, however, that they are seldom more than 9 months engaged in weaving; that is,

from Martinmas to the end of August, or beginning of September, when the lint-harvest commences. The scarcity, and the consequent high wages of men servants, are chiefly owing to the numbers now employed in weaving, tempted by the profits made in this branch of manufacture.

By 1803 water-powered mills were churning out linen and cotton more speedily, more consistently and more cheaply than traditional handloom weavers like Hume could ever match. After a cold, hungry winter of fieldfares, woodcock and wild geese, with no other options left but to stretch out a desperate hand, he took the King's shilling.

The 'Gallant 42': the 42nd Regiment of Foot, the Tay's regiment, the Black Watch. Who were these men flowing out of the country, selling themselves for a bounty to escape the restrictions of life along its banks, for themselves, for their children, for the benefit of their families? What pressures were put on them to enlist by His Grace, the hereditary Duke of Atholl, his factors, ministers, neighbours, high politics, industrial economics? What we do know is that in Hume's company the majority of privates were labourers and weavers, those at the very edge of the breadline whose lives were at a low ebb desperately in need of a lifeline.

Labourers and weavers, a blacksmith, a courier, a couple of tailors, two carpenters, a mason, a shoemaker and more weavers and labourers are recorded in 'Description Roll of Captain Richard Smith's Company 2nd Battalion, 42 (Royal Highland)'. It tells us facts about them, but, like water, light dapples momentarily and then it is past. Hume's 'Person' is 'well made', his 'Head' is 'round', his 'Face' 'long', 'Eyes' 'grey', 'Eyebrows' 'thin', 'Nose' 'small', 'Mouth' 'wide', 'Neck' 'short', 'Hair' 'fair', 'Shoulders' 'round', 'Arms' 'short', 'Hands' 'small', 'Thighs' 'thin', 'Legs' 'thin', his 'Feet' are 'small'. Scanning the roll my eye catches the colour of the eyes of these men who flowed out and away, migrating across the world from the confines of this land of mountain and flood: brown, grey, blue, hazel, grey, black, blue, brown, black, grey, grey, hazel, brown, black, brown. But like looking into the moving river, it is impossible to penetrate the surface. The cuckoo cries, eyes fill with tears.

> . . . I never will forget the day his regiment walked past
> The pipes they played a lively tune but my heart was
>   aghast
> He turned around and smiled farewell, and then from
>   far awa'
> He waved to me the tartan of the Gallant Forty Twa.

The 'Black Watch' was created as part of the early eighteenth-century reforms General Wade brought in, in tandem with his road-building scheme. The regiment's dark uniform earned them their nickname 'Am Freiceadan Dubh' in Gaelic; their hearts, it was said, as dark as the tartan of their kilts.

> Enlist my bonnie laddie an' come awa'
> And it's over the mountain and over the Main,
> Through Gibraltar, to France and Spain.

Pit a feather tae your bonnet, and a kilt aboon your
knee,
Enlist my bonnie laddie and come awa with me.

What happened to Hume? The battalion was to fight
Napoleon in the bloody Peninsular War in Spain, with
many casualties.

It seems that David Hume, my fourth great-grandfather,
did not return. And what of Isobel and their children?
Weaving was an occupation that employed a whole
household not just the man: 'the earnings of the man and
woman cannot be separated, as they are both employed
in manufacturing the same piece of cloth'. The annual
income of these 'industrious poor' families in the parish
could reach £23, against an expenditure of £15 in the
good years, an £8 surplus. The signing fee for the Black
Watch would be £10. A further £10 was paid to recruits
later, but how this or part of this was transferred back to
Isobel and families like theirs, if at all, is unclear.

Following that journey downriver from Dowally to
Caputh taken by Isobel Borrie, the river is no less wide
but the landscape closes in about you. At Dunkeld and
Birnam the river becomes accessible again as it scours
a path through the last of the Highland hills to form a
gorge. This narrow pass is forested, craggy, often mist-
shrouded. It is a gateway. Here in the mile or so of the Tay's
western bank, between the outflows of the river Braan
at Inver and of the Inchewan Burn at Birnam, much is
compressed into a short stretch of the Tay, geographically,

historically, culturally. If my family connection to the wider Strathtay now feels tenuous here, other cultural influences feel stronger, run deeper, seem more relevant to who I am.

Plowtering about in my bare feet in the Inchewan Burn, I listen to the music of the river, watch it paint the pebbles with the colours of Scotland. I see the sunlight capture the momentary movement of the water, see it reflect the dramatic branches of Macbeth's oak, mirror the holiday home of Beatrix Potter in its surface, hear the lament of Highlanders passing out of their homeland forever.

Whilst the poorest of his tenants became cannon fodder, His Grace John Murray, the 4th Duke of Atholl, used artillery pieces to fire an estimated twenty million tree seeds over his vast Tayside estates. If Hume and his fellow conscripts found themselves touring Europe in the brutal company of the Duke of Wellington, for the British upper classes the Napoleonic Wars had the opposite effect, cutting off travel to the continent. Grand Tourists started to stream to Scotland, soon enticed further by Walter Scott's bestselling poem *The Lady of the Lake* (1810) and then his blockbuster Jacobite novel *Waverley* (1814). Where money went, artists and poets followed. The painter J. M. W. Turner toured widely in Highland Scotland in the early years of the nineteenth century, painting upriver at Tummel Bridge and, in a sketch now in the Tate Gallery, on the Lyon at MacGregor's Leap. Scott's writings were presenting a vision of Highland Scotland that appealed to the romantic. It was a vision so strong it not only captivated sentiment across Europe at the time but persisted and grew throughout the rest of the nineteenth century. The trickle of tourists along the Tay became a flood after the purchase of Balmoral by Prince Albert for his wife Victoria, and the mid-century development of railways opened up access to the Highlands for the burgeoning middle classes.

Dundee celebrated the Queen's visit of 1844 by erecting an elaborate Royal Arch by its docks. While royalty could afford original artworks by Turner or Landseer, these were out of the reach of the middle classes. For the rising numbers of tourists a new technology offered them a way of memorialising their visit. The Queen's favourite photographer, George Washington Wilson, is known for his Highland travel photographs and mementoes of Scottish excursions. His training as an artist informed the composition of his landscapes in the new medium of photography. While drawings and engravings illustrated the early nineteenth-century travel guides to Scotland and provided regular income for Scottish landscape painters, photographs were to replace them from the middle of the century. Wilson was a leader in developing this new form, his skill not only in replicating the oils, watercolours and engravings of traditional artists, but exploring the possibilities of this new media that combined art and science at an affordable price. In *The Salmon Leap, on the Tilt, Blair Atholl* or *Birnam Falls, Dunkeld* (*c.* 1860), Wilson structures the images as an artist would. In *Birnam Falls*, at the top of the photograph a Highland cascade pours from a tree-lined gorge. The waterfall is positioned in the centre; we view it from the pool, looking up, giving the impression of its height. The black solidity of the rock is contrasted with the white liquidity of the water. What the new medium offers, though, is the feeling of, and indeed the actual capturing of, time. While the ancient rock remains immobile, the impermanent water flows. The real-time process of uncovering the camera's blackened lens and allowing light to flood onto the photographic plate captures the actual movement of the water in a way that most painting could never achieve. The blurred white of the falling water has an ephemeral quality separate from everything else in the picture, not only the immemorial rock but the seasonal delicacy of the leaves on the trees. The trees for a few decades will fringe the river – their trunks and twigs a thin, black reflection of the linn's many branches – but they will rot and die. The photograph of the waterfall I take today standing where Wilson stood 160 years ago captures exactly the same water, the same rocks, though the surrounding vegetation is different. Where the free-falling water stops in the pool at the bottom of the image, it changes tone as it slows, now fading to grey, neither still nor torrent but moving gently, easing our eye out of the picture and on, like the river, beyond these moments with the course of our journey.

The sensation of movement captured in the photograph thrilled Victorian viewers and was developed further by innovations such as stereoscopic cards, where double images placed side by side gave a binocular feeling of depth and space, such as his *Fall on the Braan at the Hermitage Bridge, Dunkeld* of 1863. By the 1880s Wilson was further experimenting, printing his images onto glass plates that were then hand-coloured and could be viewed as 'magic lantern' slides, Wilson himself presenting lectures to accompany a showing. By the time of his death in 1893 his photographic publishing firm was employing forty people and accepting images from photographers from all over the world. His only rival operating on the same scale was James Valentine in Dundee.

The art/science of photography was not limited to the professional. By the 1870s amateurs such as the Rev. MacKenzie from Kenmore were capturing life along the Tay. Raised on the remote islands of St Kilda, his fascination for the everyday has left us a unique portfolio of the people, buildings and animals on its banks. As well as the collapsed crannog, he seems to have been particularly interested in Highland cattle (perhaps having not encountered them on Hirta). Local history also interested him. He recorded the early Christian handbell at Fortingall and, on an excursion south to the Sma' Glen, picnickers by Ossian's Stone, showing that domestic tourism along the Tay was thriving in the Victorian age.

In Birnam and later at Dalguise, amateur photographer Rupert Potter encouraged his daughter Beatrix in the medium whilst on their Tayside holidays from 1871. It made a change from having to endure her father's angling stories – all about the ones that got away – while he fished with his friends, but she had her revenge later, turning him into a frog named Jeremy Fisher in one of her books for children. At the Beatrix Potter Exhibition in Birnam Arts Centre, a bronze statue of Jeremy Fisher sits beside the pond, fishing, at no risk from being eaten by a trout.

Many of Potter's characters were based on people, creatures and activities she encountered during childhood summer holidays in the area.

Scott's romantic vision of the Highlands attracted the Potters north and continues to define our image of the upper Tay today. The reality for those who lived in the Highlands was very far from 'romantic'. At Inver at the beginning of the century, Niel Gow, a natural musical genius who Robert Burns described as 'a short, stout-built, honest Highlander figure, with grayish hair on his honest social brow; an interesting face, marking strong sense, kind openheartedness, mixed with unmistrusting simplicity', played for tourist pennies. In the 1870s Sergeant Donald MacDonald, who did return from the Napoleonic Wars and lived with his sister, Kitty, at Milton of Kincraigie, regaled holidaying visitors like the Potters with his patriotic tales of battle, while Kitty had the unenviable job of laundering their dirty clothes.

Beatrix Potter describes Kitty as 'a comical round little old woman, as brown as a berry [who] wears a multitude of petticoats and a white much'. Kitty was transformed by her into Mrs Tiggywinkle, a hedgehog.

Inside the Birnam Arts Centre today, children delight in trying on a Mrs Tiggywinkle costume: white linen cap, long skirts and petticoats, complete with wooden 'spines' projecting from the back. In a game, a whole life cycle is played out – child becomes adult, worker and servant, then becomes an old woman. Children dress up as part of their learning about the world, act out roles, then return to being themselves in preparation for adulthood.

Clothing or uniform identifies us with our tribe or clan – tartan, tweed, petticoat or mutch: they signify class and role in life. Potter uses animals to explain to children how her world works and how they should behave. It can be a brutal world. Peter Rabbit's father in seeking to take food from the Victorian middle-class is himself turned into food and baked in Mrs McGregor's pie. The continued popularity of Potter's stories tells us much about our own world.

Our animal nature lies beneath the surface; we cover ourselves with our clothing. But our clothes are soiled, dirtied, tarnished, impregnated with marks of our physical existence and have to be cleansed. The Potter family paid for Miss MacDonald to launder their clothes, to lather away signs of life unmentionable in polite Victorian society: sweat, incontinence, menstruation, fornication. To beat out the stains of life's acquired sins: greed, lust, inebriation. It reveals much about the clothes wearer – things perhaps we'd rather keep secret – but it's an unpleasant task, one we'd rather not have to do ourselves. If you can afford to, best to get someone else to do it.

That role fell upon those at the lowest end of Tayside society: poor women. Laundresses would either come to houses to do the washing in basement rooms or outhouses, or to take it away with them, out of sight using the Tay's pure water to wash away the stains of Victorian life.

Even the act of cleaning can be tarnished. The male gaze sought sexual gratification in watching women launder clothes. George Cruikshank's 1810 print *Scotch Washing* depicts women tramping clothes in tubs by a river with their dresses tucked up to reveal their legs. It is a motif Scott inserts into his bestselling novel, where Waverley 'observed two bare-legged damsels, each standing in a spacious tub, performing with their feet the office of a patent washing machine'. This became a subject for many a 'saucy postcard'-type print, where the height of the skirts rises and the amount of leg shown increases. The central figure is depicted like Botticelli's *Venus* emerging from the waves, embedding the notion that those who service the visitor's domestic needs can also provide for other wants. With typical Victorian ambivalence, those women deemed to have 'fallen' would be sent to workhouse laundries. But rather than rising from the warm Mediterranean waters like a goddess, or Scott's 'damsels', the reality was that a laundress's work required them to trample clothes even in the depths of winter in freezing water. Their legs and feet were mottled with the cold (known as 'tinker's tartan'), their fingers worn red raw from washing.

Potter notes how wrinkly laundering makes Tiggy-winkle's hands. Later the washboard replaced the need to beat linens against the riverside rocks to force the dirt-soaked water through the fabric. All along the river's length the wood, zinc, glass-ridged surfaces of women's washboards glinted and dripped and sang to the rhythm of hard, dirty work.

Potter chose to depict Miss MacDonald as a hedgehog, a small, timid creature but with prickly defences – an eater of slugs, different from them. Kitty was not just small, she was stunted from a childhood of malnutrition and poverty. Potter wrote of her:

The simple fact is that people, even the Scotch who are still tolerable savages, cannot with the modern ideas of decency and comfort subsist like rabbits.

This old woman living all alone, the last of her race, might be expected to look back with sentimental love for the past, but the circumstances most insistent in her memory appeared to be 'the stinting' which she endured and which stunted her growth as a girl.

Kitty's father had a small croft but died soon after she was born. Aged seven, she was sent to an uncle's hill croft, where she tended sheep and cattle in the high pastures. Life was frugal. Kitty never forgot the privation.

Unlike the Potters' fine linens, Kitty and her family 'were content to wear the coarse worsted of their own flocks, their scanty stock of hand-spun linen lasted practically a lifetime'. The cloth was produced for personal use in the cots of home weavers like the MacDonalds. Linen for sale, woven on the handlooms like the Humes', or in water-powered mills, was manufactured all along the Tay. Wool came from the sheep that during the post-Jacobite period replaced people cleared from the Highlands to make way for them. Cotton came from the slave lands of America; flax was imported from the Baltic States and woven into sailcloth for the warships protecting the shipping lines, expanding the Empire, and for merchant ships importing the cotton from America and later jute from India. It was woven into osnaburg, a cheap form of linen used to clothe the slaves picking the cotton, and all financed by the flow of money from Scotland's banking systems.

These connections were like the very cogs and gears driving the watermill-powered cotton-spinning factory you can visit today at Stanley. The inventor of the cotton-spinning water frame, Richard Arkwright, was one of the original investors in the mill. While the waters of the Tay were used to drive the mill wheel, it was the people – mainly women and children – working thirteen-hour shifts, feeding the machines slave-picked cotton, repairing breaks in the yarn, that made mill owners their disproportionate profits.

Bleaching was also an important part of the Tay's cloth industry – and a beloved metaphor of generations of Presbyterian ministers and their adherents along the river. A bleaching works operated at Stormontfield outside Perth from 1787 to 1971, its lade filtering the waters of the Tay through a number of sluices to keep it pure. The mill would take delivery of huge rolls of raw brown cloth from all over Britain, Ireland and even from India to be boiled, bleached, rinsed, then tinted to the shade of white or, if necessary, dyed in the sister works at Huntingtower. The cloth was then cut to the width required and dispatched all over the world, oftentimes to emigré Scots.

As tourists flooded in, native Highlanders were cleared out. Potter continues her biography of Kitty MacDonald, writing that Strath Braan was once full of people but, like Kitty's uncle, they emigrated to America in a convoy. The old crofter farms would never return.

Orphaned, unprivileged, Scottish, Highland, single . . .
spines projecting through her clothes, revealing her animal
nature, just as her speech, her poverty, remind them that
she is not as human as they, even though Mrs Tiggywinkle/
Kitty MacDonald is dressed in Victorian fashion. As the
washer of their clothes, she knows their dirty, shameful
secrets and so is both patronised and feared, indulged and
kept in her place.

Within a week of returning to Birnam as an adult in
1892, Potter had already collected the local gossip on
Kitty before paying her a visit: 'She became confidential
and told me the history which I already knew, of her reasons for leaving Kincraigic . . . that her neighbours teased
her for a witch.'

On revisiting the past, sometimes things are gladly
remembered, others best forgotten. Potter noted: 'Her
memory goes back for seventy years and I really believe
she is prepared to enumerate the articles of her first wash
in the year '71.'

Kitty lived out the remaining years of her long life in
the old ferryman's cottage at Inver. The ferry had been
painted by Alexander Nasmyth, but had fallen into disuse
after Telford's bridge was built at Dunkeld ( a bridge that
for all its elegance houses a prison cell under its eastern
bank). Next door to Niel Gow's cottage, it was now the
village poorhouse, as Miss MacDonald ended her life as
she had spent her ninety-two years, 'stinting'.

If you regard fellow humans, to use Potter's words, as
'savages', then you allow yourself to treat them inhumanly.

*

On the northern border of Atholl in 1798, Donald Campbell (known in Gaelic as Dòmhnall Phàill, Donald son of Paul) was born in Dalnaspidal by the river Garry. A shepherd and poet in the Ossianic tradition, his verses and songs were composed and recorded in his head. But just as each pool of a river relies on the one before and the one after it to continue the river's journey, so the bardic culture relied a continuous line of poets working in the oral tradition to memorise and recite their works. It also needs a society with a culture of listening. Whilst today we use the word 'ceilidh' to describe a formal dance, in the original Gaelic it just meant a gathering in a domestic setting where there would be music and dancing but also songs sung, verses recited, news and gossip exchanged. The Highland Clearances came so suddenly and savagely upon that society that as a result only five of Campbell's songs are known. As the introduction to these few remaining verses notes, 'Nobody thought of taking them down at the time; and in his latter years the old bard could rarely be prevailed upon to sing the songs of his youth.'

What was the point of singing a song when the culture that was integral to its creation had been destroyed? His most famous song is 'Guma Slàn Do Na Fearaibh' ('Here's Good Health to the People'), known as 'The Emigrant's Song', recording the leaving of their homeland by cleared Highlanders. Unlike his contemporary, the Poet Laureate Robert Southey, who we will encounter later on our journey and who composed his 'Inchcape Rock' before he ever came near it (and then when he did, only viewed it from the shore six miles away), Donald Paul witnessed the events he describes first hand as they happened. Just as his Highland predecessors would stand and observe a battle, a gathering, an execution, a funeral and compose verses, so, on the feast day of St Columba in 1838, he participated in the climbing of the hill of Creag Bheag, where tears flowed and musicians played as the emigrants bade farewell to their ancestral homes. He joined them on their long walk to Fort William, where they took ship to Oban and thence left Scotland forever for Australia. Of the 326 who left, ten died on the four-month voyage and five babies were born.

Donald had been going to join them, but in the end he turned back after composing this:

*Gu 'm a slàn do na fearaibh*
*Thèid thairis a' chuan*
*Gu talamh a' gheallaidh*
*Far nach fairich iad fuachd,*
*Gu 'm a slàn do na fearaibh*
*Thèid thairis a' chuan.*

A health to the fellows,
Who'll cross o'er the sea!
To the country of promise,
Where no cold will they feel.
A health to the fellows,
Who'll cross o'er the sea!

When we're gone from this country,
Our rents will be trifling;
And Martinmas will not

Bring blush to our cheek.
A health to the fellows,
Who'll cross o'er the sea!

We'll depart from this region,
Where nothing will flourish,
The potatoes are ruined,
And won't grow for the cold.
A health to the fellows,
Who'll cross o'er the sea!

There we'll get silk and ribbons
We'll get wool in abundance;
And the wives will make cloth
In the style of the North.
A health to the fellows,
Who'll cross o'er the sea!

They will not arouse us,
With the bell of Kingussie;
Nor will it much matter,
Though we wake not so soon
A health to the fellows,
Who'll cross o'er the sea!

To the country of promise,
Where no cold will they feel.
A health to the fellows,
Who'll cross o'er the sea!

They would be blushing on Martinmas (11 November),
one of the old Scottish term days when rents would be

due, when cattle were either slaughtered or moved into the inbye near the home, and the harvest stored for the coming winter, but such was the paucity of food that they could neither afford to pay rents nor provide for themselves. So they look forward to a better life in a new land, the open optimism covering a deep, deep undercurrent of sadness and loss.

Ochain, ochain, ochone.

I am standing again on that wee bridge at Birnam gazing at the Inchewan Burn as it gurgles below me to meet its destiny with the Tay. At this first and last of Atholl's crossing places – between upland and lowland, Gaelic and Scots, the past and future – the Highland Tay itself is about to end and the Lowland river begin.

Water does not flow upstream; the past cannot return, nor would we want it to, but the river – like people – carries within itself memory of what it has been to enable it to be what it will be in the future. Somewhere nearby, perhaps in the branches of Macbeth's oak, a birdsong echoes. 'Cuckoo, cuckoo . . .'

# Glen Almond

## *A Tryst*

By the old ferryman's cottage at Inver, the Braan flows into the Tay. Follow it uphill past the Hermitage and Rumbling Bridge, then cross the watershed and meet the Almond as it flows south, before it angles east to join the Tay at Perth.

The Almond is a discreet river. The upper river keeps itself to itself in a quiet, steep glen away from main modern routes, avoiding towns and cities. A mere 30 miles long, its lower stretches are an epitome of a certain Tayside mix, being home to an industrial estate which houses the Perth abattoir and the Inveralmond Brewery (Ossian Ale, its signature brand), and country villages that are now almost exclusively occupied by urban commuters. Suburban villas, country houses, country house hotels, shooting estates, an exclusive boarding school in Glenalmond College, a dog-training centre and kennels all line its banks. Recently an illegal puppy farm was raided by police and the SSPCA. More traditional working farms – pasture in the west, arable in the east – line the river's banks.

From the green iron-girdered bridge spotted with rust over the river at Millhaugh, an azure blur is a kingfisher rising from the water, the dying fish in its sharp beak a semi-circle of silver. In the fields where the Almond joins the Tay, the previous course of the river can be traced in the dark crop marks which, when the golden barley is tall enough and the wind blowing, can make the river seem to flow over them again. Crop-markings also reveal where once the angular walls of a Roman fort stood: Rath inver Amon, or Bertha, according to the fourteenth-century chronicler John of Fordoun. New forces are building roads here now, moving the earth, bridging the river, changing the flow of traffic as the current westward expansion of Perth mixes with the widening of the A9. New roundabouts like eddies spin traffic down new channels, feeding into new tributaries of the city cut straight as a drainage pow.

An alternative route north lies twelve miles along the Almond. A ferocious series of rapids and waterfalls at the Buchanty Spout divide the upland and lowland river. Past Buchanty, the hills close in tightly and the Highlands are almost upon you. The Highlandman Loan from Strathearn joins up with General Wade's Old Military Road of 1730 as you head into the Sma' Glen. My journey is slowed by a shepherd driving his flock along the road to new sprouted upper pastures. His border collie flows like the wind to his sharp whistles, his crook reaches out and hooks a lamb from the roadside ditch with an instinctive movement that is millennia old in its effectiveness and grace.

The Almond and the road run side by side through the glen, snug between the steep slopes of the Highland foothills. Through winter-browned and wind-toasted heather, green brackens are thrusting upwards, pushing at the edges of bare, grey scree fields, trying to establish a foothold, a precarious task: at any time the rocks can give way and even in late May a hail of stones can rain down. The river courses south; my course is north. Where the glen widens, the river slows, dividing its channel between garths of raised beaches of bleached white stones. Where it narrows, the river speeds up and the road is forced to climb the side of the hill. A thin band of pines separate our routes.

Bluebells are now wilting after an exhausting display unmatched in vivacity in recent years. Pale white honesty flowers with the innocent hope of youth in the dappled shade of birches. Rowan and ash still open out their papery new season's leaves, reaching out over the boulders that line the river, deposited there by river, hill and glacier – water, gravity or ice. Cold but inviting, I slip off my shoes and socks and succumb to its winking allure. Amongst these riparian boulders the river's waters are slow, brown, clouded with peat, but in mid-stream they run with that pure, clear, slightly blue opacity of many Highland mountain streams: icy, bubbled as handcrafted glass. I step from stone to stone out into the river. Looking down, the water's surface is contoured with ripples as it flows over the boulders it has rounded underneath my feet. Thriving on them are slimy water-weeds. The power of the river forces them to cling on tightly to each rock so that they look like the hills above, as depicted on the mid eighteenth-century military map of the glen by General Roy. Around them smaller stones of different sizes are blurred by the flow; peach, buff, grey and pale blue, some speckled like a clutch of eggs collected from all the different nests of the glen.

Along the glen lies another boulder, a massive one, its history wrapped in opacity. The so-called Ossian's Stone has been a waymarker for travellers for millenia, but in the early eighteenth century, when General Wade was driving his military road along the Almond, he decided that it was in his way and had to be moved. The Hanoverian government of the newly unified kingdom of Great Britain had decided to go beyond the Roman policy of containment, of controlling access to and from the Highland glens with forts at their Lowland ends; instead, they took an offensive policy of military roadbuilding into the heartlands of potentially and actual rebellious clans who, despite the failure at Sheriffmuir, still supported a separate Scottish state and/or a Stewart monarchy. The sixth verse of the British national anthem beseeches:

Lord grant that Marshal Wade,
May by Thy mighty aid,

Victory bring.
May he sedition hush,
And like a torrent rush,
Rebellious Scots to crush,
God save the King!

A show of strength, a touch of cultural vandalism. On levering the stone out of its position Wade's soldiers discovered a small stone cist grave containing burnt bones. Presuming that only the Romans would have the technological skill to lift such a huge and heavy object, it was declared that this was the grave of a Roman officer and the bones would be kept as a military souvenir. The Highland soldiers under Wade's command were appalled; it was obvious to them that though they did not know whose bones they were, to deserve such a burial they must be of a great ancestral person worthy of the utmost respect. They insisted on reburial, firing their muskets over the new grave.

By 1805, the stone had become to the early romantic tourists, like William Wordsworth in his poem 'Glen-Almain', the very grave of Ossian himself:

In this still place, remote from men,
Sleeps Ossian, in the NARROW GLEN.

The name Ossian became known throughout Europe in 1762, when the Scottish poet James Macpherson 'discovered' the poems of Oisín, first with the epic 'Fingal' and the following year with 'Temora'. Both of these works were supposedly translations from third-century Gaelic originals. Actually, although based in part on genuine Gaelic oral ballads, the works were largely the invention of Macpherson. They tell the tales of Ossian and his father Fionn/Fingal and his son, Oscur, in the dim and misty Celtic past, where bravery and just cause are eventually overwhelmed by the indifference and anarchy of the world, of fate.

The poems were published in Edinburgh within twenty years of the Battle of Culloden, the death knell of traditional clan culture. The reworked poems were hugely popular – admired by Jefferson in the newly independent States, Goethe in Germany, Napoleon in revolutionary France, who carried a pocket edition in his uniform coat. People saw in them an alternative tradition that could inform different futures from the ones they were rebelling against and change the course of history. Claims that the published Ossian works were fake misunderstand Highland culture. Macpherson saw himself working within the oral, bardic tradition that James MacGregor had written down and recorded in the *Book of the Dean of Lismore* we encountered earlier. The teller of a story does not read a printed text where the words are immobile on a page.

Nor is it an instruction manual like the medieval *Murthly Hours*, designed to regulate and unify practice and belief across Europe from Papal Rome. The Tayside village of Murthly gives its name to this thirteenth-century Book of Hours, once owned by the Stewarts of Grandtully, now in the National Library of Scotland. Its pages are beautifully handwritten and illustrated with miniatures of scenes from the Bible, illuminated letters and marginal drawings. Almost certainly created in Paris, it has been added to with further illustrations in England before coming into the possession of the Stewart family probably sometime in the fifteenth century when Gaelic text was added. The 'hours' are the monastic divine offices – Matins, Lauds, Prime, Terce, Sext, None, Vespers and Compline – each marked by a bell ringing the changes of prayer and worship throughout the day. The book also contains a calendar, a list of Saints days, penitential psalms and the Offices of the Dead. It instructs the lay reader, almost certainly a noble woman, in the timings of daily, monthly, yearly and life rituals and devotions, but it also instructs her how to be a good Christian.

History is claimed as fact but 'Ossian' is from that reciting and listening culture where verse becomes a poetic work of the moment, of the time and the place of the telling; fluid. The Tay may not be called 'Tay' at its source on Ben Lui – it is fed by waters from lochs and burns, each with their own character – but it is still the Tay. All Macpherson did that was different was to write his interpretation down, merging the spoken and written into one as that ancient oral tradition ended.

Across Europe cultures were being challenged by the rise of the nation state, colonialism and industrialisation. The Scottish painter David Allan had captured the remnants of an similarly ancient culture of the rural communities on the island of Mallorca and on returning home in the 1780s turned his eye to the duality he encountered in Scotland. He painted both the smelting of iron ore in the factories of the Lowlands and, along the Tay, the remnants of Highland culture in paintings such as *Highland Wedding at Blair Atholl*. It depicts the great fiddler/violinist Niel Gow. Gow collected tunes as well as playing them, interpreting them through the lens of his own genius, just as the great bards had done. Just as the bards were patronised by the McGregors and their ilk, Gow had a patron in his clan chief, receiving an annual retainer of £5 from His Grace the 3rd Duke of Atholl. He had inherited the Dukedom from his uncle only after a dispensation from the House of Lords, as his father had been attainted as a Jacobite. It was this duke who built the Hermitage above the falls on the river Braan just beyond Gow's humble cottage in the village of Inver. The select visitors to this Ossianic Hall were greeted by a life-size portrait of the Celtic bard, which through a system of pulleys slid aside to reveal a room reverberating with the thunder of the Black Linn waterfall beyond, the mirrors on its walls reflecting its torrential flow, a trompe l'oeil – a trick of the eye – a folly. Today the Hermitage is in the care of the National Trust for Scotland. Its mirrored walls are etched with reproductions of scenes from Ossian by Alexander Runciman, who like Allan had travelled to Italy to develop his art in the classical style in the mid eighteenth century but who, on return, was captivated instead by Macpherson's book.

Here is a very clear example of how the Highlands – both landscape and culture – has been, and still is, viewed. A place that has been a threat, opened up with military roadbuilding, modern mapping, technologies which destroy it – then we lament the passing of the very culture that has been destroyed. This, you may think, has been a historical act no longer relevant. History, perhaps, does not matter; it is to be melded and blended with our idea of the past to suit our present. *Outlander* generates huge tourist income that feeds families and secures jobs all along the Tay today, but its storylines are criticised for the use of sexual violence against women, a lack of character depth, that it has no poetry, is mere folly.

> How hast thou fallen like an oak, with all thy branches round thee! Where is Fingal the King? where is Oscur my son? where are all my race? Alas! in the earth they lie. I feel their tombs with my hands. I hear the river below murmuring hoarsely over the stones. What dost thou, O river, to me?
>
> – Ossian, in 'Fragments of Ancient Poetry',
> James Macpherson

*

Modern roads either follow Wade's, as in Glen Almond, or run parallel to it, as at Dalnaspidal. Further to the west, a series of ancient routes run parallel to the modern A9. They cross Atholl's mountain passes, connect to waterside places from where ferries once crossed lochs, and bridge and ford rivers that feed into the Tay. One of these, known today as the 'Kirk Road', links Glen Lyon to the ancient Black Wood on the shores of Loch Rannoch. It is a journey of seven miles over rough track on foot, but the equivalent journey is twenty-nine miles round mountain and loch by modern public roads. The kirk in question is the one at Innerwick, where the back road from Loch Tay over Ben Lawers meets the Lyon.

The kirk was built in the 1820s to a design by Thomas Telford on the site of a much older church originally established by holy men from the west. Inside it houses a relic of these saints – an eighth-century handbell, trapped silently now in limbo behind bars since its companion at Fortingall was stolen ten years ago. The road winds uphill from the kirk, taking you over the hills to Loch Rannoch through a lingering remnant of the ancient Caledonian Forest. War marks this landscape. A plan to completely harvest the trees during the First World War fell through but did not spare the young men of these hillsides and glens. A rust-red squirrel, scampering, twists in parallel up a Scots pine and leaps into another. Between them an auburn burn steps down, burbling, over weir, echo-ing under a fir plantation. Past the 1,500-foot summit lie the remains of old sheilings in muirburnt heather. Once in lush high pastures, these circles of fading stones no longer ring with summer laughter, women's man-free talk or teenage wooings. They fall further each decade into the bell heather, with no one to toll their loss, lament. Water and frost crack open and splinter the walls of both sheiling and hillside. Dry rock cries scree-slides of rocky tears. The road traverses the Lairig Ghallabhaich, the Way of the Lowlander. These sassenachs may have been cattle drovers or soldiers – certainly General Wade drove one of his roads through here, opening up to Lowlanders the previously inaccessible Highlands to government observa-tion and fast deployment. The military still use this route.

Suddenly the reverberations of four turbo-prop engines send waves of sound down the glen as an RAF Hercules flies low over the land. I am blinded as it crosses the sun, so look down and follow its shadow's journey undulating along the valley floor – over empty sheiling, cattle-less track, war memorial. In a few seconds it has passed out of sight, then out of sound, leaving behind the tinkling of silver birch leaves in its aeronautical wake.

The velvet glove of water and its iron-fisted companion, frost, have burst open cracks in the skin of these hillsides. They have scratched through thin soil, etched into bed-rock under gravity's merciless command, opening deep trenches in the never ending combat between land and season in this spinning world. Antlers of water, they gouge this land. Autumn after autumn the hunted stags that are tolerated here for 'sport' retain the energy, the life drive, for a bit of internecine gouging themselves. Belling, in a display worthy of Highlander and Lowlander, they lock horns with each other instead of turning their firepower on those who would slaughter them and their kind, chase them down the hill, rip the arses out of their tweed-clad sassenach breeks. The ancient bell tolls for the stag on the hill, the lassies at the sheiling, the drovers on their way to the slaughterhouse, the youth to the killing fields of Flanders, and the ancient woods once saved which have now gone to the sawmill: 'How hast thou fallen like an oak, with all thy branches round thee!'

People have long become the rarest creatures in the upper catchments of the Tay. From the bleakness of the

Lowlanders' Way, I am soothed a little coming under the canopy of the ancient Black Wood of Rannoch on the shores of the loch. Its seeds, at least, are being used to regenerate other Caledonian Forests. Who knows what they will grow?

Nature writer Jim Crumley speaks movingly of the ancient trees, so aged that they still have memory of when wolves roamed here. Many advocate the reintroduction of wolves. The local Gaelic once spoken at the sheiling with tales of Ossian and preached in the kirk founded by St Adomnán is long gone, too, and it seems unlikely that it shall ever return, but the wisdom of the past remains. Later, flicking through a copy of *Perthshire Gaelic* in the clearance box in a local bookshop I come across a warning: '*tàlaidhidh am biadh fiadh na beinne*' – 'hunger makes the wolf come out of the woods'.

For now, it is time for feasting. For celebration, not stinting. Back on the banks of the Tay music is drifting over the river opposite the old ferryman's cottage at Inver, where Braan and Tay join. A tryst, a meeting, a coming together. I am at Will and Vikki's wedding on the riverside at Dunkeld.

Family, friends, community, celebrating a union. The Scone bride and Blackford groom have, like their guests, come from different sources, followed separate streams, but are now joining their hands together in marriage by the banks of the Tay. The music at the ceilidh is by Niel Gow, whose cottage at Inver is just across the river. The fiddler is excellent: '*an ceòl a' dol an casan nan cailleachan-dubha*' ('the music would bring nuns to their feet'). Gow, the undisputed genius of Scottish fiddle playing, was the natural inheritor of the traditional music Burns was collecting. Among his most famous compositions are 'Miss Stewart of Grandtully', 'Dunkeld Bridge' and 'Niel Gow's Lament for the Death of his Second Wife'.

A tryst, a meeting, a coming together. When Lowland Burns pledged his troth to Highland Mary, they are said to have done so by exchanging Bibles over a flowing stream.

On the bridge over the Inchewan Burn that separates Little Dunkeld from Birnam, a plaque marks the traditional boundary of the Highland Gaelic and Lowland Scots languages: allt/burn, Uisge Tatha/River Tay, leum-uisge/ waterfall. It is the falls on the Inchewan that Washington Wilson photographed. As it flows down the hills behind Birnam the Inchewan is first spiked by pine/*crann-giuthais* needles, then showered in golden coins of silver birch/ *beith* leaves, then those of the copper beech/*faidhbhile*.

As it enters the Tay an ancient tree known as 'Macbeth's oak' stands. It's old but not Macbeth old (*c.* AD 1005– 1057) – but had Shakespeare visited the area in 1589, as some claim, it would already have been a centurion. James Dorret's 1750 map delineates 'Inchewan' and beside it 'Birnamwood in K. Mackbeth's tragedy'. Today, across from the mouth of the burn stands the East Ferry cottage, its working life ended by Telford's bridge just upstream, and Eastwood House, one of the Potter family's holiday lets. One of Rupert Potter's photographs depicts the painter Millais, full tweeds and plus-fours, the epitome of the sporting English gentleman, perched on a coble between shore and river, with a salmon, a trout, rods and ghillie.

Salmon fishing is *the* thing on the Tay. Like land, the river is divided into separate areas of ownership known as beats; there are thirty-eight in total. These are highly prized and charge fees accordingly for anglers to fly fish on their pools with varying degrees of success. One of the most famous is the Glendelvine beat between Murthly Castle on the south bank and Spittalfield on the north. It has pools named the Garth, the Minister's and the Boat. It was in the neck of the Boat pool in October 1922 that Georgina Ballantine, daughter of a ghillie, landed the largest ever salmon to be caught by line and rod in the British Isles at 64lb. The capture and landing is described as 'Homeric' on the beat's website today. Following its capture and killing, a cast was taken by a taxidermist from Malloch's in Perth. The fish's body was then donated to and eaten by patients and staff at Perth Royal Infirmary. The stuffed fish was then added to the sculpted monuments to the dead going up all along Tayside between the two world wars.

In the century since Ballantine's feat, no larger fish has been caught on the Tay. The declining number of salmon had already been recorded a century before, the *Old Statistical Account* noting:

The fisheries of this parish are of considerable value, and are mostly all held in lease by a Company in Perth, who preserve the salmon in ice, and send them fresh to the London market . . . It is observed by old fishermen, that there is not now 1 in the river here for 10 that were in it 50 years ago; but this scarcity is . . . owing . . . to the many fishings carried on in the lower parts of the Tay now where formerly there were none.

There were still enough fish in the river in Millais's time for him to sketch his daughter in *Mary with a Huge Catch of Salmon*. Throughout his life, the Tay was to provide inspiration for his work, with riverscapes like *Chill October at Kinnoul*, *Glen Birnam*, with an old cailleach walking through the snow by the Inchewan Burn, or the sentimental *Flowing to the Sea*, depicting a sergeant in the Black Watch departing for service overseas by the Waulkmill Ferry. This picture resonates more deeply with me, having discovered through writing this book my own family connection to that scene.

What I saw once as late Victorian melodrama in his painting *The Flood* – a baby in a wooden cradle cast adrift on rising waters – takes on new meaning in today's climate crisis. The child is oblivious to the danger it is in, entranced by the light refracting rainbow colours through the droplets of rain on the branch of the old tree above, however, we the viewer, like the parents urgently punting across the flood waters, are all too well aware of the danger. We are not innocent of our fate as the waters threaten to rise and engulf us. The Bible tells us that after Noah's flood God promised: 'Never again will I curse the ground because of humans, even though every inclination of the human heart is evil from childhood. And never again will I destroy all living creatures, as I have done.'

As a society we do not have the faith of the Victorians;

we know that it is us, humans, not God, causing the waters to rise today. As we persist in our inaction as water levels rise that tryst, that meeting with our fate, comes ever closer.

At the Inchewan Burn, the imminence of that coming together, despite the recent Scottish Parliamentary Flood Risk Management Act/Achd Riaghladh Cunnart Thuiltean, is manifest. On the burn's side and at its mouth, people continue to build in an area of high flood risk: hardly one garden in five here has not been paved over for driveways; bricks installed as part of flood prevention work along the burn are already flaking into the water; more houses are being built right up against it.

The Scottish Environment Protection Agency estimates annual average damages to residential properties alone in the Dunkeld and Birnam area is nearly £200,000. In addition to the economic impact following flooding the weight of the branches of Macbeth's oak are in danger of splitting the tree's main trunk asunder: to save the ancient wood it has been proposed to saw branches from the tree.

The sound of those many waters is not, as stated in the Bible, the voice of God, but that of the rising tide of our own self-inflicted fate.

# Strathmore

## *Isla and Ericht*

Strathmore, the big valley that runs south-west from the North Sea to Perth, collects the waters of the western Angus Glens and feeds them into the Tay near Meikleour. Its principle waterway is the Isla, itself topped up by the Ericht, flowing from Glenshee and Blairgowrie, and the Dean Water, from Forfar. These west-flowing tributaries are separated from the east-flowing Tay as it widens to its Firth by the Sidlaw Hills and the Carse of Gowrie. Despite its Gaelic name, Strathmore is very much more Lowland than Highland.

Hunting, gathering, fishing, tending beasts, growing crops, paddling a boat – the mechanics may have changed but across Tayside they are human activities that continue uninterrupted today from our prehistory. From Bronze Age to the age of iron, metalworking has also endured.

There really isn't very much at Eassie in the centre of Strathmore except a few houses and a smiddy – a blacksmith, a still-necessary throwback in this mechanised and digital farming age. In a garden nearby, a retired farmer is dressing his lawn as carefully as he ploughed his parks (no satellite technology matches his sure eye). In the kirkyard, a representation of ploughing on a gravestone – in modern polished granite, a tractor is silhouetted against a peach setting sun. Each new dawn brings a new day. In a reversal of fortunes, inside the protection of the now ruined kirk an Old Red Sandstone slab seven feet high, three feet wide, that was cast down by Reformation iconoclasts in the seventeenth century, has been fished from the Eassie Burn. On it the ancient dwellers of these lands carved a hunter, his hound, a deer, a stag and three cows. One of the cattle has a curved horn and a bell hanging from its neck. Whilst decorated cow horns may have been used as war trumpets or to sound the alert of cattle-raiders descending on Strathmore, they have also a more bucolic use. In the Strath's burghs you may find a 'Toutie's Neuk', where the local cowherd would blow their horn and gather the townspeople's cattle to take them out to the common grazing land. In Alyth, my grandfather would go 'up Toutie' to visit his grandfather and in the museum on the other side of the Tay in Abernethy there is a fine example of a 'tootie' cow horn that would be blown morning and evening to summon the cattle out and home.

The simplicity of pastoral music and its instruments greatly appealed to Robert Burns. He collected the traditional song 'Hey Tutti Tati', where the human voice echoes the sound of a trumpet or horn, for the book *The Scots Musical Museum*. Burns's passion for the music of Scotland went airt and pairt with his idea of himself as Scotland's bard, leading a metaphorical national cei-lidh, with poetry, storytelling in verse, music and good company. The Ayrshire farmer poet, having been feted by Enlightenment Edinburgh society, travelled into the Highlands to absorb the bardic tradition, 'a book I prize next to the Bible . . . Mcpherson's Ossian'. Acclaimed by all classes of people in the Lowlands and capital, his visit to Niel Gow binds him to the native genius of the Highlands. In a direct link to that ancient past he collects a fine example of a shepherd's stock and horn by the Tay.

In a letter to George Thomson, dated 19 November 1794, he writes:

I have, at last, gotten one, but it is a very rude instrument. It is composed of three parts: the stock, which is the hinder thigh bone of a sheep, such as you see in a mutton ham; the horn, which is a highland cow's horn, cut off at the smaller end, until the aperture be large enough to admit the 'stock' to be pushed through the horn, until it be held by the thicker or hip-end of the thigh-bone: and lastly an oaten reed exactly cut and notched like that which you see every shepherd boy have, when the corn-stems are green and full-grown. The reed is not made fast in the bone, but is held in the lips, and plays loose in the smaller end of the 'stock', while the 'stock' and horn hanging on its larger end, is held by the hands playing. The stock has six or seven ventiges in the upper side, and one back ventige, like the common flute. This one of mine was made by a man from the Braes of Athole, and is exactly what the shepherds were wont to use in the country . . .

Many of the huge Old Red Sandstone slabs like the one at Eassie had originally been transported around the valley in ice. The glaciers and rivers flowing down from the Highlands at the end of the last Ice Age seem to have affected the movement of the glacier that scoured Strathmore, undermining and directing it eastward. On its southern border the flanks of the Sidlaw Hills show the scrapes of its passing. In Dundee's museum you can view a glacial erratic, a stone both scratched and smoothed by the ice's flow. Meltwaters have marked this landscape. Deposited mounds of smaller stones and gravels normally associated with rivers are found where no rivers now flow, but where the impenetrable glacier redirected long-gone flow.

Over the Strath's berry fields, the horizon is turning pale peach and orange. In the middle distance the hills enclosing Strathmore, losing all definition, are mauve. On the tips of my nose and ears, I feel the cold from the white peaks of the not-so-distant mountains. I smell the ice yet on the wind. The white rumps of two, then three fallow does emerge from the furrowed field. Sensing me, uncertain whether to walk or run, they move stiff-legged and awkwardly, like Forfarshire farmers in high heels at a country ceilidh, hooves clacking over the tarmac track.

Once in the safety of the trees – not so far away – they stop and look back with moist doe eyes.

Earlier in the day I had encountered other deer. While climbing the steep sides of Barry Hill on the north of the Strath, another fallow doe had bounded off as I summited.

Steadfast after two and a half millennia are the earthworks of the hilltop's fort. Curving lines of ramparts ripple out from lozenge-shaped stonework battlements; prickly yellow whin in bloom forms another line of defence. Below the peak in a natural hollow the circular well now lies stagnant. The thirty-foot-thick walls were interlaced with timber, which when set alight have vitrified. Evidence of this is all around: screes of red rocks fallen from the battlements are glazed and glittering. In a gap between stones a small black-bodied spider has spun its dewy web, while other gaps and crevices are entrances now to safe homes for numerous insects, small rodents, rabbits. Dropping down from the Highland massif the river Isla bends a protective arm round the defences in a deep ravine called the Den of Airlie.

The 400 million-year-old red sandstone colours this landscape. Below the fort, tractors are ploughing deep troughs of the plum/brown soil for potatoes; in its purple mud pigs wallow, protecting their delicate pink skin from the strengthening spring sun which sparkles on their semi-circular corrugated metal styes, makes the red sandstone houses of Alyth blush in its glow. This wedge of Devonian rock runs diagonally across Scotland from the Firth of Clyde in the west to the North Sea coast just to the east of here. Lavas of sandstone mixed with strange compounds of gravels and quartz hint to greater liquefactions of rock on this, the edge of the Highland Boundary Fault. A mile further up the road that runs along the foot of the hillfort, the ground beneath your feet metamorphoses into Dalradian rock from the more ancient Cambrian age, about 5,000 million years ago.

That road bridges the Isla just upstream of the Reekie Linn. In a rocky gorge, 130 feet deep, lined with mature mixed forest, the river drops from hard Highland volcanic rock over two waterfalls into a black pool. When the river is in spate, these two combine into one impressive fall, which has been sculpting this gorge out of the softer Lowland sandstone, undermining it, in a constant attack, an infinite act of siege warfare. The waters fall, pulsing like a creeping barrage; the constant roar is dizzying, the unremitting speed and uncontrollable power alters everyday perceptions. The steepness elicits vertiginous fear. Emotional responses are whipped up by this natural phenomenon – 'romantic', 'sensational', 'awesome'. The spume and spray of the falls ('linn' in Scots) create a watery smoke or 'reek'.

A waterfall is a transitional place. In our book *The Wonderful World of Nature* my brother and I learnt that it is a geological feature, where flowing water that has scoured as deeply as it can along hard bedrock drops onto a softer strata of rock, eroding it. But it is also a magical place – a doorway of mist on a mountain, a mysterious window's watery curtain, an unpolished lens obscuring what lies behind. The wall of sound thundering in your ears further disorientates. The spume and sunlight combine to create watery rainbows. Keek through and who knows what you might find . . .

Water drips through rock, seeping into a cave. All is silenced: the weather outside, the sound of the river. The metronomic drips of water infiltrate; the pulsing of my heart is a drumbeat echoing in the cavern, ringing in my ears. The light flickers on the cave walls, oscillating, animating, making them dance with a life that is not life, just as water gushes down the river like a living creature, yet is not alive. The light of the torch moving in my hand catches and illuminates the ripples the dripping water creates on the surface of a groundwater pool, reflecting them back onto the wall, superimposing a weft and a weave of watery plaid, spinning them into the moving shadows. Fire and water, opposites yet the same. The torch batteries start to give out. What was once powerful, reassuring – a lighthouse beam in a storm – dwindles to a pale sepia vignette, a Victorian calotype. Beyond all is the most absorbent of black in a dark, dark room. Timeless, lifeless, the blackness of space. No stars.

At the bottom of the Reekie Linn, hidden behind the falls, is such a cave. Local legend has it that an outlaw fleeing justice took shelter there one night only to encounter in the transient chamber the very devil himself in the form of a black, inky tyke. Chided, he fled and handed himself over to the earthly forces of law and order, the local laird, the Earl of Airlie.

Re-entering the daylit world the sun offers redemption. It catches the linn's reek forming rainbows, reminding the religious of God's covenant with his people after the flood, and the rest of us, of spring after winter.

Reach out to smell a blossom. Pull the skeletal branch to your nose and a droplet of rainwater runs down a dry riverbed finger of your delta hand.

Salmon, for all their amazing leaping ability, are unable to pass the Reekie Linn. Their spawning grounds, therefore, lie in the stretch of water downstream from it known as the Slug of Auchrannie within the ravine of the Den of Airlie. There was concern there recently when proposals were submitted by the landowner, the hereditary Earl of Airlie, to install an underground hydro-electric scheme in this section of the Isla between waterfall and fort. During the planning process it emerged that it was not the salmon that was the main species under threat from the development but tiny river jelly lichen (Collema dichotomum), extremely rare and which flourishes in upland rivers such as the Isla. Here it grows in mats semi-submerged like an olive-green seaweed. The British Lichen Society made representations to ensure it was protected during and after development. The scheme also identified invasive species that would be cut back and removed – sycamore and rhododendron – leaving room for the surrounding ancient woodland to expand. Alder, then oak, then ash trees now grow unimpeded on the different levels of the Den, intermixing with formidable ancient yews, tiny liverworts and – as spring progresses – more and more woodland plants, like the rare whorled Solomon's seal. Lamphreys and otters, badgers, bats and squirrels all flourish in this ravine. The proposers and planners believe that the underground run of the river scheme, in operation only when water levels are high, will not affect the hydrology of the Isla nor the unique natural history of the gorge.

On the eastern edge of the Den other underground works were constructed nearly two thousand years ago. The Barns of Airlie is a particularly well-preserved souterrain – a long curving stone-built passage running for sixty feet, six feet wide and six high (from the French *sous terrain*, meaning 'under ground'). Typically these structures built just below ground level will have walls constructed of large boulders, giving way to curving courses of smaller stones and then huge flagstones in the roof. It was formerly thought that souterrains were defensive dwellings with the 'terminal bulge' – a wider space at the far end of the passage – used as a storeroom, but current thinking is that they were a form of storehouse and byre for livestock. Serpent-like figures and rippling grooves are carved into some of the blocks used in its construction, but whether they are part of this or from a more ancient monument that has been reused is unclear.

Close by, another contemporaneous underground chamber was discovered next to Airlie school, an Iron Age grave containing a Roman glass cup.

Back above ground, evidence of ancient practices recently used: a protective line of holly bushes planted to prevent cattle straying into the Den over a hundred years ago have now grown into trees. Their trunks are smooth and thick, their branches oddly serpentine, their sharp shiny leaves as sparse as the hairs on a centenarian's head. They have that peculiar quality of beings that have lived beyond the normal span. Where not cut back, the glossy leaves of another evergreen, rhododendron, reflect the sun's light. Buds have formed on their branch tips, but it is too early for them to flower yet.

After winter the rocky outcrops above the gorge are blessed with a profusion of delicate wood anemones (*flùr na gaoithe*, windflower in Gaelic). Six or seven palest white tepals form a halo around yellow anthers about an inch in diameter, fluttering on the breeze. An indicator of a woodland's long-term health, they flourish here in the trees' leaf litter. Spreading via rhizomes, it takes a century for them to grow the length of a human. In early spring, a hover-fly pollinating is welcomed, but the seemingly timid plant has defences as strong as a hillfort, being poisonous to both people and animals.

Among the riverside trees are many tiny birds. High up in branches, quick of movement, they are difficult to identify by anything but their sound. The 'whoo-eet' of the willow warbler, the 'chiff' then 'chaff' of the newly arrived chiffchaff, the 'shrupp-tup' of the long-tailed tit. Perhaps because of the noise of the water falling, I am able to advance close to a group of four birds low down in the branches of a birch. The nearest is a female siskin, her colours so pale that they remind me of a grey mountain rock, scree flecked with snow and pale yellow green lichens.

In the Isla above the Reekie Linn large speckled mountain rocks have been left by the ice. They disrupt the water flow, turning the dark river white with miniature rapids across its forty-five-foot width. In the lea meadow a recumbent monolith bears the scrape marks of glacial gougings, the soft hair traces of cattle's itching, splattered by bovine shitting and speckled by the snow-white drop-pings of the birds that perch on them. The Isla in spate leaves its watermark on the parchment bark of a stand of silver birches. It has rumbled and clacked the pale, dry riverside stones until they are rounded by ages of sculpting, each liquid polishing bringing hidden colours briefly to life. But the thoughtless river in flood drowns or makes homeless the creatures that inhabit the souterrain holes in the sandy cliff bank. It overwhelms the mid-stream island, and in the aftermath desecrates with the cliff's sandy mud skat the pure celandines growing there who curl up their heart-shaped leaves in protection. Above the exposed cliff-face the soil is stabilised by thin alders – for now. Two of their number bridge the riparian zone, sprawled face down in the river, undercut then drowned from the last spate, roots in the air. Through the horizontal tree trunks four or five deer delicately tiptoe away.

Where the Isla enters the Tay near Meikleour there is a special monument. In a chain-sawed clearing in a wood the trees around me are the usual plantation mix of Sitka spruce and Scots pine with a few silver birches on the fringes. They are the latest crop to make up the North and South Woods. Detailed maps of the area have been produced over the past two centuries and on them it is possible to track the trees' ebb and flow – in the nineteenth century, mixed deciduous woods predominated, and by the mid twentieth century most of the South Wood had been felled and conifers planted in the North Wood, each felling and replanting a ring on the forest's family tree.

Today birch saplings, whin, broom and heather are colonising the open space on top of cushions of mosses and tiny early spring flowers. A chaffing coal tit (in Gaelic, *cailleachag a' chinn duibh*, meaning 'the little old woman with the black cap') is agitated by my presence but keeps hidden. I hear the sound of red squirrels scampering up a snakeskin trunk of a Scots pine to hide in the canopy; see mountain bike tracks patterning the muddy path; through the undergrowth suggestions of animal routes, deer droppings. Unlike the cartography, all is merely hinted at or partially glimpsed, traces of what has been; difficult to decipher, unclear.

Under my feet is one of Scotland's most ancient monuments. The Cleaven Dyke is a huge earthwork embankment that runs across the Perthshire landscape for one and a half miles. It consists of a pair of parallel ditches 150 feet apart, with a bank twenty feet wide and three to six feet high in between, known as a cursus. There are a number in Britain and Ireland, and they are very old, of the Neolithic (New Stone Age ) period; this one was built around 3600 BC. It must have taken a huge amount of labour to construct but its purpose is unknown. Very little archaeological evidence of its use has been discovered. Possibly it could have been some kind of ceremonial route, though there may have been between two and five gaps along its length. It may then be a series of long barrow-type structures built over a long period rather than a single entity. The 'dyke' runs along a north-west to south-east orientation but is not obviously aligned on any geographical or celestial landmark, though it is near the confluence of the rivers Isla and Tay. An area of strategic importance later to house the Roman's largest legionary fortress in Scotland; indeed, until the 1990s the cursus was believed to be part of the Inchtuthil fort, which lies a mile or so south of it. It could perhaps be a boundary marker, but there is no evidence of it being a defensive structure, and while the eastern end may have bordered the river Isla there is no evidence the western end ever connected to any river, hill or fort. It has been suggested that other cursuses demarked an area between sacred and agricultural land. Could it be a series of mounds that mark a line of kinship, ancestry, family?

It lies like a whale or a pod of whales in the landscape. This whole area is on a geological boundary, north/south, Highland/Lowland, but if the cursus marks a boundary it is a human one perhaps, between the transient hunter-gatherers and herders, and the settled agriculturalists. This structure was built as the Stone Age was coming to an end but before metalworking had begun; the Neolithic farming village of Skara Brae in Orkney is from roughly the same time, older than the Callanish Stones and the Maeshowe chamber tomb. It has been proposed that societies were adopting more hierarchical systems of working together during this period and the structure may be linked to that, but in what way is unclear. What is certain is that rituals around death, burial and the placing of large objects or structures in the landscape, with possible religious or tribal significance – whether solitary standing stones or groups of them, the engraving of stones with 'cup marks', or the construction of mounds or cairns

– all begin to happen in this period of our history. If the Cailleach and her shrine are domestic, her stones a family, tactile, intimate, these later structures and monoliths are engineered by larger communities. A small cursus on the north bank of the river Earn at Broich near Crieff shows signs of a Neolithic palisaded circular structure being constructed upon it.

Cursuses were used, perhaps added to, as at Meikleour, sometimes reused, as at Brioch, by succeeding generations of Taysiders. How were they constructed? While a pick made out of deer antler was discovered in excavations of the cursus near the site of Stonehenge, no tools have been found here. Neolithic digging implements found elsewhere – ranging from rough stone blades and the pelvic bone of an ox attached to a wooden handle, to early Bronze Age finds of wooden spades – suggest possible excavation methods.

Walking along its ridge, I come cross a rusting metal bucket filled not with water but drowning in a pool of sphagnum mosses. Presumably its woven or wooden ancestors would have been used to carry the spoil of loosened earth from the ditches to form the embankment, but like water from a holed bucket the people who built it, its purpose and its meaning have flowed out of all knowledge.

The river flows. Like ancient hunters and herders it is always on the move; it cannot rest. Its imperative has the power to cut through rock. Humans had the foresight to channel that power. The earliest mill wheel would probably have been small and portable, perhaps used to grind flour from nuts and seeds. As new grains and the knowledge to grow them trickled into the area humans were able to settle more permanently and the same local knowledge of seasons used to harvest wild foods, animals, birds and fish was applied to crops. Oats and barley, a little wheat and flax possibly, for oil, were grown. Grains were selected on productivity and disease-resistance. By the Iron Age the hulled, six-row barley (Hordeum vulgare var. vulgare) was the dominant crop cultivated. The river's fertile plains nourished these crops, its tributary waters channelled to irrigate fields, its power used to grind flour, its glacial clays fired to make vessels for storage. The houses and homesteads of the earliest farmers built of timbers, walled with woven willow and mud, thatched with heather or reeds, have left nothing behind but postholes, quern stones and potsherds. The new interchange linking Strathmore to the A9 sickles through these fields. Stay temporarily in the B&B at Newmill, the latest farm on the site where an ancient timber roundhouse once was, where a stone quern was found, a grave with a clay beaker pot. Beyond and above, the land is growing ever more mountainous, the speed of the water flowing off it once harnessed by mill wheels from the eight-spoke wood-and-iron wheel of Aberfeldy's watermill on the Moness Burn, the flour mill at Blair Atholl, Barry Mill at the Firth and the whirling turbines of hydro-electric schemes across Tayside. The invention of the mill wheel freed the arm-deadening, mind-numbing tedium of grinding grains into flour for some women – always women; for others the drudgery ground on until achingly recent times.

A clay pot is a fragile object. It is unsuited to being carried by people on the move compared to the stitched animal skin sack of a hunter-gatherer, or the CamelBak water bottle of a modern day hillwalker. It is an object that speaks of settlement, of permanence, and even though it is liable to break, it is easily replaced with local clay, fired in a blazing hearth. It can store a household's grains and flour, meat and cheeses, preserved fruits and berries.

# PERTH

*The Sound of Many Waters*

Ploughing his high parks at Upper Muirhall a mile due east of Perth city centre in 1984, John Dow uncovered a simple stone cist chamber containing a beaker pot and a scattering of teeth. Examination of the teeth showed second permanent molars and eruption with early wear, wisdom teeth with enamel not completely formed. An adolescent about the same age as James Mitchell was buried here. A life spilled, gone before it could be fulfilled. Where have they gone, where were they expected to travel?

Though fragile, the pot is a vessel, is a boat. Did it travel to the setting or the rising sun? The pot, high-bellied, everted neck and indented with horizontally banded decoration, was empty but for some unidentifiable half-moon stain colouring the bottom, its circular base scored with four lines in the shape of a cross similar to the sun disc decorations of the Bell Beaker people found along the Rhine, who travelled the rivers and seas across Western and Atlantic Europe between 2800 and 1800 BC. It has now travelled across the river to Perth Museum.

The Tay runs north to south here. Perth sits on its western bank, the land rising sharply to Kinnoull Hill on the east. On a stone in Old Kinnoull kirkyard a carved ferryman punts across water. Crossing the Tay by the Queen's Bridge, I stop and look down. The surface of the water has many forms. Its lights and colours are not a uniform plane but multifaceted, contoured by wind, by flow, by bridge piers, rocks, stone beach, embankment wall, flood defence, island, weir – but not directly by tide, though a slackening beyond the city can affect it here. Lithe, quick, wafer thin, yet the surface of the water also has the texture of layers of thick, old gloss paint in one of the unmodernised Victorian villas that overlook it at this spot. In places it seems that a blowtorch is bubbling it, melting and re-liquefying it from solid; waves of heat pushing waves of paint of various thicknesses before them. A moment later it's a sandy desert, the ever changing flow of dunes creating wave and trough, trough and wave, whipped by the sirocco.

The dazzling light of the midday July sun is flooding over the water. In places the river is impenetrable, here reflecting it straight back in blinding compact-mirror circles, there in the troughs of a cross-hatched pattern made by counter flowing ripples, puffs of white light, like clouds seen from high above the deep blue seas of Earth from a ship travelling through space. Yet a metre away its rays have entirely penetrated the water, illuminating gold the base stones of the riverbed, alchemically. As the water deepens the light has further to dive and is broken up by the river's constant movement; it is caught and refracted through the translucent carapaces of freshwater shrimps, dissipated by flecks of ombrotrophic peat washed down from moor and bog, becoming opaque as a freshwater pearl. Gold turns to amber to copper to rust, foretelling the coming seasons' flow in its crystal glass as all goes inky and black in unseeable depths until it restarts the whole process by dancing lightly over the surface again.

My eye is caught by a movement midstream and looking up I see a small pale disk of river-borne foam and a scattering of white petals swirling, spiralling by. Behind it – an accompanying trail of bubbles – is confetti swished by the train of a summer bride.

The river is ripening, full, wide. Here the Tay has more than a county town on its banks; in the city of Perth (albeit a small one, a city nonetheless), it is coming to the end of being a country river. It has been joined by all but the Earn of its main tributaries – and that soon. With her bridesmaids, the goddess Tatha is preparing for her marriage with the sea. On Cirsten Bisset's 1747 gravestone in Greyfriars Cemetery a three-masted ship is in full sail. Within the confines of the city, the Tay will taste the salt of the tide, feel the weight of North Sea-going vessels in its harbour; hear, perhaps, the distant cries of blubbery seals, her future children.

Like these maritime mammals, small islands have formed, half of the land, half of the water, precarious to the river's change of mood or direction but for now bound together by the roots of opportunist trees.

Giggling drunk with youth, love, lust and sun teenagers free of school have crossed the stepping stones of a causeway. On the tip of the island, the sun catches the whiplashings of their rod and line as they cast glinting flies out into the water: 'Silver Stoat', 'Blue Charm'. Bluebottles are iridescent. River and sky are blue; the one hot, the other cool.

Behind, just along from Old Kinnoull kirkyard, stands Bowerswell House, once home to the Ruskin family. John James Ruskin as a boy had received drawing lessons from the painter Alexander Nasmyth. He in turn encouraged his son, also John, to appreciate fine art, and from this paternal encouragement he went on to become the foremost Victorian art critic. Mass production was anathema to Ruskin, Turner's young champion. In his hugely influential *The Stones of Venice*, Ruskin posited that the factory-manufactured glass of industrial nineteenth-century Britain – clear, uniform and soulless – was inferior to the hand-crafted Venetian glass which though sometimes 'muddy, inaccurate in all its forms, and clumsily cut' could occasionally be 'so lovely in its forms that no price is too great for it'. 'The difference between the spirit of touch of the man who is inventing, and the man who is obeying directions,' he wrote, 'is often all the difference between a great and a common work of art. How wide the separation is between original and second-hand execution.'

Ruskin's nostalgia for the hand-crafted drinking vessels of the past is understandable. The handmade Roman glass unearthed at Airlie is magical in its beauty. But its Iron Age Tayside owner and his heirs, people of high tribal status who coveted its beauty, removed it from the world of the living into the selfish underworld, never intending for the likes of you or I or Ruskin to see it. Ruskin's appreciation of aesthetic beauty must be balanced against the benefits that the uniformity of mass production was going to deliver to wider society: enough cost-effective glasses and cups, and sinks, baths, toilet bowls and plumbing for efficient sanitation to lift the vast majority of people living along the Tay out of squalor and disease. After all, what value a handcrafted Murano glass to today's Venetians – dwellers in that city of elegant crannogs – when they suffer human sewage being discharged into their putrescent canals?

As for 'common works of art', on their glass plates Wilson and Valentine were demonstrating a modern nineteenth-century technology, like photography could produce works of vitreous beauty, moulding light in a way that was both artistic and accessible (and affordable) to the masses.

Precociously gifted since youth, John Ruskin also wrote poems and romantic fairy tales. In *The King of the Golden River* the king tells the hero: 'the water which has been refused to the cry of the weary and dying is unholy, though it had been blessed by every saint in heaven; and the water which is found in the vessel of mercy is holy, though it had been defiled with corpses.'

He had written it for and presented it to a twelve-year-old Perth girl called Euphemia Gray, lucky her! The Ruskins had sold Bowerswell to the Gray family, and it was there seven years later in 1848 that Effie and John made their ill-fated marriage. While within Effie the desires of heterosexual love flowed, in John they did not and the marriage was never consummated. As a champion of the Pre-Raphaelite Brotherhood of artists, Ruskin invited John Everett Millais, one of its leading painters, to holiday with Effie and himself in the Highlands. Ruskin and Millais shared their fascination, drawing and painting the turbulent mountain streams and tortured twisted rock formations against a backdrop of a passionless marriage and the growing love between Effie and Millais. Ruskin's supposed horror of his wife's pubic hair, of her moist sex, his self-proclaimed destruction of Turner's erotic drawings after the artist's death can be contrasted with the mutual passion of Effie and Millais which was to result, after the annulment of her marriage to Ruskin, in remarriage and eight children. The fecundity of their love is beautifully illustrated by that sketch Millais made in oils of their daughter Mary on the banks of the Tay surrounded by a cornucopia of salmon.

Millais, famous for painting *Ophelia* as she floats in the river, and whose whole Pre-Raphaelite concept was of a return to a medieval quality of craftsmanship, was not above learning from the new medium of photography. Often a guest of the Potter family when they holidayed at Dalguise, the artist would engage the young Beatrix to take photographs of the landscapes he was painting as an aide-mémoire when he worked them up later in his studio. In *The Sound of Many Waters* (1876) Millais is clearly adopting in oils the vision of flowing water revealed by photographers like Wilson – the waters flow as if time-exposed. While Washington Wilson's workers were mechanically tinting glass plates, Millais was using all his craftsmanship and skill to paint the colours he saw in the Braan at Rumbling Bridge. 'Scotland,' he wrote, 'is like a wet pebble, with the colours brought out by the rain.'

In Old Kinnoull kirkyard, smooth white marble marks the grave where Effie now lies. But in death also sweetness. In a corner of the graveyard a hive has buzzing to and fro, a stream of bees drunk with pollen and nectar from the summer blooms of Rodney Park, Branklyn Gardens, suburban borders, tenement window boxes and waterside weeds. On wasteground running up from the river near Bowerswell House, thin, straggly dog roses struggle to bloom, Ruskin-like, but here was once the nurseries of Dickson & Brown, famous for their cultivation of the pure white Scotch rose.

Fated to die young, the increasingly bedridden Perth poet William Soutar tasted the sweet nectar of a brief summer blooming:

'The Tryst'

O luely, luely, cam she in
And luely she lay doun:
I kent her be her caller lips
And her breists sae sma' and roun'.

A' thru the nicht we spak nae word
Nor sinder'd bane frae bane:
A' thru the nicht I heard her hert
Gang soundin' wi' my ain.

It was about the waukrife hour
When cocks begin to craw
That she smool'd saftly thru the mirk
Afore the day wud daw.

Sae luely, luely, cam she in
Saie luely was she gaen;
And wi' her a' my simmer days
Like they had never been.

The name 'Perth' is from the Pictish/Gaelic for 'woodland'. The growth of the town into an important place for trade, both internal and external, developed from the early years of the second millennium. Around AD 1100 an Irish-style round tower, one of only two in Scotland, was being raised at the Celtic church just downriver at Abernethy. It has fine views along the south bank of the Tay, but if it was used as a belfry, then it signals, perhaps, a final flourish of the Celtic church, which had its roots in Columba's Iona and St Fillan. By the 1120s Augustinian monks had taken possession of the Culdee church at Scone on the river north-east of Perth and built their own priory on the site. They were part of a gradual usurpation of the ecclesiastical power along the Tay by a church that looked south to Rome rather than westwards for direction.

St Martin plays a significant role in this spread of Latin

Christianity. He was a Roman soldier who on seeing a beggar shivering by the roadside drew his sword and cut his cloak in half to share with the man. Another of the stories told of his life is that despite fierce opposition he persuaded a Druidical community to convert to Christianity. He told them that they must cut down their sacred tree to complete their conversion from paganism. 'Only if you stand before it as we cut it down,' they said. He agreed, and the ancient tree was felled but miraculously missed the saint. Martin became Bishop of Tours in France; he cast down pagan temples and altars and founded monasteries that spread across Europe. In Scotland, the rival Culdee tradition was assimilated or overthrown.

Along the Tay the oral, bardic tradition of prehistory and the early saints merges with the written word of the lingua franca, Latin, washed in from the continent. It was the Latin of the invader that described the fleeting ebb and flow of ancient Roman influence on the Tay. The spread of monasticism and later university education were to establish its firm foothold. On the lower reaches of the river those who could write preserved their stories, set them in stone. In the Middle Ages the stone buildings noted for their absence by Roman invaders began to rise in the towns forming along the banks of the Tay. Churches lay at the centre of these burghs. Perth was chiefly known as Sanct John's Toun, named after the church dedicated to the Baptist at its core, an image of him blessing with water cast on a bell in its tower. A range of ecclesiastical houses of continental European origin become established in and around it, like the Augustinians at Scone.

These holy orders dapple like light on the waters of the Tay – Blackfriars (Dominicans), Whitefriars (Carmelites), Greyfriars (Franciscans), Carthusian monks and nuns (their order originating, like the sacred axehead, in the Alps), the nuns of St Leonard's Priory and of St Paul's, the house of the Bishop of Dunkeld washing away the vestiges of the old Celtic Christianity of the previous millennium. Around these religious houses the town grew, trades and crafts became established along its vennels, the river Almond was diverted to provide both a lade to power the burgh's mills and a moat to strengthen it defences.

Archaeological excavations in the medieval town revealed fragments of pots: Scottish redware, Scottish gritty whiteware, Yorkshire ware, Rouen ware. One of these vessels had a decorative band of scallop shells. Crossing the Queen's Bridge I turn up the Watergate. The entrance to a vennel on the old High Street has fragments of the medieval past in plain sight: the sculpted head of a holy man or bishop plundered from some religious house and repurposed is flanked by a pair of scallop shells. The shells speak of the sea, of pilgrimage, of St James, that fisher of men. Turning north along Tay Street, I pass Smeaton's Bridge, the Auld Brig, its dressed red sandstone blocks etched with the dates of the Tay's great floods. Like deaths on a family gravestone, the dates are memorialised: above the Roman numerals XVIII, 'height of flood 15th June 1931' is etched, then progressively higher: 1894, 1990, 1950, higher still at 22 feet in 1847, 1993, the carving still sharp till the height of the great flood of 12 February 1814, when 23 feet is reached.

The January 1993 flood is still sharp in the memory. A thaw after midwinter blizzards had caused an unprecedented amount of water to flow into the Tay from across its Highland catchment. People had to be rescued from their homes by the army in boats; helicopters that the previous week had lifted people off snowbound roads were winching people off the roofs of their houses. Perth and surrounding areas were the worst affected, Muirton, north of the city centre, bearing the brunt of it when the river burst its banks. Ian Rutherford's newspaper photograph of a resident up to his waist in water dialling the emergency services from a public phone box is an iconic image of the event. After the floodwaters had receded, a massive programme of flood defences was undertaken along the North and South Inches, the town's traditional flood plains. The barriers on the North Inch that adjoin Smeaton's Bridge are impressive. The pair of bronze gates with panels designed by David F. Wilson are etched with flowing motifs and images that capture the river's power – a power that can destroy but also rejuvenate, nourish and enrich. Among the images is that of the Cailleach, the winter queen, who used her staff to swirl the waters to create storms and floods but who, come spring, would also cast the same staff onto the frozen land and rivers to break the spell of winter. The floodgates now protect Perth from flooding – but only if they are closed. In October last year, despite flood alerts, they were left open and the Tay flooded properties bordering the Inch.

On Perth's North Inch today all signs of that flooding have gone. I wander into the sedate tree-lined parkland which for now is dry underfoot. The river will inevitably flood again but when it does one hopes those with responsibility will identify the risk and act faster. Knowledge of who were the actual combatants at the Battle of the Clans, fought here in 1396, will never be identified for sure. Andrew of Wyntoun, who may have been an eyewitness, writes:

A thousand and thre hundyr yere
Nynty and sex to mak all clere,
Off thre score wyld Scottis men
Thretty agane thretty then
In felny bornyt of auld fed,
As thare fore elderis ware slane to dede.
Tha thre score ware Clannys twa,
Clahynnhe' Qwhewyl*, and Clachinyha†:
Off thir twa kynnys ware tha men,
Thretty agane thretty then.

And thare thai had than chifftanys twa:
Schir Ferqwharis sone‡ wes ane of tha,
The tothir Cristy Johnesone.
A selcouth§ thing be thai wes done:
At Sanctjohnestone# besid the Freris

The North Inch (the name half English/half Gaelic, *insch* meaning island, or island in boggy or wet land) was at the time marshy ground outside the burgh adjacent to the Blackfriar's Monastery, Wyntoun's 'Freris'. The

---

* Clan Wheel? † Clan Chattan; ‡ Sir Farqhuar's son
§ extraordinary; # Saint John's Town (Perth)

Dominican friars' house was a favourite place of King Robert III. A welcome staging post, Perth was a convenient crossing place to hold court on his progresses round his kingdom. This transient ground outside the burgh and bordered by the Tay lay across the river from Scone, the site of his coronation and the source of his regal authority. The river, the backdrop for this most remarkable event, having collected its waters in the Highlands, is about to complete its journey in the Lowlands.

Unable to stop the constant inter-clan warfare between Clan Chattan (a confederation of smaller clans, including MacThomases, MacPhails and MacBeans) and Clahynnhe Qwhewyl (Clan Wheel?), the king bid them fight it out before him. Who Clahynnhe Qwhewyl were has never been satisfactorily resolved but they may have been either external clan enemies, such as the Camerons, or an internal grouping struggling for control of the confederation. Summoning the disputants before him, Robert hoped that this quasi-judicial 'battle' would resolve the dispute and reinforce regal authority.

In the *Computum Custumariorum burgi de Perth*, which lists the king's expenditure records, is the sum of £14 2 shillings 11 pence 'for timber, iron and making of lists (joust enclosures) for 60 persons fighting in the Inch of Perth'. But the idea and the 'battle' itself was a shoddy parody of the medieval ideal of noble knights jousting or of the combat described by the classical historian Livy between the three Horatii brothers of Rome and three Cuiriatii brothers of their Italian rivals the Albans: 'they should fight, three against three . . . as the champions of their countries, the victorious to have dominion over the vanquished'. The three Curiatii brothers slayed two of the Romans but were then in turn each vanquished by the last of the Horatii.

Allowing sixty men, un-mailed and dressed only in their long shirts, armed with bows or crossbows, swords, battle-axes, daggers and only round leather targes or shields for defence, to fight it out in a gladiatorial arena was a clear statement of the ruling Lowland Scots' contempt for the Highlands and very near to a judicially authorised massacre.

Walter Bower, writing fifty years afterwards, says that the debacle was 'like butchers killing cattle in a slaughter-house'.

Centuries later Sir Walter Scott opens *The Fair Maid of Perth* with this romantic re-enactment:

The trumpets of the King sounded a charge, the bag-pipes blew up their screaming and maddening notes, and the combatants, starting forward in regular order, and increasing their pace, till they came to a smart run, met together in the centre of the ground, as a furious land torrent encounters an advancing tide.

Blood flowed fast, and the groans of those who fell began to mingle with the cries of those who fought. The wild notes of the pipes were still heard above the tumult and stimulated to further exertion the fury of the combatants.

At once, however, as if by mutual agreement, the instruments sounded a retreat. The two parties disengaged themselves from each other to take breath for a few minutes. About twenty of both sides lay on the field, dead or dying; arms and legs lopped off, heads cleft to the chin, slashes deep through the shoulder to the breast, showed at once the fury of the combat, the ghastly character of the weapons used, and the fatal strength of the arms which wielded them.

Whoever the combatants, all sources agree that Clan Chattan emerged victorious with ten survivors (sometimes they are mortally wounded), but of Clan Wheel all died – except, that is, for the one man who leapt into the Tay and swam to safety.

If the combatants were Chattan and Cameron, then the king's bloody ploy didn't work. In 1429, in revenge for a cattle raiding spreagh the two clans were butchering each other in a Highland church in the Battle of Palm Sunday. And Robert's successor, King James I, found no sanctuary within the walls of Blackfriar's. On the night of 20 February 1437 kinsmen of the Earl of Atholl entered the monastery and, having pursued the fleeing king down a sewer, assassinated him.

Drip, drip, drip. Duncan, Macbeth, James. Spilt blood drops into itself. See in slow motion it form a liquid crown, but in real time it dissolves into itself . . . and is gone.

# Strathearn

*Romans, Christians, Jacobites*

Curving south of Perth and back into the Highlands is the river Earn. It is the southernmost of the Tay's main tributaries, the pinkie on your hand map of the river. Flowing out from Loch Earn at the village of St Fillans, it passes through gently undulating hills and rich farmlands. It is countryside, but commutable enough to Perth and the Central Belt to have a suburban feel in places. It has to be forded to reach the Central Lowlands and is bounded by the Ochil Hills, which have to be crossed to reach Edinburgh or skirted to pass through the gap at Dunblane to Stirling and Glasgow beyond.

Just south of Perth that road climbs out of the hollow of Strathearn over the Gask Ridge and into the valley of the Tay. It is a route I have travelled all my life (though we have both changed on the way). The current dual carriageway was being constructed as I moved from the west to study in Dundee, from childhood by the Clyde to the beginnings of adult life by the Tay. The new road climbs Cairnie Brae to the east of the old at a gradient adapted to articulated lorries, tourist buses and electric hybrids, but the road I am walking down just now is even older, two thousand years old. Its gradient was determined by the two-ox cart and experience gained in an empire that stretched from Tibbermore to the Tiber, the Jordan to the Danube, the Nile to the Taus.

This road is a masterpiece of strategic planning. It starts from the fort at Ardoch on the southwestern slopes of Strathearn, marching to the one at Strageath just below Crieff, then runs parallel with the Earn until it cuts northward to Tibermore and on to Bertha, the legionary fortress at the confluence of the Almond and Tay on the northern outskirts of Perth. The whole of this fertile valley, once a heartland of the southern Picts, is both traversed and observed. Watchtowers – ditched and double-ditched – are placed along its length, ensuring constant and speedy communication. The road is straight but not dogmatically so; where it was prudent for it to deviate, then it did. Experience gained first in the valley of the Tiber, then throughout the mountains and plains of the Italian peninsula and into Europe, Africa and Asia led to the speed of the mastery of this landscape and construction of the road, all within a few short years around AD 75–86/7. A huge amount of military construction was completed in a very short timescale, but just as quickly it ended. A greater threat to the Empire on another river frontier – that of the Danube – led to the withdrawal of the legions, the Caledonians sufficiently, if not entirely, vanquished.

The Romans left a template of how to subdue Scotland: drive supply routes east and west through the Southern Uplands, secure the Central Belt and have naval forces on the Clyde and Forth, send a fleet round the north coast, and build forts at the entrances to Highland glens, blocking off access to the rich pasturage and farmlands of the Lowlands. As the Tay collects the waters of the Southern Highlands along its length, the Romans constructed forts at the junctions of its tributaries – Carpow at the mouth of the Earn, Bertha at the Almond, Inchtuthil at the Isla.

The section of this Roman road I'm walking along is now a forest track. The warm southern sun has shrunk winter puddles along the rutted path, leaving timelines of concentric tidelines of February's storm-tossed pine needles and, within them, spring pollen. In a square clearing among the trees of Dupplin is the round earthwork remains of one of these lookout stations. While the timber framework has gone, the double-ditch of the defensive earthworks is clearly visible, bog grasses growing in the damp moat, rich mosses and heathers on the raised platform. Clumps of heather and bog myrtle suggest where once wooden posts may have stood; last autumn's pale leaf litter from the silver birches that fringe the site is withering among the woody stems and lichen-mottled twigs.

A sudden movement catches my eye as a more observant lookout reacts to my invasion of its territory. Too quick, it is gone. I approach the next clump with circumspection.

There on sentry duty is a common lizard, warming its blood in this northern outpost's sun like one of the Syrian archers who was stationed here two thousand years ago. Lulled by my commando stealth, hibernation, post coital torpor or the live young growing inside its warm womb, it sits seemingly unmoving, but as I watch I can see its sharp eye taking in my every move, its tiny claws tensing, ready to surrender its black-tipped tail should I make a grab for it (the tail would grow back but shorter than the original). The straight line of its back is yellow brown, its flanks rust, both semaphored by a morse code of paler dots and dashes. Flattening itself, its armoured flanks ripple like water, drinking in the sun's vital warmth.

Moist, pendulous bilberries are spring's tiny pink fruit offering, paired with a vermillion ladybird wandering amongst the heather. Nearby a mulberry and gold metallic shield bug marches obliviously on its verdant way; a uniformly black-and-gold-striped bumblebee drones on an aerial route dictated by the vagaries of patches of flowering purple milk-vetch and heath milkwort.

The Gask Ridge sits like an old frog in a boggy pond edged by hills and mountains. South and east lie the Ochils with their pre-Roman vitrified forts, Gleneagles and, beyond, the Allan Water, which flows away from the Tay through the gap in the hills at Dunblane and into the Forth. To the south and west, due to the sweeping curve of the Highland Line, you look back on to the high peaks of the mountains of the Trossachs and into the southern Highlands. Westwards, then to the north, the Perthshire hills with the snow-capped Grampians beyond

– their name an erroneously medieval transcription from the Battle of Mons Graupius, which Tacitus describes as the crucial victory of the Roman general Agricola over the united tribes of Caledonia. Led by Calgacus, the first named Scot, Tacitus has him declare in a speech before the battle that the invaders 'create desolation and call it peace'. The road, forts and signal towers, and a further large fort at Dalginross, south of Comrie, are integral parts of that Pax Romana, but despite two further incursions into Tayside in the reigns of emperors Antoninus (AD 142) and Septimius Severus (208), it was over a thousand years before southern influence began to alter this landscape.

A long-held but erroneous belief was that Pontius Pilate, the Roman Governor of Judaea who washed his hands of Christ's crucifixion, was born at Fortingall, where the ancient yew was already a thousand years old. Search the internet for 'Inchtuthil' and it won't be long before you are offered 'Roman crucifixion nails' to purchase. Over 850,000 square-shafted nails of varying lengths have been recovered from the site of Scotland's largest legionary fort at Inchtuthil in the parish of Caputh, near the cursus on a plateau close to the confluence of the Tay and Isla. That so many iron nails were buried by the Romans when they abandoned the fort shows both the scale of their building and their scrupulousness in leaving nothing behind that could be smelted and used against them. The pit in which they were buried was elaborately concealed under the fort's huge workshops. At other abandoned forts, wells were infilled with metal objects and dressed stones that couldn't be carried away.

Construction of the fort began in AD 83, but it was abandoned four years later. Five and a half thousand troops could be accommodated within its double-ditched ramparts. Its accommodation ranged from basic barracks that held eighty men of the auxiliary cohorts to more comfortable rooms with sophisticated underfloor heating sytems for the legion's elite troops and master-craftsmen, a welcome luxury in the freezing Perthshire winter. There was stabling for the 120 horses of the units' cavalry, and at its centre stood the administrative headquarters, where soldiers' pay would be stored and the legion's eagle and gods housed. The fort was testament to the practiced efficiency of Imperial Rome. Six granaries held tribute from local tribes, and ovens to bake hundreds of loaves of bread were built. There was a hospital to tend the expected or actual large numbers of injured or ill. Although nothing but ramparts remain above the surface, the fact that, uniquely, no town developed upon the site means its archaeology is the most complete of any legionary fort in the whole of the empire.

Four stone steps are all that remain of the bath house in the officers' quarters. Drains and sewers were dug, which Historic Environment Scotland suggest would have required the diverting of water several miles upstream of the fort by some form of aqueduct to be able to service the fort on its elevated plateau. The Romans were certainly capable of engineering that, but they abandoned the site before work could begin. As for its discharge, the Roman practice was, as the Cloaca Maxima sewer on the Tiber in the centre of Rome demonstrates, to flush their privies and bathwater into the nearest river, sacred or not.

The fort was to be a vital component of the Roman's strategy of containing the north and securing the southern half of the island of Britain. By building a series of forts at the mouths of the Highland valleys from the north bank of the Clyde in the west to Stracathro north of Montrose in the east – commonly known as 'glen-blockers' – any incursion by the Caledonians could be held up until reinforcements came, either from the XX Legion at Inchtuthil or, if needed, southern troops of the II Legion at Chester could arrive via the Gask Ridge. These forts follow the geology of the Highland Fault and the catchments of the Tay. Whether or not there were any plans to go beyond the mere containment of the Caledonians and invade further into Highland Tayside, the urgent withdrawal of the II Legion to reinforce the Danube frontier saw the XX redeployed to Chester and Inchtuthil abandoned before it could be completed. Until recently this was thought to have been a sudden withdrawal, but a denarius coin of the Emperor Domitian, dated AD 86, was excavated from the site, suggesting this happened over a longer period.

Which Taysiders withdrew with the legion? Soldiers recruited forcibly or voluntarily for auxiliary units to be posted on the far side of the Empire, like the Syrians and Germans who served in Scotland? Servants, slaves, wives, children, camp followers – who went with the legion south? Hostages, semi-captive high-ranking tribespeople, 'guests' of the Empire to ensure compliant behaviour? Those seeking a new life – escape, adventure?

The Goddess Fides, holding ears of grain and a basket of fruits, is depicted on the reverse of the Roman coin. She personifies the obligation soldiers owed to the state, a reminder to the troops that while they are rewarded in silver for their service, having accepted Caesar's denarius, they also owe a duty to Rome. The mere presence of the powerful military camp was also an all too obvious reminder to the locals, enough to prevent further conflict. Tribute from Taysiders of ears of grain and baskets of berries to the occupying forces, and gifts to tribal chieftains, would have kept a degree of peace along the river's lower catchments. Diplomacy was usually preferred to war.

The clear glass cup excavated at Airlie has passed from occupier to occupied. It is like water solidified, a simple yet magical thing, wonderful to its Caledonian possessor – not an object to be kept in the world of the living but a vessel withdrawn to another world, to the gods. If the Romans were dutiful, logical and pragmatic, efficient at planning, building and administrating, makers of glass, they were also highly superstitious. A ritual pit lies at the centre of the fort, but whether used to take auspices before the fort was built or used by legionaries during its occupation is unclear. Perhaps offerings were made to a local deity, for, as well as their own Roman gods, the gods of the auxiliary troops from across the empire would also be worshipped in this frontier land and the troops would respect local gods, often assimilating them into their pantheon – Caledonian gods would have travelled with those recruited into the legions. It may be that offerings were made to Tatha by these armies from over the Alps four thousand years after the jadeite axehead had made a similar journey.

The fort at Carpow at the mouth of the Earn is from the later campaign of the Emperor Severus at the beginning of the third century. According to the historian Cassius Dio, aware that Roman emperors were both made and unmade by the favour of their soldiers, 'Severus, seeing . . . that the legions were becoming enervated by idleness, made a campaign against Britain.' His goal was to subdue the Maeatae, who controlled the lands between the Antonine Wall and the Tay, and the Caledonians north of the river. He raised an army that may have numbered as many as fifty thousand troops. The fort at Carpow seems to have been the northernmost port of a naval supply chain that provisioned the invading legions along the east coast from the Tyne to the Forth to the Tay. It was a substantial construction, a double-ditched, stone-built headquarters, with roof tiles which bore the boastful imprint of the Sixth Legion Victrix PFB – Pia Fidelis Britannica (Dutiful and Faithful Victors over Britain). The intention seems to have been for this to become a base from which a longer occupation or suppression of the north could be achieved. His son, co-ruler and successor Caracalla, famous now for his baths in Rome, minted a coin or medallion in AD 209 which depicts troops crossing a pontoon bridge, a method probably used to ford the Tay. The Severan campaign, though, was short and only partially successful. Cassius Dio, who was writing contemporaneously and had personal experience of governing in a Roman province, reports:

Severus, accordingly, desiring to subjugate the whole of [the island of Britain], invaded Caledonia. But as he advanced through the country he experienced countless hardships in cutting down the forests, levelling the heights, filling up the swamps, and bridging the rivers; but he fought no battle and beheld no enemy in battle array. The enemy purposely put sheep and cattle in front of the soldiers for them to seize, in order that they might be lured on still further until they were worn out; for in fact the water caused great suffering to the Romans, and when they became scattered, they would be attacked. Then, unable to walk, they would be slain by their own men, in order to avoid capture, so that a full fifty thousand died.

But Severus did not desist until he approached the extremity of the island. Here he observed most accurately the variation of the sun's motion and the length of the days and the nights in summer and winter respectively.

Having thus been conveyed through practically the whole of the hostile country (for he actually was conveyed in a covered litter most of the way, on account of his infirmity), he returned to the friendly portion, after he had forced the Britons to come to terms, on the condition that they should abandon a large part of their territory.

If the Romans first showed invaders how to subdue Scotland, the Caledonians' tactic of waging guerrilla warfare was a blueprint for how to resist, enraging the Emperor, his fury murderous, alas (*ochone*) also a blueprint for future invaders.

He ordered: 'Let no one escape sheer destruction / No one our hands, not even the babe in the womb of the mother / If it be male; let it nevertheless not escape sheer destruction.'

Yet 'the water caused great suffering to the Romans'. Severus caught some (water-borne?) disease and fell ill. Retreating, he died at York. Caracalla hurried back to Rome, his father's ashes in an urn of purple stone, to secure the succession. Like the Agricolan and Antonine campaigns, Imperial ambition to control the lands north of the Tay ebbed away southwards.

If the Roman gods are looking favourably on my account, the bird of prey that is circling imperiously over Carpow as I write this would be an eagle, but it's just a lazy local buzzard scanning the Strathearn fields, the shrill piping not the harassing guerrilla tactics of painted Caledonians rattling their spears but a pair of noisy piebald oystercatchers seeing it off their riverside territory.

Literacy allowed the Romans to communicate their experience directly to us. The story of their occupation, the forts and roads, excavated from the earth or seen from above in the summer parched fields by eagle-eyed aerial archaeologists along the river, further deepens our knowledge. We can admire the Romans' learning and knowledge, foresight and organisation, their regimented engineering, but also question their folly, their strange beliefs. We don't have to take their vision of us as fact. Cassius Dio, though writing contemporaneously, was doing so from far away beside the shores of the Mediterranean for a readership who were the imperial ruling class. This is not dispassionate reportage:

There are two principal races of the Britons, the Caledonians and the Maeatae, and the names of the others have been merged in these two. The Maeatae live next to the cross-wall which cuts the island in half, and the Caledonians are beyond them. Both tribes inhabit wild and waterless mountains and desolate and swampy plains, and possess neither walls, cities, nor tilled fields, but live on their flocks, wild game, and certain fruits; for they do not touch the fish which are there found in immense and inexhaustible quantities. They dwell in tents, naked and unshod, possess their women in common, and in common rear all the offspring. Their form of rule is democratic for the most part, and they are very fond of plundering; consequently they choose their boldest men as rulers. They go into battle in chariots, and have small, swift horses; there are also foot-soldiers, very swift in running and very firm in standing their ground. For arms they have a shield and a short spear, with a bronze apple attached to the end of the spear-shaft, so that when it is shaken it may clash and terrify the enemy; and they also have daggers.

They can endure hunger and cold and any kind of hardship; for they plunge into the swamps and exist there for many days with only their heads above water, and in the forests they support themselves upon bark and roots, and for all emergencies they prepare a certain kind of food, the eating of a small portion of which, the size of a bean, prevents them from feeling either hunger or thirst.

So, can we believe what Cassius Dio tells us? The Caledonians and Maeatae do not till the land, he says, yet, as we have seen, farming was established across the Tay catchment for at least three thousand years before the Romans. Indeed, plough marks were discovered in the archaeology under the Roman fort at Boathill on the Tay.

Stone-built towns would not have existed, and certainly there would have been pastoralists, herders, hunters and foragers who lived in tents, but they were unlikely to have gone naked. Plundering, as we will see, in historical times, would certainly have formed part of some Highland communities' culture. We know little of personal relationships but a certain clannishness would have been the basis for social structures, just as it was for the Romans. Severus had himself posthumously adopted into the family of the Emperor Marcus Aurelius. No spear with bronze apple rattle is known to us.

It seems unlikely that these people existed in bogs, with only their heads above water, for many days, but they would most likely have been able to survive very well by foraging and would have carried some kind of emergency rations whether at war or peace.

Perhaps the most startling line is 'for they do not touch the fish which are there found in immense and inexhaustible quantities'. This seems remarkable, and he gives no reason for this statement. If this was the case, how widespread a prohibition across society was it? Did it apply to the full week or year, or only seasonally or at festivals, and was there some kind of religious element to it? The salmon etched on Pictish stones across Tayside immediately after the Roman invasion show a detailed knowledge of their physiognomy. Lack of evidence of fishing up to the medieval period neither proves nor disproves the claim: an excavated bone needle may be used to sew a net, but was the net used for capturing wild fowl or fish? The recently introduced practice of finely sieving soil on Iron Age archaeological sites is able to detect fish bones and may provide that evidence in future. Shells, being larger and sturdier than fish bones, are found in abundance in Iron Age middens and are the same as those found today along the Tay's intertidal zones – mussels, cockles, clams and razor clams. The shells and claws of crabs that come inshore seasonally from the deeper waters out in the Firth would have also formed a minor part of the diets of the river's coastal communities.

Evidence of the use of whale bone and thus by implication also their meat, oil and blubber exists, but as to them being actively hunted we cannot say. Today whales become stranded on Scotland's beaches as they must have done in the past. As we shall see later, occasionally one enters the river itself and it could be conjectured that in, such an instance a whale may have been pursued and killed. Oil and blubber, and waterproof skins, were certainly obtained from the hunting of seals.

Recent large-scale isotopic analysis of 137 skeletons from the Pictish settlement further north on the coast at Portmahomack, starting from the sixth century, found that neither river nor sea fish formed part of the people's diet. So perhaps there was some kind of taboo on the eating of fish. Until we have more data we cannot know. The invaders didn't miss out on their favourite seafood, though: garum, a fish sauce popular with the Romans, was imported in clay amphoras stamped with a maker's mark from southern Spain and found at Carpow.

Whilst the Romans minted coins etched with images of pontoon bridges spanning the rivers of their earthly Empire, on its northern fringe the people along the Tay carved on monoliths salmon with a different kind of knowledge, swimming in another world beyond human measurement and control. That knowledge has now slipped like a fish through the fingers into the dark depths of the past.

Another symbolic fish with origins at the far end of the Roman empire was to succeed in unifying the peoples of the Tay and the Tiber, where emperors had failed. Cassius Dio, though thoroughly Roman, wrote in ancient Greek. In that language, 'Jesus Christ, Son of God, Savior' produced the acronym ICHTHYS, the word for 'fish'.

Across Tayside, there are many Pictish stones, richly ornamented. These enigmatic stones were carved in eastern and north-eastern Scotland between the sixth and ninth centuries. We know very little about them, but they have been roughly categorised into three types, however inexact this may be:

Class I: rough stones, incised with symbols, pagan, sixth to eighth century.

Class II: dressed stones, carved in relief with at least one large Christian cross. Animals or other symbols fill the spaces around the arms of the cross, and on the other side of the stone, eighth to ninth century.

Class III: so wide in its scope that almost any sculptured work from the later eighth and ninth century can be encompassed within it. One defining feature is that all these stones have no Pictish elements.

Moving out of the area of Strathearn to Meigle in Strathmore for a moment, the museum in the converted Victorian schoolhouse has a most impressive roll-call of complete and fragmented stones of different classes: a late eighth-century cross has imagery copied from an monastic book; a repurposed standing stone with a ringed cross based on a piece of jewellery is majestic in its beauty; zoomorphic creatures interlace with the huntsmen and warriors who gallop across their surfaces; biblical scenes swirl next to mythological imagery – Daniel is assailed on four sides in the lion's den, a centaur beside a felled tree brandishes an axe in each hand; an ox is devoured headfirst by a beast; salmon swim fossilised across red sandstone.

They are made by a culture rich in visual expression. Despite postulations that it was a society where matrilinear descent played an important role, it is one that has left us very few representations of women. Neither has it left us many of its words. What could we have learned from listening to their bards and priests – roll-calls of their ancestors, tales of resistance to the salmon eaters from the south in their fish-scaled armour, the coming in coracles of holy men from the west with their tales of Daniel's piety beside the Euphrates, Christ's baptism in the Jordan? Alas, all we have is the second- and third-hand mentions in later texts of a language more akin to Gaulish than Gaelic, and in fragments of place names: aber, the mouth of a river; carden, a thicket; pit, a share or portion. Pitkelly, the share of the bard or storyteller.

Back in Strathearn, it's the last weekend in April and the fields around the river are ridged with new furrows. Tractors bounce along narrow lanes where, under high hedgerows, a carpet of discarded copper is the first sign of beech coming into fresh, green leaf. The lane's meandering course follows the twists and turns of the river in stark contrast to the arrow-straight directness of the Roman road to the west. This geography of curving rivers and connecting roads makes the area around Forteviot and Dunning an ideal meeting place, and this has made it a place of significance throughout history.

In the damp soil by the river, meadowsweet is starting to grow again as it has done here for millennia. When a 4,000-year-old tomb was excavated in the early years of the twenty-first century here, a clearly identifiable sprig of it was found, a grave gift among offerings of white river pebbles and interwoven birch bark. The massive capstone covering the grave was discovered to have been repurposed from earlier human use, bearing carved cup marks and etched with a meandering spiral.

The river eddies, too, sending blossom petals spiralling under the span of the bridge. History spins in this riverside landscape where many paths cross. Imagine rituals, ceremonies and processions, possibly by torchlight, circling the huge Neolithic palisaded timber enclosure that occupied the valley floor here, or bards reciting the genealogy, the leaps over moats, the epic combats of the warrior chief as his remains are interred in a Bronze Age grave, paeans ring out 'Ochain, ochain, ochone'.

This significance is the reason why the Romans drove their road straight past it, keeping a watch on the area from the Gask Ridge. It is why the Picts set up a massive and elaborately carved cross on a natural plateau above the river at Dupplin around AD 800. Relocated just a few years ago to inside the local kirk at Dunning for its protection, the magnificently sculpted cross is nine feet high, with arms three feet wide. It is thrust, symbolically, into what appears to be a pagan altar stone. Current thinking suggests that it was placed here because it marked an important boundary.

From the spiralling river of time, the name of the tomb's occupant, once remembered by a successive stream of bards, is now forgotten. But on the Dupplin Cross a name is etched in stone and survives.

During or soon after the reign of King Constantine (fl. AD 793–820), a partially legible Latin inscription was carved into the Dupplin Cross, which seems to read 'Custantin filus Firgus' (Constantine son of Fergus). This combination of a king named after the first Christian Roman Emperor, the father's Gaelic name, the Pictish decoration and the Biblical iconography seems to inform the carvings.

On the front, Constantine is depicted on horseback, his head enlarged, a nod to that of the later King Malcolm Canmore (Gaelic: *ceann*, head; *mor*, big). Under him march a line of smaller warriors, rhythmical with spear and shield, a bodyguard, Praetorians. Round on the left flank are more soldiers, bigger than the warriors, smaller than the king, possibly Angus, Constantine's brother, who was to succeed him, and slightly smaller again, perhaps his son Domnall. Facial hair as well as scale seems to be a marker of rank. The king is heavily bearded, while Angus is significantly more moustachioed than his nephew. The warriors are clean-shaven. Returning to the front a triumvirate of hunting dogs bound beneath the warriors, hence the idea that the stone maybe signified a border of royal hunting land.

The panel above nephew and uncle is of two horse-like beasts entwined, their hooves in each other's mouths. It has been suggested that this symbolises unification of the two great kingdoms: Pictland of the east and north, and Dalriada of the Scots of the west under Constantine. Constantine himself is named after the first of the Roman emperors to convert to Christianity and at the bottom left corner of the stone a simple piece of three-stranded knotwork hints to the Holy Trinity. On the right-hand side another knotwork panel, when studied closely, reveals a snake pierced with its own tale. The origin of this is undoubtably the Viking symbol of eternity, but under Constantine the Vikings seem to have been driven out of his kingdom, at least temporarily, hence it is stabbed by itself. Soon after his death, they were back.

A king who protects his people is the message on a decorative scene on the rear of the stone. It comes from the Old Testament and shows David, before he slew Goliath, as the shepherd defending his flock from bear and lion. Higher up we see David again, this time with his harp in hand, composing and singing the psalms. In the non-literate Pictish world the bard was not only musician, storyteller and ancestor-reciter but priest-magician. In the figure of David, priest and king merge. As Tay and Earn merge, and the Scottish kingdom starts to form, both temporal king and spiritual priest are vital to the formation of the new nation.

At Forteviot, an arch was constructed. What is an arch? What does it do? What is its significance? It vaults the space between two separate objects, makes a gateway, forms a bridge. The Forteviot Arch was recovered from the Water of May (a tributary of the Earn at Forteviot) in the early nineteenth century and is now an exhibit at the National Museum of Scotland. This elaborately decorated stone arch once formed part of a Christian altar. A cross carved at its apex has been defaced, but the figures on either side are still clearly defined, if awkwardly positioned into the curving space. To the left of the cross a large male figure, moustachioed, possibly bearded, is holding a staff or rod or oar in both hands. A horned ox is at his feet.

Beside the defaced cross a lamb sits on its hind legs, and to its right two moustachioed, hooded and robed figures, smaller than the first, also bearing staffs, are curved into the arc. While we can postulate that these are kings or priests, or Christ and two disciples, the message seems to be that they are working together on some strenuous task, bending their backs into it. Are they powering a ship of state or a fishing boat on the Sea of Galilee, or possibly pile-driving stakes to form an enclosure or palisade around a church or a palace, or both? Their task is real and symbolic. They are shepherds of their flocks, drovers of cattle, herders, protectors, leaders – people of power. The arch was part of a statement of power. So confident in that power were the builders of the arch that it was located on the flat valley floor, down by the river, among the relics of ancient ancestors, rather than on a defensive hilltop.

Another interpretation of the figures is that the largest is the king and the two hooded priests or bishops represent the Pictish and Gaelic communities, joined together in the symbolic and sacred act of bending their backs in creating a holy site at the centre of a new state. The iconography is a blending of the Pictish and Dalriadic.

The church, on land magnanimously donated by the king, housed both the arch and a special holy relic, perhaps a bone of St Andrew, who was to become Scotland's patron saint.

The site is associated with Kenneth MacAlpin (Cináed mac Ailpin), King of the Gaels of Dál Riada, who became King of the Picts and the first king of both (848–858). The previously held view – that at Forteviot the kingdom and

Christian practices of the country became one – is perhaps more symbolic of a gradual coming together of western Gaels with the northern and eastern Picts under one governance than the immediate formation of a complete entity. This history is mirrored in the area's geography: the coming together of the Highland Tay with the last of its major tributaries, the Earn, and their meeting with the estuarine Firth.

Here, fresh and saltwater meet with time and tide, keeping both in brackish flux. This new kingdom was being called Alba by the reign of Constantine II (*c.* 879–952). In AD 906 he met with Cellach, Bishop of the Scots, at Scone, where they 'pledged themselves that the laws and disciplines of the faith, and the rights in churches and gospels, should be kept in conformity'.

This concord mutually strengthened the positions of the two most powerful elements of the newly formed state, making Crown and Church more secure. Beyond its political significance at the time, and how it has influenced history since, it gives some insight into how ancient places along the river may have been used. The site where king and bishop pledged their fraternal support is an artificially constructed lozenge-shaped embankment above the Tay, its shape recalling the cursuses of the distant past, the platform on the stone circle at Croft Moraig. It is used as a meeting place, a place for the display of power. At Scone's Moot Hill, the king, with his nobles and supporters, affirms the rights of the bishop with his clerics and priests, and the hill henceforth becomes 'the Hill of Belief' (*Collis Credulitatis* in the Latin of the Church). When the king dies and a new king is to be crowned, the ceremony takes place here at this place of mutual support – royal power is reaffirmed by its partner, the Church.

The Stone of Scone, a rather dull lump of Tayside rock in comparison with the many beautifully carved red sandstones in the area, is believed to be a relic from these enthronements. It has now returned to the Tay under the principle of restitution. Today it continues to play a ceremonial role in the coronation of the monarch of the latest edition of these united kingdoms but on the banks of the Thames rather than the Tay.

On the Tay, place-names like Breadalbane – 'Upper Alba' – reflect this history. Over the next few centuries, as the new state forms, the Gaelic of the Scots becomes dominant and is used in the documents in which the Crown records and thus controls the lands along the river. In the place-names recorded in Strathearn, traces of the early Church can be found.

Amulree in Gaelic is Ath Maol Ruibhe, 'the Ford of Maolrubha': he was a monk of St Columba's Iona who lived around AD 650. He crossed the water, bringing the good news of the Gospels. Safe passage must have been offered for those who prayed to St Patrick before crossing the river Earn via the Dalpatrick ferry. Gleneagles is not of the valley of eagles, but Gleann na h-Eaglais, 'Glen of the Church'.

Madderty is a combination of *meadair*, meaning a wooden bowl, and Ethernan, the name of an Irish monk who died among the Picts in AD 669. Where did this bowl come from, what was its purpose? A communion vessel transporting earthly wine into the spiritual blood of Christ, or a baptism cup whose water transformed sinner to saved? Where is it now?

The valley is itself a bowl, cupped in the hands of these holy men. We will soon hear of other holy wooden vessels – the now lost 'Mayne'; the preserved 'Brechbannoch', its shape like the Temple of Jerusalem in the *Book of Kells*, illuminated at Iona. When the resurgent Vikings plundered the western seaboard, Iona's great treasures were dispersed, many coming to Dunkeld only for them to be lost to the Danes, who in their shallow-draft longboats raided far up the Tay in 903. Perhaps another reason why Constantine and Cellach cemented the union of Scot and Pict.

In spite of the avarice of Vikings and zeal of Presbyterian reformers, these Celtic holy men are remembered and celebrated in the valley's churches today.

On the north side of Strathearn at Fowlis Wester, St Bean's church holds within itself a unique link to an all but disappeared past. The main road no longer runs through it, but like the Roman road over the Gask Ridge the passage of history remains constant nonetheless. Inside the church an ancient nine-foot-high carved stone cross is given sanctuary from the weather. Previously it had stood outside and was anointed with hot oils to protect it.

On one side, its panels are an intricate interlacing meditative knotwork, giving way to zoomorphic designs of beasts and birds. Then at the base, figures. On the other, a complex iconography of Pictish symbols, humans and animals. It is unique in its design. The horizontal bar of the cross projects beyond the profile of the stone, unknown in Scotland but common in Ireland. At some stage in the more recent past it has served also as an object of punishment. There is a chain of iron, which has held a collar or joug, once put around offenders' necks for public humiliation and punishment, to be rained on, snowed on, spat on, pissed on, flagellated, just like Christ.

If our perceptions of Christian behaviour today are different from those of the past, so too is our vision of Christ himself. On the ancient stone, the cross is meditative, contemplative, the eternal knotwork is infinite – pick a thread and ponder its endlessly stony flow. On the reverse, Christ is depicted as an earthly lord on horseback, caped, at the head of his followers, a noble hunting party, beneath him a phalanx of his troops armed with shield and spear. A horned cow is led by a harness, a bell round its neck, just like at Eassie – a sacrificial offering, a unit of wealth driven to market, a timeless rural daily or seasonal event.

Well over a thousand years separate the making of the stone and the stained-glass window a short distance across the aisle of the church. It depicts an Edwardian Christ in bleached white robes teaching the parable of the sower. In the background the landscape is the red-furrowed fields of the Strath, cupped in the bowl of purple mountains, another timeless rural scene. In this neat, ordered church the perceived depiction of Jesus carved on the stone or etched in the glass is not of an agonised, bloodied victim figure bound to a cross, but as a leader – a noble lord on horseback or a wise, lean, self-possessed teacher. He could be any one of the lairds, lords, earls, thanes or abbots that have controlled this land and people, commanding them to bend their backs into draining marshes, bridging streams, ditching fields. The impression is of quiet rural comfort, conservative wealth. After the cruelty of winter, Viking invasion, fighting both human and nature, this is a softer vision of life, a pause from the mountain stream and the rapids, a time to meander, water, nourish and grow.

In the years after the foundation of the new kingdom the flood plain of the river Earn saw new monastic establishments set about engineering a different physical and political as well as religious landscape. Sitting on an island in Methven bog was Inchaffray Abbey, an Augustinian establishment on the site of an older Celtic Christian community. A bronze seal from the fourteenth-century abbey depicts the figure of St John in the church, on the reverse his winged eagle. The inscription in Latin, not Gaelic, reads:

S'COMVNE:ECCE:SCI:IOh'IS:EWANGELISTE: DE: INSVLA: MISSARVM

('Common seal of the church of St John the Evangelist of the Island of Masses')

In this watery boundary land between Highland and Lowland, the Abbot of Inchaffray in the early years of the fourteenth century was Muireach (in Gaelic; Maurice in English and French, or Maurus in Latin). Like Bishop Cellach before him, he combined his spiritual role with high politics. He was a trusted supporter of King Robert the Bruce in the Wars of Independence. First he was sent by the king south on a diplomatic mission to negotiate with the English, then, when that was unsuccessful, to hold a service of blessing of the Scottish army on the eve of the Battle of Bannockburn. It was said that he had in his possession a reliquary – 'the Mayne' – which housed a sacred bone of St Fillan. It was probably similar in design to another carried at the battle, 'the Brechbannoch', a silver gilt box made of yew about AD 750, decorated with Pictish designs. Fearful of defeat and of losing the holy relic to the enemy, Muireach left the bone behind at Inchaffray. Raising the Mayne above his head for all the troops to see, he heard from inside it a rattle and when he cautiously opened the lid, there inside miraculously was the venerable saint's holy bone.

In the relative peace that victory brought, Muireach's successors and their neighbours set about improving the physical as well as the spiritual conditions of the people who lived by the Earn. The monks and their earthly superiors set about river management to prevent flooding of arable land and creating more by draining bog and marsh, planting trees to soak up the moisture.

Hints of this waterlogged geography remain in the strath's place names, too: Blackmoss-side, Blairs, Laigh of Cultmalundie, Muir o' Faulds, Sparrowmuir Wood. Behind the site of the abbey today runs Sweep's Stank (in Scots, a drain) and in front the Pow of Inchaffray, a unique waterway. 'Pow' is an Old Scots word for a drainage ditch, dating to the Middle Ages. The Pow must have been in existence since at least the early fourteenth century, for as part of Robert the Bruce's measures to restore the country after years of war he granted the monks at Inchaffray permission to extend it. Uniquely in Scotland it has, since the end of the seventeenth century, been managed by a drainage commission with the terms updated as recently as 2019 by an act of the Scottish Parliament. The commission is responsible for the upkeep of the Pow's nine miles of water and the further five miles of tributaries of which there are about ten major ones, draining the land and keeping its banks in good repair to prevent flooding to neighbouring properties. The thankless task of a dedicated cross-party group of MSPs has been to identify who is responsible for the maintenance and the cost of maintaining the Pow — those who live by it benefit but none willingly pays. Even finding statutory bodies and non-governmental organisations prepared to play a part has been a struggle, let alone appointing commissioners to oversee it. The unplanned reintroduction of beavers into the watercourse has posed a challenge in this delicately balanced environment.

Over the course of writing this book beavers have become established both on the river and in the public mind. A period of calm seems to have settled but resentments and fears still swirl around those opposed and could rise to the surface in future. Whilst the Tay and its catchments flow across many different council boundaries, all its waters lie within the jurisdiction of the Scottish Government and are monitored by SEPA.

Throughout the Tay's catchment and beyond, many are today concerned by the power of unelected non-governmental bodies that prioritise nature, often in alliance with private landowners who decide to 'rewild' without consultation or proper concern as to the future flow of the river.

Along the banks of the Pow everything is thrusting with life. Fields of carrots planted early are unwrapped from their protective membrane sheeting. Muddy rolls of it have been bundled up, sloughed off like a lizard's old skin. Not quite a cloud or a swarm, but there are plenty of repellent black flies swirling around. Stinging nettles are flourishing, dead nettles in creamy white flower, an abundance of ladybirds feasting on aphids, a peacock butterfly tempts but never rests long enough to show its eyes in detail. Every metre there are dry snail shells like boiled sweets that crunch underfoot. Hawthorn, gorse, prickly thistles. It is an abundant place, if not a very beautiful one. Across the Pow a concrete ramp leads down to the waterside, where a fence of thick bull bars allows cattle to slake their thirst without destroying the bank. An irrigation pipe stands sentinel, waiting to be attached to a compressor and pump, to water the dry fields later in the summer – if necessary. A stand of willows help themselves: they are lush on the waterside, but annually flailed on the other, where they impinge on the carrot field. Flies spot the water with tiny ripples where the Pow is sluggish. Downstream of a bridge, a small trout waves and ripples to keep stationary in a faster current, then in a dart is gone into dark water.

Dollerie means 'at the dark water meadow'. Dollerie House, which had been in the Murray family since the mid fifteenth century, sold recently, a feature being its crooked bridge over the Pow which was designed not for any engineering purpose but to prevent its crossing by witches (it being believed they would not venture over water if they couldn't see the far side). Romans, monks, witches – Strathearn has always been a crossing route north and south, east and west.

Traversing the valley is Highlandman Loan, leading due north to Aberfeldy and Loch Tay. We will take this route soon.

For now, I take the road west as it follows the Earn to its source, travelling out of the fertile Lowland plain to the edge of the mountainous Highlands. This stretch of country is transitional ground. Crieff was the location of a once huge and thriving cattle market where drovers from all points of the Tay's catchments would come to sell their beasts. It was integral to Highland Tayside's ancient transhumance economy and where it met with the hard cash of mainstream European capitalism.

Coins, roads, maps, written records and taxes all helped bring the lands along the Tay under centralised governance. Here in Strathearn the abbey at Inchaffray was an attempt to control the temporal and spiritual life of this river valley. The physical landscape was altered with the Pow, but a subtler change was also part of their mission: Muireach/Maurice and his Augustinian brethren's mutual support to/from the kings (now not of Alba but of Scots) had a political as well as spiritual intent, bringing their pan-European Christianity into the realms of powerful clan chiefs and a Celtic/Pictish Christian tradition.

By the small stream at Fowlis Wester the practice of the Christian religion continues today but not in the Latin form practised at Inchaffray. Just as the Church of Rome took control from the early Celtic church, it too was superseded by Protestantism. The church here may retain the name of Celtic St Bean, and sometimes be Latinised to St Beanus, but inside the ritual is greatly altered from that practiced by the Augustinian brothers. Gone is the purifying smoke of the swung censor, the clear call of a small round 'sacring' bell rung as the host is raised, as it once was here over an altar at a medieval mass. Then it was believed the communion bread turned into Christ's actual body, the wine into his blood. Now the congregation only see them as symbolic. Faith? Belief? In this church I recognise a place steeped in devotional worship, but the neo-Celtic pews, the carved communion table and pulpit are wooden to me; the geometric monotony of a framed collection of communion tokens in the vestry leaden.

But in this vestry is evidence of an emotional, even violent, religious belief and ritual that is not part of history but very much alive. The instruments of Christ's crucifixion – a large replica cross, ropes to bind someone to it, a jagged iron crown of thorns, a copper-tipped spear – bear witness to a medieval passion play. Beneath the surface of this conservative country kirk, a devout religious belief seethes and swirls. And hidden in its walls was revealed another link to ancient, passionate belief.

During restoration work a hundred years ago, another sculpted stone was discovered entombed in a chamber within the wall. Under the arms of a finely carved knotwork cross are two figures seated on thrones – kings, bishops, both? There are Roman weapons – a sword and shield – hounds, an angel and a figure being devoured by a beast. We do not know or understand the specifics of the iconography, but it is a representation of Christian devotion here that goes back to the ninth century. On the stone there are two further objects carved. A staff with nine buds perhaps represents a shepherd's staff or bishop's crozier or the Old Testament rod of Aaron, which God made flower to show that his tribe were the chosen ones. The second maybe represents berries on a bush or fruit on an apple tree, or perhaps a bough hung with bells, pearls of dew . . . or a river and its tributaries?

*

From Fowlis Wester I follow many of the Tay's tributaries north, and eastwards for 40 miles. First I head up the Highlandman Loan, the cattle drovers' road following the river Almond, then I cut east along the Braan to Dunkeld. Continuing north along the Tay at Ballinluig, I branch off along the Tummel, then head east again up past the Edradour Burn and distillery, finally flowing down to Kirkmichael with the river Ardle.

In 1715 the Earl of Mar raised the standard of the Jacobite cause at the cattle trading field at Sillerburn, Kirkmichael. By choosing this site on the banks of the river Ardle, he allowed the significant numbers of supporters of a restoration of the Stuart monarch from Aberdeenshire and the North-east to link up with those from the Highlands.

White Jacobite roses in their bonnets, they then

followed the Tay to Perth and from there descended into the Lowlands singing 'Hey Tutti Tati' on their way. The site is now known as the Bannerfield.

Today a ringing bell from the village's riverside primary school is a call not to arms but to play, as a small cohort of pupils emerge from its grey stone walls and into the lunchtime sunshine for banter and young pretending. I follow Mar's Jacobites south again, this time following the Tay all the way. At Tibbermore, outside Perth, the deconsecrated parish church retains its eighteenth-century interior of wooden boxed pews and raised pulpit. I am taken aback on reading in its visitors' book, 'Burn the witch!'

Later, having completed my circular route, I am looking across Strathearn back towards Tibbermore from the standing stone and stone circles on the grouse moor above the Fowlis Wester kirk. Musing on its gruesomely realistic passion play props, I am startled out of my reverie by the arrival of two eighteenth-century German tourists – not Hanoverians but super-fans of *Outlander*, dressed in period costume. Diana Gabaldon's massively popular books and TV series have a huge following across the world and it is not uncommon to encounter fans dressed the part across Tayside. The story, in case it has passed you by, centres on the adventures of a twentieth-century nurse transported back to the Highlands in 1743 through the portal of standing stones, the 'Burn the witch!' quote a reference to a plotline filmed in the Tibbermore kirk.

The passion is nothing new. In the nineteenth century, similar romantic notions of Scotland's Jacobite past were conjured, as we have seen, in Sir Walter Scott's novels.

Fired by this Romantic vision, the young German novelist Theodor Fontane wrote this poetic re-imagining of the early life of one who was there in the Bannerfield at the raising of the standard, James Francis Edward Keith, a Jacobite from the North-east who fought at Sheriffmuir in 1715 and later served as Field Marshall to Frederick the Great of Prussia.

> Where Scotland's mournful river,
> The Tay, from the mountains spring,
> Where still in cave and valley
> Men of Bruce and Wallace sing;
> At Tay, where every piece of soil
> Is sacred by victories,
> There stood your modest cradle, too,
> Field marshal Jacob Keith.
>
> Your Highland nurse with battles
> Would sing you into sleep,
> And tell heroic stories
> Of clan and family.
> So while your chin still bare
> From beard – a man you were,
> And virtuous as a man you fought
> At the battle of Sheriffmuir.

The indecisive battle was in reality a defeat and the Jacobite forces who had flowed so optimistically out of Tayside got no further south than the Allan Water in which many were drowned. The retreating troops returned to their homelands back up the routes that marched in time with their rivers – Highlandman Loan in Strathearn; by the Almond in the Sma' Glen towards Aberfeldy; Campbell's men back to Glenlyon; the Aberdeenshire contingent back along the Ardle past the Bannerfield, the white Jacobite roses wilting in their bonnets. For Keith, like the man they would have as king, his journey ended in exile over the sea.

For Allan MacDonald, 14th Chief of Clanranald, from South Uist in the Outer Hebrides, who had led his clan at Killiecrankie when aged just sixteen, his journey ended south of the Tay. It is told that coming home late the evening before joining the uprising he saw under a bridge by the burn an old *cailleach* washing clothes. Climbing down to the water's edge, he tapped her on the shoulder, but when she turned around he saw that she was not a real woman at all, for her nostrils were closed. She was one of the fairy folk.

'What are you doing there?' he asked her.

'It is your shroud that I am washing,' she replied, for she was *nigheag bheag a bhroin*, 'the little washer of the sorrow'.

Fatally wounded at Sheriffmuir, Clanranald was carried to Drummond Castle, where he died the next day and was buried in the chapel at Innerpeffray.

The retreating Highlanders employed a scorched earth policy, razing Auchterarder, Blackford and Dunning – excepting the kirk – to the ground in January 1716, taking what food and beasts they could, the blood of the caterans still in their veins. Ranald MacDonald, who succeeded his brother as Clanranald clan chief, assisted Lord Drummond's factor in the burning of Crieff (the town had disobeyed its owner and not come out to support the Jacobite cause). A few days earlier in a pale reflection of ancient ceremonies, the Old Pretender was crowned James VIII and III at Scone, but on 4 February he fled Scotland for France, where he was joined by Clanranald in exile.

The chapel at Innerpeffray, where Clanranald's brother was buried, had been acquired by the Drummonds following the Reformation. Formerly the collegiate church of the Blessed Mary, it sits on a promontory above the river Earn near Crieff. It is an imposing site, high above the river, well chosen by both spiritual and temporal powers as a place to make a demonstration of their authority. The suffix 'inbhir' in Innerpeffray is Gaelic for 'confluence', but the river word 'peffer' is older, possibly pre-Celtic, and the site has probably been of significance to the people of Strathearn long before.

By a quirk of fate, however, in the chapel today, among the Drummond lords' tombs, the marble reliefs with faithful hounds and bold diamond funerary escutcheons, it is the monument to the lowly and humble Faichney family that is the most remarkable funerary monument. Dating from the fatal year of 1707, it is among the most elaborate of 'folk art' gravestone carvings in Scotland. Created by John Faichney, a mason, it poignantly celebrates his love for his wife Joanna and their ten children, all of whom are portrayed on the stone, all of whom pre-deceased him. Along with more trumpet-blowing angels, a portrait of Joanna with her jaw already bound next to a skull, an hour glass, a Bible, coats of arms, a castle and poppy-headed finials, representing the opiate of Death, it is a naive, weird and wonderful confection of mortuary exuberance and personal sadness. It was brought in from the graveyard outside for protection in the 1990s and now upstages its former masters.

Around the time the monument was erected, the chapel became the home to Scotland's first public lending library. David Drummond, 3rd Lord Madertie, beneficently allowed local people to come and browse and to borrow from his varied collection of books on travel, history, medicine, witchcraft and natural history, written in Latin and English. The original Borrowers' Register is still held in the library, enabling visitors and local genealogists to see the flood of knowledge and of readers in a continuous flow down the centuries. Books were lent to adults and children, farmers, weavers, blacksmiths, laundresses, teachers, ministers and masons. One of the many notable collections is copies of the first forty-five years of the *Scots Magazine* (from 1739 to 1784). The oldest magazine in publication in the world, it is still published in Tayside today. The early editions, covering the 1745 Jacobite uprising and Culloden, are particularly popular with browsers. In 1762 the purpose-built neo-Palladian library that still houses the collection was built beside the chapel. The master mason was a John Feichney.

In one of Strathearn's angular fields, created from the Pow-drained moss today, the bulls are quite safe, for now. Having sired this year's calves, they sit sated. Drained of machismo aggression, they bear each other's company in uneasy union. One bull sat near the road is a huge triangular mass, the living image of the Gask Ridge. The sun glosses his midnight black coat with a rich sheen, varnishing the massive heft of him and his powerful musculature – the lord of all animals in this valley. He turns slowly to consider me, revealing a manure-splattered head. How human, and I think, how long before he will be led in that short ritual procession to the organic butchery on the hill behind? That fate in this place has been journey's end for generations of cattle. To market at Crieff, or further on down Highlandman Loan to Falkirk, has been the route of many a beast over the centuries. Unless there was famine and disease in the south, the Highlandman didn't ever get a good deal: the drover couldn't return north with the cattle, as there wasn't enough winter silage to feed them on the subsistence farming of the croft. It wasn't only in business that the Highlanders were taken advantage of. Here is a nineteenth-century bothy ballad version of an older, machismo traditional folksong:

There wis a butcher wha lived in Crieff
An' in came a bonnie lass tae buy some beef,
But he took her in his airms and down she did fa'
Aw the wind's blawn the bonnie lassie's plaidie awa'

For the win' blaws east, the win' blaws west
The win's blawn the bonnie lassie's plaidie awa
For the beef wis in her basket an' she couldna rise ava
An' the win's blawn the bonnie lassie's plaidie awa'.

At the recycling centre at Balnagowan, by the side of the Pow Water, the environmentally conscious separate their clear Strathearn gin bottles from those of their green Buckfast Abbey wine and brown bottles of Caesar Augustus ale. The drunken swirlings and staggerings as first the Cowgask then the Jessie Burns join it here divide the surface of the water into splintered fragments. Now it is clear, now green, now brown.

# Perth to Dundee

*North-east Fife and the Carse of Gowrie*

Outside of Perth the Tay is widened by the tide, but it retains the shape of our conventional idea of a river. Snaking round Kinnoull Hill on the north and Moncrieff Hill to the south, it has a Rhenish air, with forested cliffs and a hilltop folly. It soon straightens, is joined by the Earn, then expands into a three-mile-wide and twenty-mile-long tidal basin. To the south, on the Fife side, it lies hard against the Ochil Hills as they slope eastwards and diminish towards the sea. On the north side, the Sidlaw Hills angle away from it northeastwards, leaving a wide fertile plain or carse. The reedbeds that line its muddy banks here are the most extensive in these islands. The two banks narrow again past Wormit and Invergowrie to a point a mile wide where the river is bridged by railway and then road at Newport and Dundee.

It's said that gorse in bloom smells of coconut, but today its aroma is more like vanilla. Both yellow-flowered gorse (whin, in Scots) and broom grow here, but the pricklier gorse is more abundant on the slopes under the ancient fortification on Castle Law above Carpow. On the cusp of the season the Tay below me is about to transform from river into estuary.

A passing buzz is a honey bee, all sweetness, inspecting the first daisies. Morning too progresses, as do the seasons. Today is one of these days when you realise winter has finally withdrawn and you find under the blue March sky even a fly is beautiful in the welcome spring sunshine – iridescent, silver-winged. Birdsong welcomes me to the new season. I look up into a semi-blossomed tree to find a chaffinch. Its position on the branch means that I'm examining it in reverse, tail to head – its undersides white blushing into pink, above the striped wings a white shoulder patch, then quivering throat, before a tiny beak opening in song: 'pee-ink, chwink'. A silent buzzard glides over the hill's crest.

There is crawing from the old quarry. The dilapidated brick shed at its entrance is a remnant of past industry, of hard labour, Victorian winter. Inside is more recent debris – a glass vodka bottle reflects hard drinking and, in the soft, stained mattress, discarded sheath, hard couplings. Under the cracking timber floorboards, what has been hibernating? The bee, or a hedgehog, as prickly as gorse? The building itself has a defensive feel: tumbled bricks from the tops of the ruinous walls have left them crenellated.

Jagged whin is rewilding the hard-cut rockface, picks now as much history as Picts. Choosing my steps carefully, I negotiate the hill's natural defences. Skylarks, even when not climbing high to protect a nest, have that parachutist quality to their flight. Coming to a brief rest on the gorse, a couple take a break from their dizzying courtship flight. An old saying goes, 'When gorse is out of blossom, kissing's out of season.' It's a stiff ascent towards the top of the hill. Pechin', it is my turn to rest.

Now I am higher than the birds. I look down. The wings of silver crows glint as they patrol the lambs' field. The larks' courtship out in the open – no secretive human thrustings on a stained winter mattress in an old shed, but aerial acrobatics in the pure spring air. Yet among the prickling whin, the same life-creating imperative takes over and there is consummation.

Advancing up the slope, I spot fragments of egg – a recent death, or last year's Easter celebration of a resurrection? A snail shell, a defensive structure spiralling back so far in time as to make you giddy, lies vanquished. Tumbled down from the summit, a slew of rocks from the fort's once massive, timber-laced walls – twenty-feet thick, built two and a half millennia ago. Whether intentionally set alight by invaders or by design, when these timbers were burnt and fanned by the wind it created such high temperatures that the rock fused together, forming a glass-like bond. This process has given these – almost exclusively Caledonian structures – the name vitrified forts. To the west, not far along these same Ochil Hills, is another at Castle Law, with more on the north side of the river at Aberlemno, on the Law in the centre of Dundee and on the one visited earlier on Barry Hill at the entrance to Glen Isla. It has been suggested that, given Castle Law was dismantled and covered over some time in the distant past, the firing of the walls may have been part of a ritual closure of the site.

The Old Red Sandstone of these hills has undergone more than mere humans could affect, forces and extremes of heat beyond our imagination. Volcanic eruptions have uplifted and faulted, deposited and submerged, glaciated and eroded, sculpting the landscape under and before me. On this thin crust I see the once bubbling asphalt that has cooled into straight lines of motorway and tarmac road, iron ore smelted into the rigid rails on the train track, quivering marsh and bogland fringing the river now gridded by causewayed farm avenues, drainage pows, plough rigs, polythene tunnels of berry bushes, spruce plantations, wind turbines, housing developments, Roman fort and medieval tower.

But the river cannot be straightened. It is too powerful here, with its tidal ally the sea. The serpentine River Earn allows itself passively to be bridged, crossed, temporarily banked, but its sliding, concertina journey into the Tay cannot be halted. Together flow and tide mould and remould slithering mud and sandbanks. These sand and mudbanks have their assortment of names – descriptive, historical, mysterious, lost in the mists of time, cautionary: Channelhead Bank, Reckit Lady Bank, Dispute Bank,

The Turk, Eppie's Taes, Sure as Death Bank. Today their watery surfaces are sky blue, scudded by ever-changing cloud reflections. The wind blows up white caps on their intermingling waves, river and sea. To the north-east, three rococo curves of sand – concave, convex, concave – swish across the widest breadth of the estuary from the Fife shore to Invergowrie Bay. Beyond all is water from here to Norway. These narrow sandbars are like floating bridges, depending on the sailor's luck – leaping off points to jump to shore or to heaven, or elsewhere.

As I gaze the miles down the Firth, the estuarine waters are blown by distance into a vanishing smirr of sea and sky on the far horizon. A mere movement of the eyes, not even turning my head, brings into vision the snowcapped hills of Glen Isla, the Cairnwell at the head of Glenshee fifty miles away. These snows will melt and journey past here. I turn slightly and over Moncrieff Hill I can just discern the pyramid tip of Schiehallion – the fairy mountain of the Caledonians seventy-five miles away. Invisible beyond it, the waters of Loch Laidon, Loch Rannoch, Dunalastair, Loch Tummel. All of these will eventually flow to the sea past here.

On the summit of the hill millennia of human interventions have created a miniature landscape. They have sculpted, like volcanoes or earthquakes, or like the river, this piece of land: gouging glens (embankments) and gorges (moats) and gullies (drains); creating a loch (well) and, in a cairn, a tiny modern triangle of mountain, built one rock at a time by human hands.

Descending to a lower plateau I pass clumps of umber

bracken, silver birch pinking in the spring light, copper birch fringing a little bogland formed in a neuk of the hill. These are the colours of the day. An uprooted tree trunk has excavated out of the soft, wet ground still-living plants – greening foxgloves and young nettles strong enough to sting a misplaced hand are among its roots, forming an air garden. Branches broken by cutting winter winds crackle morbidly as a gentle spring breeze sways the sprouting, resurrecting buds and blossoms that have survived into the new season. In the boggy pool there are ripples caused by more than the breeze: a toad swims balletically away. Last year's bleached white bog grass is interlaced with pearly strings of toad spawn. A robin comes closer to investigate me, his duller human namesake. On the other side of the pool he is perched on a branch, then flitting to another, then another, gradually making his way closer until there are four of us – above and below reflected in the water, two sets of twins made of water, made by water. Brothers, sisters, family. The ever-chattering of a skein of geese 'V' over its surface, joining the leaves, grasses, sphagnum mosses and the branches of trees on, over, under its mirror surface until a puff of wind scatters us in a flurry of zigzags and S's to oblivion.

The fort's stones have been cast down upon the hillside. Water finds its own way down, often using human and animal paths, surreptitiously softening the ground under dead bracken and new sprouting wild garlic, greening the hillside that is grey under last autumn's wind-fallen leaves. The gossamer threads of a web are jewelled by dew on the blooming hawthorn's branch, where soft and round buds are forming among crowning spikes. On the flat flood plain, a digger is drilling like a woodpecker, crows squabble, my ribbed corduroys 'whee whet' along, a train horn toots before a level crossing. To gasps from a team of archaeologists, a prehistoric log boat squelches out of the river mud at Carpow after three thousand years. Plum trees silently blossom.

A track leads up from the river at Carpow to Ormiston Hill behind Newburgh. This old route is said to be the path Macduff took, fleeing Macbeth. The view from the hill affords vast panoramas westwards across Strathearn, north to the Carse of Gowrie and east down the Firth to the sea. In a field of cattle there is a low, circular platform made up of undressed boulders perhaps fifteen feet in diameter and at its centre a weathered, now featureless stone stump, the remnant of what was once said to be a carved cross dating from the mid eleventh century. It is known locally as MacDuff's Cross.

Atonement and the cleansing of sin are associated with MacDuff's Cross. The traditional story goes that if you were a MacDuff and a fugitive from the law at one time you could have escaped justice by tethering a cow to each of the four corners of the cross.

The cross was destroyed by a zealous mob of iconoclasts during the Reformation, so no one can prove that the following verse was actually inscribed upon it:

An altar for those whom law pursues, a hall for those whom strife pursues, being without a home. Who makest thy way hither, to thee this paction becomes a harbour. But there is hope of peace only when the murder has been committed by those born of my grandson. I set free the accused, a fine of a thousand drachms from his lands. On account of Macgridin and of this offering, take once for all the cleansing of my heirs beneath this stone filled with water.

Macgridin is one of the early Irish evangelist saints (possibly St Adrian) who is associated with north-east Fife. The Duffs were certainly a powerful local family, probably inheritors of the southern Pictish kingdom, once even kings of Alba. It explains why, when fleeing Macbeth, Macduff supposedly came by this path. His clan were hereditary abbots of the Celtic abbey at Abernethy below, and Thanes, then Earls of Fife. Macbeth's wife is said to have been a Duff called Gruoch. If the chains attached to the cross here were symbols of atonement via a financial penalty, and on the cross at Fowlis Wester of payment with physical suffering, both link earthly transgression to divine justice.

When we transgress the appointed order, there are consequences. In Shakespeare's play, Macbeth usurps Duncan, bucking the 'natural' order of things. He is tempted by the 'supernatural' witches; his ambition is put into words and reflected back to him. He has doubts. His doubts are quelled by the fierce spirit of his wife, who reassures him of his ambition. Regicide, overturning the current flow, will change the course of history. The flow of blood, its staining of the guilty, their vain attempts to cleanse themselves of the sin with water fails to assuage for their crime.

'Will all great Neptune's ocean wash this blood clean from my hand?'

Lady Macbeth reassures him: 'A little water clears us of this deed.'

But the guilt cannot be so easily washed away. The irresistible tide of natural justice is not so easily turned. In the final act, she sleepwalks – in neither the real world nor the world of sleep, nightmarishly she cannot cleanse herself of the guilt blood of the king nor of the other innocent victims of their lust for power, her kinswoman Lady Macduff and family.

'Out, damned spot; out, I say . . . Yet who would have thought the old man to have had so much blood in him.' Macduff slays the usurper. By giving fealty to Malcolm as king, Macduff returns to the status quo. The world is rebalanced, proper order is restored and respected by him. Whatever the implications for Shakespeare's or our times in the early medieval period, the Macduffs, perhaps symbolically, retained the hereditary right of crowning the monarchs of Scotland upstream at Scone where 'the laws and disciplines . . . should be kept in conformity'

At Newburgh other fruit trees are in flower. Orchards and gardens tell the town's story – Roman apples, monastic pears, Victorian cherries, wild plumbs. The Blossom Festival brings a hint of the Far East to the east coast of Scotland, where viewing the sweet blossoms offers the promise of fruit to come. New buds opening, spreading like fingers, the pure fragrance of cherries, the sensuous scent of plumb blossoms. The flowers may herald new life, offering a glimpse of the future, hope for the coming year, but they soon fall from the black skeletal fingers of the tree's branches. Spring may, just, be here, but summer is yet a long way off.

The sharp odour of pink redcurrant blossom is one of the smells of the day. Can you smell that muck-spraying tractor, the other spreading silage? A third deep-ploughs waves of soil, clouds of seagulls following as if it were a trawler. Pass beyond them to the river's edge, sniff a whiff of the stagnant estuarine mud at low tide. A Tay coble, the preferred boat of the river's wildfowlers – filled with rainwater on which three decoy ducks float – gently squelches in that mud as it is rocked by the wind. The walls of Newburgh harbour are interlaced with timbers like those of a vitrified fort high above. Bricks impressed with the names of long gone works have been cast down, fly-tipped into the river. They testify to both an ancient and a more recent industrial heritage, names impressed on to them: 'WEMYSS', a derivation from the Gaelic for cave, *uamh* – the caves there a treasure trove of Pictish carvings; 'LOCHGELLY' and 'BALGONIE COLLIERY', synonymous with heavy industry and coalmining on the south side of the Tay, but also 'PITFOURIE' on the north bank at St Madoes opposite, a brickworks that used the river's glacial clay deposits. It is a cuneiform tablet that links us back to our cultural origins by Tigris and Euphrates. The prefix 'pit' denotes a place of Pictish origin. On the hill behind, quarrying still goes on and has, as recently as the 1960s, cast down the Pictish fort on Clatchard Craig.

Drip. Drip. Drip. Resistant to flow, the liquid reluctantly drops into the waiting pool below. I'm not atop

Ben Lawers, nor beside a Highland waterfall. I'm in my kitchen doing a lateral flow test, squeezing the sides of the plastic vial that contains a mixture of extraction fluid and snot from 2.5cm up my nose. Waiting in a white plastic rectangle, the litmus paper starts drawing up the tiny wetness, turning pink as the liquid flows up this miniature canal, a stream under cherry blossom trees. Absorbed, I watch as it passes the 'T' line with no visible reddening, seeping closer and closer to the 'C'. Within a few minutes a test that is the difference between carrying on with my life and not. Stagnating.

I delivered the first draft of this book in January 2020 just as stories of Covid started seeping into the news and into our consciousness. A few days later came the first people in Scotland to be tested for the disease. Soon everything ground to a halt – work, socialising, travel. Our worlds closed in on themselves. Life became detailed; we became small ponds, disconnected puddles. So when restrictions started to be eased a little in June of that year and we were allowed to travel up to five miles from our homes, the first place I headed for was MacDuff's Cross.

Coming up past the cat rescue home at Whinnybank Farm and seeing the panoramic view over the Tay for the first time in months was genuinely breathtaking. What seemed like celebratory bouquets of white dog roses garlanded the hedgerows; the vista encompassed the confluence with the Earn, the old salmon netting bothies, the berryfields, Perth's suburbs and the Strathearn hills beyond, and shimmering in the vast distance the triangular peak of the Highland Shiehallion in the azure distance – a distance that was intoxicating. I loved the indistinctness, its lack of detail, its Turneresque impressionism, and at the centre, snaking its way through the landscape, the liquid otherness of the river. Walking round the north side of the hill, the experience was of a slow motion panorama viewed through a fish-eyed lens. The reedbeds on the north bank re-greening after a huge fire destroyed over two miles of them in spring (closed within my bubble, I had seen the black smoke clouds rising ominously from over the hill, the eerie, spectral light adding to the widespread sense of doom). Beyond the already yellowing fields of the Carse, waves of heat shimmer the Sidlaws, the tips of the Angus Glen hills beyond watery against a Pacific blue sky. A lone white sail venturing downriver minute against the three-mile-wideness of the river between Balmerino and Ninewells, a flag of hope. The Bruegel hugeness was exhilarating.

Yet there was also a stillness, an absence. There was hardly any traffic on the roads on either bank, no planes coming and going from the riverside airport at Dundee, no sound of water. Rivers contained within their banks flow silently at the centre of our landscapes. Often we do not even notice them, and then they flood or evaporate or become polluted and we realise how important they are to us. Similarly when we lose our freedom to act, are suddenly constrained, we notice its absence more keenly. I think of the bedridden poet William Soutar, his failing body restricting his ability to experience the cuckoo by the waterfall, smell the delicate scent of the white dog rose in the hedgerow.

Above Newburgh my eye is caught by a tiny movement and between the dewy white blooms and pricking thorns of the roses a zebra spider is spinning a web. Its black-and-white prison uniform is so delineated, clear, certain. Looking up, I refocus through the web to the river beyond, and in the distance I see the crenellations of Castle Huntly, where the open prison inmates daily experience the strange existence of withdrawal, constraint and gradual release that I am experiencing now.

Beyond Dundee Law and the bridges, the Firth, the open sea, where the tides ebb and flow, whatever our human concerns, refreshing and replenishing. In the far, far distance I can see clouds forming and a haar starting to creep in. Turning back, hung on a farmer's fencepost is the corpse of a raven.

Death in life continued despite the easing of restrictions, and not everything continued to flow as before. During the writing of this book Malloch's in Perth closed after 149 years of trading. It was with a Malloch rod that Georgina Ballantine landed her record-breaking salmon, and Malloch's taxidermists who memorialised it. John, fourth son of Effie Gray and Sir John Everett Millais, designed their trademark logo – a kingfisher. The founder, Peter Duncan Malloch, is said to have been the first to understand that the markings on each salmon's scales could be read to uncover the story of the fish's life journey in the river or at sea. How do we decipher a river's journey, a life's journey? How do we get the scales to balance before the final act, before all dreaming ends and we are dead-bait?

*

I'm floating in a star shape in the calm of the river's tawny brown waters. They are enshrouding my body like St Martin's cloak. Above, a perfect blue sky is cloudless for a seventh consecutive late summer's day. The morning sun that has over-ripened berries and un-lotioned skin bronzes the water. The only objects breaking the warm surface are my toes, monumental wrinkled sea stacks five and a half feet away. The horizon strata begins with a thin line of copper sand or lime strands of wispy duckling-filled water weeds. The tattered green of pine forest fringes the shores. At one point above the tree tops a thin column of breakfast campfire smoke fades into the pure Highland air. Beyond the geometric plantations of Scandinavian fir that tartan the hump-backed foothills, the mountains behind rise, rise in a frieze woven of ever-diminishing vegetation – tree to shrub to heather to grass to sphagnum to alpine to lichen and finally to rock. Last night a huge platinum moon pulsed over these hills before a freckle of silver stars. Patches of ice-white snow in the wrinkled rocks of the corries are like toenails; they resist the sun's warmth, testament to the harshness of this land, rock and humans ground down by hammering fists of weather and wind.

Back in the water a stroke of my gentle arms stirs up the sediment of the river's bed and as it settles tiny grinds of mica under the surface are caught in the sun's light – a shower of gold. The air brought under the surface by my swimming stroke bubbles and dapples stars across my liquid body. Flipping over on to my front, looking down through the water, everything is clear, bright, translucent. Each stone on the river bed is sharply defined, every delicate filigree of weed elucidated. I swivel my eyes a fraction and now they are out of focus, streaks of pure colour, spots of golds, reds, rusts, bronzes. Lifting my head I pinch the bridge of my nose between thumb and forefinger, rinsing my eyes in tears and refocus. Through the widening tube of an underwater viewfinder I scan the riverbed looking for but not really expecting to see freshwater mussels. They are so rare now, and so protected that the once lucrative market in Tay pearls has long gone. They can live to be one hundred and forty years old, and within the blackened and corroded shells of some of these geriatric bivalves very, very rarely a pearl can be found.

A photograph of the last Scottish pearl fisher, Bill Abernethy of Coupar Angus, in the National Galleries, shows him by the riverside armed with a prehistoric-looking wooden spear, double-tipped for foraging on the riverbed sand and gravel for the molluscs, an open-bottomed bucket by his side, and between his spread, wader-covered legs, some opened mussel shells. He said that he could tell which contained a pearl from looking at them and extract it without killing it, skills that flowed down to him from generation upon generation. His most famous find, 'Little Willie', 'the Abernethy Pearl', perfectly round and the size of a marble, displayed in Cairncross, the jeweller's, in Perth for many years, has just been sold at auction.

In the city's museum a viewer like a milk-churn with a glass bottom was used by pearl-fishers from boats to scan the riverbed. It is now a practice totally illegal; even the possession of them can lead to prosecution.

Julius Caesar forbade the ownership of pearls, except by the most affluent in Roman society. He had a passion for them and, according to the Roman biographer Suetonius, it was one of the reasons that drew him from the Tiber to these shores: 'They say that he was led to invade Britain by the hope of getting pearls, and that in comparing their size he sometimes weighed them with his own hand.'

That Caesar loved these gemstones is attested by the huge black pearl he gave his mistress Servilia, said to be worth six million sestercii (over £1 billion today), while the decadence of Caligula's reign is illustrated by Seutonius's claim that: 'In the devices of his profuse expenditure, [Caligula] surpassed all the prodigals that ever lived; inventing a new kind of bath, with strange dishes and suppers, washing in precious unguents, both warm and cold, drinking pearls of immense value dissolved in vinegar, and serving up for his guests loaves and other victuals modelled in gold; often saying, "that a man ought either to be a good economist or an emperor".'

In the Cononish the bright yellow glare of sunlit gold creates avaricious lust among miners, panners and snipers when it gleams out of the darkness of the streambed. This gold, smelted at high temperature in the chemical foundry of our volcanic, geological, creature-less past, has a raw elemental barrenness; it cannot be broken down into any constituent parts. Its attractions are raw and basic, however finely we humans work it. The shadowy, veiled brilliance of an out-of-focus pearl offers a different lustre.

No gaudy Cellini, however skilled, can match its natural allure. River-born, nurtured and tenderly grown in the warm flesh of the muscle – like us within a soft womb of a living being, created, like Adam, from the mud – it is constructed from a multitude of elements. It forms with the tender caresses of the mollusc, touching, polishing, mothering the pearl with depths and layers of lustre and sheen. Looking on a pearl, one senses the river within it, the movement of light across its surface, the glimmer of other currents beneath, flickering suggestions of movement, indistinguishable changes of colour and texture, hints of dreamscapes in its depths. To look upon gold is to see your fish-eyed self reflected back. To gaze upon a pearl is like diving into the ever-flowing river.

The health of the mussels tell us the health of the river. While greedy, wasteful and destructive pearl-mussel poaching has in the main been deterred, the diminishing mussel population is a sign of the river struggling to cope. Filtering its waters through its hairy beard, the young mussel is susceptible to pollution from agricultural run-off, changes in water quality, bank erosion, increased river speeds and rising temperatures – all the result of human intervention. When the female mussels release their larvae at spawning time in August, their hope is that of the millions flooding the river a few will manage to adhere to the gills of a young trout or salmon and grow, eventually inhabiting the slow pools and meandering shallows, moving through the fine gravels on its singular, muscular foot. If this material is washed away or silted up, the molluscs with be deprived of habitat and starved of oxygen. These human interventions equally affect the fish population, thus the symbiotic relationship that connects human, salmon and mussel has been fractured and needs urgent repair. Tree planting to provide soil stability and shade; the removal of human obstructions and concreted embankments; allowing the river to revert to its natural course; a reduction in agri-chemicals – these are all ways that the repopulation of the Tay mussel beds is being addressed.

On the Sidlaw Hills, fire covers the tops. This spring has been light on rain and the ground is dry. In the night sky the glow illuminates the black rolling clouds that are generated as the blaze burns its way through the moorland heather. Even the highest parts of the hills are utilised and here, as across so much of the Tay catchment, grouse moors are managed for the shoot. Patches of different-aged heather camouflage these hills, the result of this practice of low-intensity burning of old, woody heather. The skill is to burn off the surface without setting fire to the deep flammable peat underneath. Opponents of muirburn argue that even controlled burning dries out the top layers of peat, releasing many of the pollutant carbons that it captures and stores back into the atmosphere, exacerbating global warming on two fronts and, with the land denuded of vegetation, water runs off the hillside more quickly, increasing flooding along the river valley.

Well-managed muirburn is a legal activity that, along with legal predator control, provides good breeding conditions for red grouse, which can then be shot for profit. As a consequence of this, other species such as sheep, deer, black grouse, curlews and mountain hare also benefit (though mountain hares can also carry parasites that harm grouse, so they too are shot). Those opposed to driven grouse shooting claim that biodiversity is restricted by it and that more species are harmed either directly or by collateral damage than benefit. There is also the moral objection to killing for 'sport'. The hen harrier poisoned on the grouse moor, the eagle nailed to the barn door. Emotions run high on either side. Factors beyond questions of morals can cause the muir to burn out of control. Reduced numbers of estate workers and the unpredictability of the gusting wind can all contribute, if, sometimes, even accidentally on purpose. Alternatives to burning include cutting – cutting with machine flails – but that can be expensive and labour intensive too, and with a few recent bad seasons money is already tight.

Up on the hilltop the raging flames of the fire give off a volcanic, artificial light: the wind fanning them parts the black billowing smoke temporarily to reveal glimpses of a smoking moon. It has a Mannerist, otherworldly feel. Backlit by this dramatic, technicolour display, the communication masts on the summit of Craigowl Hill only add to the feeling that before me is Golgotha in a 1950s Hollywood epic. Such supra-natural lighting is not uncommon in the art of Protestant northern Europe. It has a heritage that can be traced back to the years following the Reformation in early sixteenth-century Germany in the paintings of Dürer, Grünewald and Altdorfer. Eerie, spectral light; bright colours; a feeling of doom; high emotion; extreme religious feeling; physical agony;

bloody crucifixion; death. For the majority of Scots and the people living by the Tay, the rich visual culture of religious art, though once an integral part of Scotland's spiritual and cultural life, has been almost totally lost because of its destruction by the hardline Calvinist zealots who directed Scotland's Reformation in the later sixteenth and seventeenth centuries. Shrines and sculptures, holy wells, crosses like that on the Forteviot arch, or MacDuff's, paintings and altarpieces – all were destroyed by religious fundamentalism on a par with Isis in Syria and the Taliban in Afghanistan.

Yet like the flower that survives the inferno, a tiny bloom, if a bloodied one, can still be found. Inside the medieval church at Fowlis Easter, between the Sidlaws and the Tay, are unique artworks from before the Reformation: a carved fleur-de-lis decorates the 'women's entrance' in the north wall and has a 'stoup' for holy water; an octagonal font sculpted with the baptism of Christ; a sixteenth-century painting on copper of the dove of peace, with Noah's ark grounded in the background; and, amazingly, a remnant of a large *Crucifixion* that has survived from *c.* 1450.

Measuring thirteen feet by five feet, and painted in tempera on eighteen oak panels, it survived only because it was overpainted with whitewash. Now cleaned, it is a unique survivor from a different past.

A poem collected by the Dean of Lismore and preserved in his book contains the lines: 'For thy son, oh Virgin most honoured / Though he has saved the seed of Adam / Not good for himself was the cross.'

Blood flows from the wound on Christ's hand, not

vertically down but along his arm to his elbow. It flows across his forehead into his beard and intermingles with his shoulder-length hair. It flows triangularly from the hole in his feet, but most of all it flows from the gash in his side that has just been pierced by the blade of a red-shafted spear thrust diagonally across the painting by a cavalryman in rich Netherlandish robes. He points to his own eye: a drop of Christ's blood has spurted out and gone into it, and suddenly all has been revealed. He can see. These eyes that were blind have been opened in the instance of delivering the coup de grâce. His name is Longinus and he has realised that this Jesus is the Messiah. The artist has painted the good centurion on the other side of the cross, saying 'Vere filius dei erat iste' ('Truly he is the son of God'). But there is no mention of Longinus in the Gospels. Instead, legend has it that rather than being converted to Christianity, Longinus suffered eternal torment for his actions that Good Friday.

As we have already seen, what was once clear becomes muddied. Time stirs up the riverbed, clouding the waters. Different currents take history's flow in unexpected directions. Traditions merge, the centurion and Longinus become one person. Christ, no longer the Pictish noble floating among decorative knotwork, is speared by the Praetorian in all too graphic detail. Among those looking on is a jester, an unusual depiction in a painting of the crucifixion, yet he seems to be there to show that, in spite of the dreadfulness of the death he must endure to come to glory, only a fool would fail to recognise Jesus is the Christ Messiah.

Macbeth in *Holinshed's Chronicles* washes his hands after murdering the king but cannot get them clean; Lady

Macbeth washes her hands to no avail. *Holinshed's Chronicles* were a multi-volume history of England, Scotland and Ireland published in two editions in England in the latter half of the sixteenth century and a source from which Shakespeare took the subject of many of his history plays. Edited by the censors of the English state they are more story than history.

Whether born in Fortingall or not, Pilate's washing of hands is synonymous with physical washing being unable to expiate morally indefensible actions. To believers through these flowing wounds, Christ's blood cleansed the world of sin.

We are not used to looking at religious paintings inside Scottish parish kirks. It is probable that this painting is of Northern European origin, but lack of extant comparable works in this country makes identification difficult. That trade occupied many along this stretch of the Tay, as it widens into the Firth.

At Lindores are the ruins of a Tironensian abbey. The mother house was at Tiron near Chartres in France and its grey-habited monks lived an ascetic life that valued hard work as well as spiritual devotion. The order was noted for the communities of skilled craftspeople it housed, and from its early days its monks traded goods along the Seine and the Loire. By AD 1200 it had expanded and grown wealthy. They established abbeys in Scotland, and Lindores was probably trading with the continent via the order's own ship. Five miles along the Firth's south coast the remains of the Cistercian abbey at Balmerino include a broad cobbled road leading down to a jetty at which just such a sea-going vessel from the continent could have docked.

The Cistercians at Balmerino traded wool directly with the flourishing textile industry in Flanders and the Low Countries. The granting of royal charters to the burghs of Perth and Dundee allowed urban merchants too to trade across the North Sea. Fish from the Tay and from the Firth, wheat from the drained farmlands of Strathearn and Strathmore, cattle hides and sheepskins and wool from pastures beside upland streams were traded via Bruges, the largest market for their goods and the location of the Scottish staple – a form of medieval freeport that housed merchants who imported these goods and sold them on to buyers from across Europe. In turn the staple acted as a hub for goods coming into Tayside – wine, fine cloths and textiles, art. As part of his scheme of national restoration, Robert the Bruce had in 1327 granted the burgesses of Dundee exclusive rights to both buy wool and skins in Forfarshire and trade with foreign merchants. In *The Flemish on the Firth of Tay*, David Dobson describes the jostling for control of continental trade to and from the Tay's ports:

Dundee burgesses had first choice of any imports, and foreign merchants could only act as wholesalers, with all goods to be weighed and measured at the Tron (a public weighing facility usually found in the market square).

King David II renewed the burgh charter in 1359, again giving Dundee burgesses the monopoly of buying wool, skins and hides within the shire of Forfar, but extended to purchasing all sorts of goods at the market of Cupar in Fife. Dundee's hinterland, over which it had a monopoly of trade, included Coupar Angus and Kirriemuir (also possibly Arbroath and Forfar). There were boundary disputes between Dundee and Montrose to its north, and Perth to its west. Dundee and Perth squabbled over trading rights on the river Tay until in 1402 the Regent of Scotland, Robert Duke of Albany, decreed that Dundee had jurisdiction over any ports between Invergowrie and Barry on the north and also on the opposite side of the river, while Perth had control over the upper Tay.

Along the Watergate in Perth, through the rounded stone arch of Dundee's Cowgate port or through the pointed Gothic arches of its abbeys, burghers and ecclesiastics along the river dealt in the weight of goods and souls. But the mixing of trade in earthly goods and heavenly souls was to lead to the abbeys' destruction. In his book, the Dean of Lismore recorded the satirical verse:

I myself, Robert, went
Yesterday to a monastery,
And I was not allowed in,
Because my wife was not with me.

Our post-Reformation churches have concentrated on the Word, reading the Bible and engaging in individual dialogues directly with God, with no intervention by priest, saint or devotional image. That dialogue has been in Scots English, English or Gaelic, rather than the exclusive Latin of cloister and priest. John Scot was probably producing broadsheets in support of the Protestant cause in Dundee from 1547, Tayside's earliest printing. Twenty years later he collected into a book Dundee burgess James Wedderburn's *Gude and Godlie Ballates*. It contained biblical texts like the 'Psalms of David' in Scots:

> At the Reueris of Babilone,
> Quhair we dwelt in Captiuitie,
> Quhen we rememberit on Syone,
> We weipit all full sorrowfullie.
> On the sauch treis[*] our harpis we hang,
> Quhen thay requyrit us ane sang,
> That held us in sic thirldome.
> Thay bad us sing sum Psalme or hymne,
> That we sumtyme sang Syone in;
> To quhome we answerit full sune[†].

And Protestant hymns:

> The warld wald sauit[‡] be full faine[§],
> And cum to gloir, but Croce or paine,
> Quhilk Christis flock must suffer heir:
> But paine thair is nane vther way
> To cum to gloir, and put away
> Eternall hellis paine but peir[#].

---

[*] weeping willow trees; [†] loud/full voice; [‡] saved; [§] gladly; [#] matching/doing this

That the faithfull must the Croce indure,
Witnes beiris all Creature,
Subdewit vnto vanitie:
Quha will not thole, in Christis name,
The Deuill sail wirk him sic ane schame,
With peirles* paine perpetuallie.

Today ane man, is fresche and fair,
To morne he lyis seik and sair,
Syne dulfullie is do meit to dede:
Evin lyke as in the feild ane flour,
The day is sweit, the morne is sour,
Sa all this wratcheit warld sail feade.

Two large gilded and framed texts of the Sermon on the Mount and the Lord's Prayer either side of the chancel are prominently displayed inside the church at Fowlis Easter, the pre-Reformation *Crucifixion* on a side wall, a historical footnote. That it is here in its original building, if not in its exact original setting, is unique in the whole of Scotland. The painting spent its devotional life as part of the rood screen which separated the nave from the chancel in late medieval western churches, forming a barrier, like the Latin of the priesthood, between laity and high altar. It seems to have survived the initial years of the Reformation, but in 1612 the local synod ordered the 'paintrie on the ruid laft' be destroyed. While the structure was taken down, the images on the panels disappeared

---

* peerless, unmatched

beneath layers of wash. Rather than being destroyed, they have resurfaced.

That zealousness which drove the Protestant mob to destroy MacDuff's Cross, chip the cross off the Forteviot arch, cast the Eassie stone into the burn and whitewash their past pervaded the everyday as well as the spiritual life on the river. Ninian Balfour is described in the 1616 port records of Dundee not just as ship's captain but 'Master under God'.

Post-Reformation trade with the continent continued, but the staple moved to Zeeland in the new independent and fellow Protestant Dutch Republic. On 31 October, Balfour's ship, *Claynge Coist* (the modern spelling: *Clear the Coast*), arrived back in Dundee from across the North Sea. The vessel's manifest listed twenty barrels of apples and 240 of 'wyngzeones' (onions). Post-Reformation, other cargoes besides 'ingins' for bridies continued to arrive along the Tay.

Bells, like people and rivers, have names. In the campanile of medieval Lindores Abbey Michael, Raphael, Gabriel and, above them all, The Lady Bell – silver etched with an annunciation and pietà – called the monks to prayer. The turn of the tide saw new names wash in from the continent – Luther, Calvin, Knox – that ended the Lady Mary's reign. But half a dozen years after the *Crucifixion* was whitewashed, the river delivered new bells from the Netherlands for the Protestant kirks of Newburgh and its neighbour, Auchtermuchty. Whilst unloading at the harbour, one fell and cracked. Cries rang out.

'Ours was marked with chalk,' said the quick Auchtermuchty delegation and there for all to see was chalk on the undamaged bell, and so it was carted off to the parish over the hill. Known as the Reformation Bell it was hung alongside the Lady Bell, which had been ecumenically appropriated from the now abandoned Lindores Abbey. They continue to ring out in tandem, calling the ebbing numbers of believers to the kirk. Back on the shores of the Tay, the irate burghers of Newburgh were feeling less than fraternal to their neighbouring parish when open-eyed they saw on the cracked bell chalk marks too, ringing in centuries of civic rivalry.

Bless, O Trinity, thy household,
King of heaven, place of jewels;
. . . By thee 'twas Adam's race was shaped
The cheek like berries richly red;

— Gilchrist Taylor, *Book of the Dean of Lismore*

By the Tay and the Isla, on the Carse of Gowrie, around Coupar Angus, by the Ericht and most famously at Blairgowrie, the berries have ripened. From hastily constructed trestle tables with red chequered tablecloths; from semi-permanent, bunting-bedecked tented pavilions; even from a booth in the form of a giant strawberry, the fruits of a hot summer are for sale. Holidaying school children and students home from university spend their days selling the family farm's soft fruit to passing trade. In punnets, in baskets, or frozen; beside bags of preserving sugar for those who make their own, or in bonneted jars of jam; with shortbread or meringues; with single cream, double cream, half-fat cream, whipping cream, ice cream – strawberries, raspberries, logan berries, red currants, white currants, blackcurrants, blackberries, gooseberries, Tayberries – all are for sale.

You can even pick your own. In fact, the farmers are really hopeful that you will pick your own as the berries start to rot in the fields. There are simply not enough pickers to harvest the crop after the demise of the Seasonal Agricultural Workers Scheme, which allowed Romanians and Bulgarians to come to the UK. With both countries gaining full EU membership in 2014, the scheme ended and workers found better-paid jobs elsewhere. The Eastern European workforce that in the first decades of the twenty-first century provided the labour to allow expansion has dried up. Attracting workers is proving increasingly difficult, but it was not always the case.

Belle Stewart's famous song, 'The Berry Fields o' Blair', describes the twentieth-century workers, where they came from and why, and their temporary dwellings.

When berry time comes roond each year,
Blair's population's swellin,
There's every kind o' picker there,
And every kind o' dwellin.
There's tents and huts and caravans,
There's bothies and there's bivvies,
And shelters made wi tattie-bags
And dug-outs made wi divvies.

There's corner-boys fae Glesgae,
Kettle-boilers fae Lochee,
There's miners fae the pits o' Fife,
Mill-workers fae Dundee.
And fisherfowk fae Peterheid,
And tramps fae everywhere,
Aa lookin fir a livin aff
The berry fields o' Blair.

There's travellers fae the Western Isles,
Fae Arran, Mull and Skye;
Fae Harris, Lewis and Kyles o' Bute,
They come their luck to try.
Fae Inverness and Aberdeen,
Fae Stornoway and Wick,
Aa flock to Blair at the berry time,
The straws and rasps to pick.

There's some wha earn a pound or twa,
Some cannae earn their keep,
There's some wid pick fae morn till nicht,
And some wid raither sleep.
There's some wha hae tae pick or stairve,
And some wha dinna care,
There's comedy and tragedy
Played on the fields o' Blair . . .

The days of Stewart's berry field workers are long gone
(hopefully along with its associated practices, such as piss-
ing into the berries to increase the weight – you were paid
by weight picked). It wasn't only fruit that was picked; as a

source of traveller culture and traditional tales and music, the ethnographer Hamish Henderson from the School of Scottish Studies at Edinburgh University likened song collecting on the berry fields to 'holding a tin can under the Niagara Falls'.

The climate and fertile fields of the lower Tay are perfect for soft fruit growing and Scotland's reputation for high quality products has seen the industry more than double in recent years. The success of growing more fruit under polytunnels has the run-off cost of the speeding up of water flowing into the Tay's rivers, which significantly impacts its health. 'Pick your own' is a smart idea, feeding a nostalgia for 'the berries' among current generations who never had the dire financial need to actually pick berries but taps into their heritage. Picking my own, I hear from the next rows the songs of today's seasonal workers on the Tay, voices not just from the east, but like ospreys they have come north from Africa.

Aw manje sthandwa sam mina ngizoku thola
kuphi

You will meet me at the river

and

Mother mother
I saw you cross the river Jordan

From Nepal, Indonesia, Mongolia, Tajikistan, Kazakhstan and Kyrgyzstan, pickers are flown in. Under plastic supported by frames bent like fishing rods, staves of a curragh or reeds in a gale, backs bend and arch to the hard work. Automation may help, but picking berries will remain a human-centred task; costly machines eat into profit margins. A cutting back of the recent growth seems almost inevitable. In the meantime by the Ericht, the Isla, the Carse, around Coupar Angus and Blair, where the air is overly sweet with the tang of raspberries, the pungency of strawberries, the wasp control advertisements are going up.

Those who toil in the fields on the valley floor of Strathearn, Strathmore, Strathtay and the Carse of Gowrie are imported, seasonal, organised by 'gang-masters', living in caravans, transported in minibuses, kept separate and sent home when work is done, for there is no permanent place for these people here.

Imported labour was used, too, to build the Tay's dams 1,500 feet above the river in the post-Second World War period of hydro expansion. Joining native Highlanders were Irish, Poles, Czechs and other displaced Europeans, and German and Italian ex prisoners-of-war, often housed in the corrugated-iron huts of the former prison camps, like the one at Cultybraggan: 12,000 in all – 'hydro-boys' and 'tunnel tigers'.

At the Glen Turret dam today, maintenance work is taking place. As well as the men with spades, mechanical diggers are at work. A modern temporary camp is constructed of stacked Portakabins. The workforce do not live here but are bussed in from Glasgow fifty miles away.

On the twisting road down from the dam, one of the few local diggers has been run over – a squashed mole. No one sheds a tear for the wee creature in this enclosed world of immaculate suburban lawns and country house grass tennis courts, second and holiday homes.

In Longforgan Kirk, on a medieval tombstone, a knight lies, arms folded, etched like a Pictish lord, his breastplate in the style of a Roman centurion – or perhaps the fossilised armoured fish excavated at nearby Balruddery.

The church stands on a raised shelf of Devonian sandstone at the eastern end of the Carse, giving commanding views over the flat plain that is flanked on the south by the deep reedbeds and mudbanks of the widening Tay between Perth and Dundee. The fields beyond it rise gently towards the Sidlaw Hills and are among the most fertile in Scotland.

Below Longforgan (meaning 'church or enclosure above the marsh') until the late eighteenth century the ground was waterlogged, boggy and claggy with heavy glacial clays. The Grays of Fowlis lorded over the Carse of Gowrie for many generations. Around 1450 King James II gave permission for Baron Gray of Fowlis to build a keep near the village, Castle Huntly. The Grays' influence spread all over the Carse; they were the patrons of the kirk at Fowlis Easter and it was they who commissioned the Fowlis Easter *Crucifixion*. Intermarriage brought the castle into the possession of the 1st Earl of Strathmore from over the hill at Glamis in 1614, and by the end of the seventeenth century his descendants were commissioning another artist to paint Castle Huntly's interior. Her name was Apollonia Kickieus. We know very little about this rarest of artists — a professional seventeenth-century Scottish woman painter.

She was born in 1669. Her father was a painter also — either Dutch or German — who worked first in London, then on decorating Edinburgh Castle, the family living in the city's Canongate. Whatever her origins, we know her ending: in 1695, in Longforgan kirkyard.

Her gravestone reads:

Interred lyes under this stone
The comely virtuous Apollone
Kickieus, a rare yea matchless one.
Exemplar for a godly life,
A constant modest loving wife.
In paintrie strange who shew more skill
Than ere Apelles could, yet still,
Tho fam'd & prais'd much, most humble.
The heavens bereav'd us of this bliss,
Now great's her gain, ah sad's our loss.

None of her murals from inside the castle remain, but they may have been similar to those upstream at Grandtully. Panels painted on wood, or directly onto the plaster on ceilings and walls. Perhaps a large central one with many smaller ones, decoratively framed. There would most likely have been the heraldry of the Strathmore and noble families that they married into, and calligraphic monograms. Grandtully has biblical figures, angels, fruit, birds, animals, fish and boats, and these elements may have been depicted here too. The subject matter may have been taken directly from books printed over the North Sea at Antwerp, as the designs on Pictish stones were taken from an illuminated Bible. The mention of the ancient Greek painter Apelles could be read as an allusion to the neo-classical style soon to be fashioned in stucco and plaster relief in the country houses built on colonial wealth along the Tay in the upcoming eighteenth century.

Along its course, the Tay transforms from Highland mountain stream to brackish Lowland estuary. Out beyond the Firth it merges fully into the waters of all the world's seas. As the tide turns, those who once ventured out into the oceans return. As evening settles, quiet falls over the Carse of Gowrie and the Tay takes on a roseate golden hue. All is calm; serene.

My first impression of this landscape as an adult was of how open and honest it was. Where were the barbed wire fences enclosing the fields? Here, set back from the tides of river and time, it seemed an idyllic country. In a painting of 1800 now hanging in Dundee's art gallery, the McManus, Alexander Nasmyth captures this atmosphere. The Tay silvers behind the solid tower, the battlements and crenellations of Castle Huntly no longer necessary, softened within the rigid structures of the neo-classical landscape tradition. Two gentlemen converse by the roadside; perhaps one is George Paterson, owner of this old bastion whose portrait by Raeburn hangs beside the Nasmyth. He was born the son of a Dundee weaver, trained in medicine at Edinburgh, London and Leiden, then joined the army as a surgeon before travelling to the subcontinent to work for the East India Company. The caption explains that Dr Paterson spent five years in India as a 'confidential adviser' to the Nawab of Arcot. A lucrative position! It enabled him to purchase a castle and estate on his return, to commission paintings by the finest artists of the day – as grand an example of the Scots nabob as you can get. He purchased the castle from the Earls of Strathmore and married the Hon. Anne Gray, daughter of the 12th Lord Gray, whose ancestor had built the tower in 1452. An active freemason, he took a keen interest in agricultural improvement on his estate, especially fruit growing, yet over a century after his death the *Dundee Courier* wrote 'society in the city and county regarded him as a parvenu beyond the pale'.

# Dundee

*City of Discovery*

In the Firth, between Perth and Dundee, salmon used to be netted, as they were all around Scotland's coast and rivers. There were three main methods. During the course of my life these have died out. One morning on a childhood holiday on the Solway Firth we were taken by a local netter to collect the salmon that had become trapped in his nets, positioned out on the tidal mudflats, overnight. The wooden shaft of an axe was his only tool.

Offshore at Ardnamurchan on the west coast, where the burn flows into the sea, my friend John used to trap net salmon. His knowledge of where metal loops are in rocks is even now passing out of memory. Taking the boat close inshore, he struggles to locate one. Finally he points out a rusty bead of iron on the headland's beard of seaweed. The trap system used a net with three chambers tethered in a special location to attract salmon but not spook them. The knowledge of techniques and locations was passed down orally, like clan genealogies and Ossianic poetry, since at least the eighteenth century. The salmon netters' boat house is now gone, the icehouse – half buried in the ground to maintain low temperature, ice collected from the frozen loch on top of the hill above – has been converted into holiday cottages.

Four herons take slow, massive flight like a squadron of seaplanes and are joined by a fifth. Black guillemot, shag and lone gannet populate the shore, cormorants and goosanders that would take a salmon. Seventeen curlews, nested on the moor at the head of the glen, fly over the yellow and white lichen-covered and crottal-encrusted black shoreline rocks, skirting the coast round towards the lighthouse. The triangular head of an inquisitive seal eyes our activity and prompts in John the story of the plain-speaking fisherman's daughter who, on her primary school visit to the seal rescue centre, shocked all and sundry with her declaration: 'My daddy shoots loads of seals every week and would shoot more if he could.'

Derrick, a former Tay netter, would sympathise. They would get into the nets and bite a lump out of every fish, he says. He blames the increase in seal numbers for the decline in Tay salmon. Their whiskers can sense the hydrodynamic wake of a swimming fish at two hundred yards. Anglers upstream may have felt like shooting the salmon netters. On the Esk, the next river system north of the Tay, the last netting station has just been bought out. During the last ten years they have averaged three thousand salmon netted to two thousand line caught – it remains to be seen what impact the buy-out will have on stocks. The end of netting on the Tay in 1996 has perhaps brought the commercial angling beats some time, but it cannot negate the deeper reasons for the decline in Atlantic salmon returning to Scotland's rivers.

The Tay netters' lives were regulated by the tide. Fishing stations located between Perth and the Firth would use a traditional coble to drag a net across the river. The Tay Salmon Fisheries motor boat, *The Fair Maid*, would come along and collect their catches and take them for sale: on the north bank, east to west from Castle Huntly to Skin the Goat to West Willowgate; on the south, at Carpow, up the Earn to Daffick and back down the Tay as close to Perth as Weal and Friarton Sand. The men – always men – from the Western Isles, Shetland and Newburgh, along with seasonal students, would live in bothies along the riverbanks, sleeping in stone-built single-storey cots, with wooden bunks and straw mattresses. Heat would come via an open fire, and there was no electricity or running water. Life was unconventional, unhygienic, basic, hard, fun, dark – a netter tells the story of how one night the body of someone drowned in the river was caught in the net. As they pulled it in, the cadaver rose up out of the river like Frankenstein's monster.

Today the pathologist from Ninewells Hospital rows silently under the Friarton Bridge – the rhythm of his oars metronomically beating time as it passes – beating out in physical labour the memory of this week's days and nights in the mortuary, propelling his skull towards the already brackish river's meeting with the sea.

Along this final stretch of the river, netters' bothies are falling into ruin with disuse. At Back Beach, Ships, California, the 'Dangerous Building. Keep Out' signs are up; metal plates support crumbling walls, birdshit stains rotting roof beams, rusting iron bars block glass-less windows; a wooden door kicked in, a blue nylon tent erected then abandoned inside. A fireplace has been ripped out but a makeshift one built using old bricks – 'BALGONIE', 'WEMYSS', 'PITFOURIE'.

From the squalor of decay, I emerge back into the light of the Carse. Outside you notice how even the nettles are green, lush, dazzling. Looking through the woven mesh of verdant reed stalks into the shallows of the river below, I see a few tiny fish, not even a shoal, flickering silver between the mud and the black rocks as the tide turns.

Behind the bars of zigzag-planted beech hedge, black-and-white striped cows make their regular afternoon journey – old lags – to the shed, the clang of iron gates, the enclosed yard, the metronomic swinging of swag-sacked udders, the ever thirsty artificial mouths of the milking machine. A short-circuiting electric fence marks out time: 'toc, toc, toc . . .'

An absconder from Castle Huntly open prison is not an infrequent news item. I think of Dickens' *Great*

*Expectations*: the escaped convict Magwitch in chains, prison hulks moored in estuaries, an orphaned Pip. On the mud flats near Castle Huntly, two white swans are fighting, huge wings beating, necks outstretched, orange beaks snapping. The story of their fight is written in the mud with whirling footprints and feather-scraped scuffings. I think of Magwitch and Compeyson struggling, the former resigned to his fate, if it also meant the recapture of his betraying partner in crime.

The move back into civic life cannot be an easy one – a fine balance between institutional regime and freedom, both with their own oppressions and rules. The river is contained within its banks, but when it breaks these bonds it loses itself in backwaters and unsustainable anarchies. The 1993 Tay flood saw the highest ever recorded river water-flow (80,000 cubic feet per second) recorded in these islands at Ballathie gauging station. Enquiries follow, public concerns and prejudices are addressed, preventative measures are recommended if not always implemented.

The swallow tattooed on the jailbird's hand is a symbol of freedom. George Waterston, who was instrumental in reintroducing ospreys, then protecting nest sites with guards and barbed wire, developed his love of ornithology whilst a prisoner of war. Yet swallow, osprey or salmon are not free spirits, leading a life regulated by weather, heat and wind on a cross-continental scale affecting such minutiae as the hatching of insect larvae or microscopic plankton blooms. They are no more in charge of fate and destiny than any of us.

Christians believe that Jesus was bound to his fate, to die so that they can be saved. Inside Longforgan Kirk the shattered remains of a font is carved with the prisoner Christ whipped, then crucified, between two thieves. He cries out, asking God why He has forsaken him, a cry echoed, perhaps often, in the room at the foot of the church tower which used to serve as a prison.

Today there is a flow of prisoners in and out of Castle Huntly, of families coming to visit, a pattern of special 'children's days' to rebuild or build for the first time positive bonds that did not exist before, recognising the value of keeping families together to prevent reoffending. Though often unsuccessful, today people working in the justice system try hard to ensure that those passing through it are not necessarily fated to return.

At Castle Huntly the river is estuarine, merging fresh and salt water; it is a crossing place where offenders start to merge with civic society, mixing back in, sometimes seamlessly; sometimes there are ripples, lines of friction, whirlpools, waves, occasional breakers.

Nasmyth was paid to paint the castle and lands in this neo-classical style in imitation of ancient Rome, giving Paterson's newly acquired estate the warm rosy glow of an imperial past, but we know how and where his money came from. Crime and those benefiting from the proceeds of crimes, legal or moral, form an integral part of the river's history. The actions of 'Grey Colin' Campbell, his appropriation of others' money and land by dubious means, are echoed today. Taymouth Castle, built on the site of his Balloch, has been the centre of a recent multimillion-pound fraud case. The lawyer acting for American investors turning the castle into a luxury leisure development persuaded them to pay £13 million for it twice. Those who enrich themselves legally but by morally dubious methods escape social justice. All along the Tay throughout the nineteenth century, in mills from Stanley to the Verdant Works in Dundee, a constant battle for better conditions for workers was waged. Owners reduced overheads by taking on women they could pay less than men; along the route of Columban saints, starving Irish, fleeing the potato famine, were employed on pittance wages; work was outsourced from the Tay to the Houghly in India, where even smaller wages and poorer safety standards increased productivity – a country of promise, of no cold for the Scottish overseers who crossed over the sea.

But others had been forcibly transported across the seas, and with zero chance of better conditions. As Professor Sir Geoff Palmer noted in his recent address to the University of Abertay: 'During the enslavement of black people as chattel slaves by Britain, Scotland changed from a poor country to a rich country. About 30 per cent of the slave plantations in the Caribbean were owned by Scots, and Lady Nugent [wife of the governor] observed in Jamaica in 1801 that "Almost all the agents, attorneys [sic], merchants and shopkeepers, are of that country [Scotland] and really deserve to thrive in this, they are so industrious . . ."

'Dundee had significant links with slavery in North America and in the Caribbean. The city produced significant quantities of coarse linen called osnaburg which was sold to slave owners to clothe their slaves. The city made millions of pounds from this business. Slavery money built schools, railways and funded different kinds of commercial activities in Scotland.'

Following the abolition of slavery, the Earl of Airlie was paid £1,362 compensation in 1837 for the fifty-nine slaves he owned in Jamaica.

At Inver, Dalguise and all along the river, pretend flies are made-up, dressed in fine feathers but projecting deadly hooks. They are cast into the river – on the Lyon, the Earn, the Tay (it matters not which one). On the grouse moors there is another form of dressing up – a uniformity of tweed, checked tattersall shirt, Land Rover, woven picnic basket – that signals a desire to conform, worn by laird and ghillie, day shooter or holidaying angler, wedded to a Victorian idea of power and money that is both conservative and stultifying in the twenty-first century. The Aberuchill Estate in Strathearn is owned by Forestborne Ltd, a company registered in the British Virgin Islands and controlled (according to the land reform expert and former MSP Andy Wightman) by Vladimir Lisin, a Russian oligarch, chair of Novolipetsk Steel and said to be worth about £20 billion. Dressed up in tweeds, he is welcomed into Perthshire's country sports community. The *National* newspaper reported on 3 March 2022, 'He is the current president of the International Shooting Sport Federation, and in that position hit out at the decision to move the European Shooting Championship from Russia in the wake of the Ukraine invasion.'

Animal, child, Highlander, angler – all are tamed, restrained, literally fashioned by their clothing, by society, to conform as they develop. So is the river. From mountainside burn to loch, its childhood may be wild but as it flows into woodland and farmland and carse it is made to conform, engineered to the adult will of humans.

Life along the Tay has been and continues to be a sair fecht. Unearthed in the 1930s during roadbuilding at Invergowrie Bay, just before the river narrows at the end of the Carse, was a late Pictish stone. Sometime during the reign of Constantine II it was carved with the unique image of a bald, bearded warrior armed with sword, shield and spear. Though his beard may suggest royalty, unlike the dashing cavalrymen of earlier carvings he does not float on the picture plain among allegorical symbols of power but plods up a solid stone slope not dissimilar to the gradient of the Roman road up the Gask Ridge. To quench his thirst (or escape this heavy world) he raises a huge cow horn vessel, its finial carved with a bird's head, to his lips. To where does he travel? Where will the liquid transport him? He looks more like a squire or sergeant than thane or king.

> Sergeant: Doubtful it stood;
> As two spent swimmers, that do cling together
> And choke their art. The merciless Macdonwald –
> Worthy to be a rebel, for to that
> The multiplying villanies of nature
> Do swarm upon him – from the western isles
> Of kerns and gallowglasses is supplied;
> And fortune, on his damned quarrel smiling,
> Show'd like a rebel's whore: but all's too weak:

For brave Macbeth – well he deserves that name –
Disdaining fortune, with his brandish'd steel,
Which smoked with bloody execution,
Like valour's minion carved out his passage
Till he faced the slave;
Which ne'er shook hands, nor bade farewell to him,
Till he unseam'd him from the nave to the chaps,
And fix'd his head upon our battlements.

*– Macbeth*, Act 1, Scene 2

In the north, the Thane of Glamis slays the rebellious Gael. In Fife, the invading King of Norway is repulsed. Scottish kings – and would-be kings – seek affirmation and authority by being crowned at Scone. The losers' head crowns the palisade on a spike.

As a lengthening spring day comes towards its end, I find myself stumbling round the many fallen trees that crisscross the path on Hunter's Hill, Glamis. Axed by November storms before their allotted span, uprooted behemoths and snapped saplings bear testament to 'the muckle forester's' power. A couple of noble beeches lie across the track that spirals round the hillside from the Devil's Cauldron waterfall on the Glamis burn, past the mill weir, and climbs on up into the woods from above the curling pond. Earlier I watched a pair of buzzards circling above the summit like wolves on the lookout for the opportunity to swoop, wary of any hawking owls. My stumbling through snapping branches has frightened off two silent deer, buff scuts and woolly brown hindquarters disappearing into the tree shadows faster than I could raise my binoculars to my eyes.

All is gloomy, dank, twilighty. A mother-of-pearl sunset glimmers opaque as a Tay pearl through the river of greening branches. A mist starts to rise, fogging the path. I weave my way round fallen trees, sometimes turning back on myself. Often the way is blocked or I find myself in a cage of boughs. It is a landscape of stagnant water, ditches and sopping mosses that, as I grow frustrated in pursuit of my goal, I carelessly allow to seep into my boots. You don't need to be in deep water to find yourself getting into difficulties. This way and that I sidewind up and down the hill in search of a clear path. Deep within the maze of the forest stands my object – the Thornton stone, the old keeper of these woods.

Reaching it at last I find its Pictish carvings cataracted by the moss and lichens of time. This lone watcher over Strathmore has seen many evenings like this, stood imperviously as morning dew, spring showers, trees, kings, centuries drop around it. On its east face the intricate meandering knotwork of a Christian cross looks to the rising sun, to the easternmost beginnings of the Tay in Forfarshire, to tomorrow, but also back to the beginning of this day and many days. I squint to follow its flow, meditating on its loops and oxbows, winding across the cross's four branches. Like the path to it or a mountain stream under snow, it is difficult to trace its course. Down the years the east of the stone has defied the wind, but the setting sun illuminates little on its western face. The three sisters of ice, frost and rain have blasted its carvings, leaving only a serpent identifiable. It snakes like a widening river across a strath, its primordial coiling a symbol of Pictish ancestry, of a pagan water god or a Viking serpent sidling in from the Norse Sea?

Down in the village of Glamis is another inscribed stone. In the garden of the manse a similar serpent writhes above a rising salmon, itself both a pagan and Christian image. A leaping salmon leaves behind the river and bridges into the upper world; under its arching body, clouds reflect on the water's surface. On the stone a circular motif common in Pictish imagery known as a 'mirror' is carved. The stone's appropriation from pagan to Christian use by the carving of a cross *c.* 900 AD was not its first; hollowed out 'cup marks' in the Old Red Sandstone at its base suggest a previous, more ancient religious use long before the Picts. I imagine water in these hollows, these miniature fonts, maybe rainwater but perhaps water drawn from a river, from a sacred well poured in libation, or the blood of a bull offered in propitiation . . . or that of a sacrificed king, offered in lustration at holy festivals, by anointed hands, in restricted rites. In their surfaces flaming torches, lightning bolts, suns and moons, eclipses, flaming comets mirrored at some time in each puddle of quicksilver liquidity. Then nothing. Forgotten years of sleet, snow, ice and rain and sun again fill and empty these cups until the monolith is sidled across the Strath not by glaciers but by human hands, sweat, and is revitalised, reborn.

The Ice Age left under the Strath a deposit of thick glacial mud, a sealant that prevents its waters draining away. The biblical Adam was born from clay, modelled by the hand of God. From the post-glacial mud hands once modelled human figures as well as sculpting stone. A *corp-crèadha* is a figure, a doll, a representation of an enemy fashioned of clay and then placed in the river to be gradually diminished and worn away. As the water dissolved the unfired clay, so the lifeblood of the victim seeped away. When a minister of the kirk discovered one of these pagan figures he broke it to pieces, thus destroying the magic. Later, it is reported, he was viciously attacked by a raven – the shape-shifting witch with whose spell he had interfered.

Swish up the riverbed and when it settles the water is all the clearer. Your eyes see things differently. Shakespeare takes a story in *Holinshed's Chronicles*, stirs it up, looks at it with the eyes of his own genius. The king is murdered whilst a guest in his noble's castle, but it's not King Malcolm, the earl isn't Macbeth. In *Holinshed* the body of the king is taken and buried in the bed of a burn . . .

And immediately, by a postern gate, they carried forth the dead body into the fields . . . they convey[ed] it unto a place about two miles distant from the castle, where they stayed and gat certain labourers to help them to turn the course of a little river running through the fields there; and digging a deep hole in the channel, they burie[d] the body in the same, ramming it up with stones and gravel so closely that, setting the water in the right course again, no man could perceive that anything had been newly digged there. This they did by order appointed them by Donwald (as is reported), for that the body should not be found and, by bleeding when Donwald should be present, declare him to be guilty of the murder. For such an opinion men have that the dead corpse of any man, being slain, will bleed abundantly if the murderer be present.

Head south from Glamis, past the Nine Maidens Well towards the city of Dundee. The valley on its northern periphery was once called Strathdichty Martin but now just Strathmartine. Martin is St Martin, who served in the Roman cavalry and was converted to Christianity; the feller of druidical yew trees, who cut his cloak to share it with a beggar. This was a favourite place of mine to escape the city when I was a student. A circular walk took me under the masts on Craigowl past a standing stone, a ruined mill, a Pictish stone and back to a beautiful girl at Auchterhouse. It is said that it is Martin who is the horseman carved on that stone that stands in the middle of a field high above the Dichty Burn, a stone he shares with pagan symbols – a zed-rod, a 'Pictish beast' and a serpent carved on its flanks. Christian and pagan, in this valley between country and city, of hill-farms, grouse moors, berry fields, farm-shops, supermarkets and suburbs, there are two ways of it. Local legend is preserved in a bit of doggerel verse that is possibly no older than the nineteenth century.

I was tempted at Pitempton,
Draiglet at Baldragon,
Stricken at Strike-Martin,
and killed at Martin's Stone.

Strathmartine place names are used as prompts to tell the story of a dragon who lusts after the nine beautiful daughters of the farmer at Pitempton. A brave lad o' pairts – possibly a blacksmith – defends their honour, fighting the evil serpent, which he first draiglet (Scots: drowned), but it resurfaces. He then clubs it to death with a hammer, but it rises yet again until it is finally slain beside the Christian saint's stone.

It's a story that could stand being remodelled to suit twenty-first-century sensibilities; nevertheless the tale and the Nine Maiden's Well in Kirkton of Strathmartine have a source beyond local legend, linking them to a pagan pan-European tradition. Like the women in the story, the *cailleach* has eight sisters. There are magical associations with the number three, and three times three being trebly propitious. The nine sisters have water associations, particularly with wells, and are ritually devoured by snakes or serpents. In the wider North European traditions, the nine are associated with freshwater and with the sea. In the mythology of the Tay-raiding Vikings, they are named:

Hrönn – wave

Kolga – the cool wave

Hefring – the rising wave

Bylgja – the billowing wave

Uðr (or Unn) – the frothing wave

Blóðughadda – bloody hair, the strands of water
    whipped off a wave crest by the wind

Dúfa – the pitching wave

Dröfn – the foaming sea crashing against the shore

Himinglæva – a name that denotes the reflective quality
of water; the heavens are mirrored in its surface

In the Celtic tradition, they inhabit an island in the western ocean, an island, perhaps, between the world of the living and the world beyond the setting sun. It is neither land nor sea, earth nor water, perhaps transient ground – moorland or heath. They are not inhabitants of this Earth, but they appear on it.

> The weird sisters, hand in hand,
> Posters of the sea and land,
> Thus do go about, about:
> Thrice to thine and thrice to mine
> And thrice again, to make up nine . . .

Mythology is littered with tales of the sacrifice of maidens, sisters, daughters, virgins to a serpent, snake or dragon, representing the world-serpent, and their rescue and its destruction by a brave warrior knight, demigod or saint – Herakles, Thor, Martin.

In these stories the woman is cast as victim and has to be rescued by a heroic male from an evil beast. But we know that that beast is always another aspect of the same male.

It has ever been the role of women, especially young women and girls, to collect water from the well, the river. Threat becomes brutal reality today in Nairobi's largest shanty town. While water is provided free in a community water-supply scheme, as more and more people sink into poverty and move there, demand has outstripped supply. The poorest of the city's population are having to pay up to a quarter of their meagre incomes to buy water. That is not the only price they pay. The sellers are men, the carriers women and girls, and sexual assaults are increasing. Sellers offer credit, then demand women pay debts with their bodies. The women and girls have fought back, not depending on some demigod but by the victims themselves organising education and counselling programmes, running an 'End Sex for Water' campaign, petitioning for women to be hired by the owners of the water tanks, taking back autonomy, regaining dignity. The women are calling out the behaviour of their male attackers, creating a new narrative, challenging the traditional story.

Victims of power struggles line the Tay's history. Bullying sex pest Henry VIII of England's troops had sacked and destroyed Dundee in 1547 as part of his 'rough woo-ing' of Scotland – an attempt to force a marriage between his son Edward and Mary, Queen of Scots. The inappropriateness of the 'woo-ing' and its roughness led to Mary marrying the Dauphin and the French helping to cast the English out of Broughty Castle two years later.

Macbeth is a regicide because of his lust for power; Andrew of Wyntoun, though, writes that King Duncan is killed at Glamis because he 'rewyist [ravished] a fair May of the land there lyand by'. History swirls like the river.

In 1537 the widowed Lady Glamis and her son were accused of plotting to kill James V using witchcraft by a man whose proposal of marriage she had rejected. She was burnt as a witch, but her son pardoned. From 'The Witch of the Carse of Gowrie':

Mare's milk and deer's milk,
Ande every beast that bears milk
Atween St Johnstoun and Dundee
Come a' tae me, come a' tae me.

Some opt for a May Day dawn dip in the river, others wash their faces in the morning dew: we all have our own rituals and superstitions. On the south bank of the river I'm chatting with Zoe Venditozzi about her popular podcast, 'Witches of Scotland', which has been at the forefront of the campaign to have justice for people accused and convicted under the Scottish Witchcraft Act 1563–1736. It is a campaign for justice, for a legal pardon, an apology and a national monument for the thousands of people – mostly women – who were tortured and gruesomely executed under this Act.

'When accused of witchcraft, people were locked up, awaiting trial, and tortured to confess. Torture in Scotland was usually by way of sleep deprivation – keeping people awake until they confessed,' says Vendittozi. 'Most of the accused were probably implicated through confessions by others accused of being witches. Some may have had psychiatric problems and made fantastical statements, others were antisocial individuals reported as witches by neighbours.'

They were people on the fringes of society: the vulnerable, the weak, those outwith normal support networks. Alternatively they could be the strong, those who wouldn't conform to that society's warped norms, challenged them, who generated mistrust, envy and fear.

One such was Grissel Jaffray, who, on 11 November 1669, was the last woman tried for witchcraft in Dundee. The wife of a Dundee burgess, she was accused of being a 'spaewife' (spae, or spay craft, was the dark art of prophesying or foretelling).

Grissel was found guilty by the town's Privy Council and sentenced to be strangled to death by the public executioner, and afterwards her body burned so as to leave no earthly trace of her. A blue plaque and mosaic mark the site of her execution. In the old inner-city graveyard, the Howff (in Scots, a 'meeting place', a fine example of Dundonian black humour), small coins are placed as offerings on a stone where the burgh's traders met to discuss business and, over time, for some reason (maybe because Grissel was a businesswoman?) the stone has become a stand-in gravestone.

Her son, a mariner who had been away at sea, knowing nothing of his mother's fate, returned to the city on the very day of her execution. Discussing with his shipmates the cause of the plume of smoke rising above the river, little did he realise it was the pyre for his mother's corpse. It is said that on learning of her execution he immediately boarded an outbound vessel and sailed away.

In *Holinshed* the witches make effigies of King Duff and set them alight, but later it is they who are burnt to death.

Another site of execution was just beyond the burgh boundary, in a natural amphitheatre called the Witches' Knowe. On the city map created by John Wood in 1821 it is still marked, the name, prophetically, running into that of a laundry stream – 'Scowring Burn Witch Know'.

The Scouring Burn, one of a number by that name across the Tay's catchment, rises at the Logie Spout on Balgay Hill in the west of the city. Like many metropolitan river courses it is now almost completely built over for the length of its passage. It once supplied water used to clean yarn, then later to power the mills of the Blackness area, including the Verdant Works, now the museum dedicated to the jute industry. On a rainy day it's the only place you can glimpse its subterranean flow beneath the floorboards. Sometimes referred to as the Mause or the Mausie, it is joined with the Dens Burn, which flowed from the east side of Dundee Law and enters the Tay at the old docks just beyond Commercial Street and the east off-ramp of the road bridge. Its enclosure and inaccessibility make it susceptible to becoming a conduit for reverse flows at high tide. I have experienced the damage this can cause. Under the arid, bookish shelves of Waterstones on Commercial Street, where I once worked, a tide line between new and old plasterwork five feet from the floor encircles the basement offices and storerooms, marking the level scoured by the burn, storm run-off and a spring tide fifteen years ago. We mark our passage in lines, some ageless others temporary – scourings by glaciers on rock, scrapings along a hull by river rock; cup marks on stone, cup marks on the table of The Three Witches tearoom by

Dunsinane; Tay flood levels carved on Smeaton's Bridge in Perth; soundings measured on a tidal chart.

Who now consults a 'water witch' to divine a hidden water course? Though modern anglers may offer a libation to the Goddess Tatha for a bountiful season, our faith is in scientific research finding the solution to dwindling salmon numbers. Yet a mile west of St Serf's kirk in Dunning, where the Pictish Dupplin Cross is housed, is another cross. It's not in the least bit as grand or well-crafted but it totters atop a rough cairn on the edge of a field, propped up by a rusting iron bar. On it are not carved priest-kings, nor is it etched with the patriarchy of early monarchs; instead it bears the simple graffitied dedication:

'Maggie Wall / burnt here / 1657 / as a Witch'

Who raised it and to whom it is dedicated is a mystery, for there are no records of anyone by the name of Maggie Wall ever existing or having being burned here as a witch. In and around the cairn various objects have been left, the kind of thing you might expect at a shrine – candles, sea shells, nuts, pebbles of unusual geology, copper coins, a small woven wreath of artificial roses, while some have black magic associations: runes drawn on a stone, a cockerel (albeit a plastic Playmobil one) – but what of the medal of St Anthony; the Minnie Mouse ears and bow, an Ikea pencil; a plastic bottle of water with a set of wind chimes dangling from it; the key for room 209 from the Lovat Hotel, Perth? Whether Maggie Wall existed or not, the point is that the burning of women as witches did take place. No matter what the objects left here signify, they mean something to the leavers, who connect to this place in a way that is different from how most now react to the sanctified cross in the closed confines of the empty church a mile away. We mark who we are by who we are not. Though we live by the same rivers, we differentiate ourselves from the witch-burners by seeking their victims' pardon. We (I hope *we*) are not the same as their persecutors.

Yet on a recent visit someone has left a haunting memorial: 'Each white stone represents a girl or a woman who lost her life to male violence' and on each white stone a name: 'Alice Laing', 'Jennifer Morgan', 'Angela McLaughlan', 'Louise Aitchison', 'Joanne Gallacher', 'Morag Carmichael', 'Andrea Douglas', 'Leighann Cameron', 'Shena Clarke', 'Emma Anderson', 'Karen Young', 'Yvonne Barr', 'Catherine Campbell', 'Ruth MacLean', 'Kimberley MacKenzie', 'Donna Black', 'Lorraine Clements and her sons Daniel and baby'.

*

How did the towns and cities along the Tay draw their water? How did they dispose of their waste? Even before the 1745 Jacobite Uprising, Dundee was having to review the public water supply. The well head now at Dudhope Castle is a square ashlar block of dressed stone capped with a swept pyramidical roof. The pump handle is missing but a metal scoop like an enlarged soup ladle is chained beside the spout, which is a cast iron lion's head – from strength flows sweetness. It was part of a 1743 scheme to improve the supply and quality of the water within the burgh. The water was sourced from the Lady Well high on the Hilltown, a rural area to the north of the city centre originally outside the burgh boundary. The late nineteenth-century Dundee chronicler A. C. Lamb notes in his book *Dundee: Its Quaint and Historic Buildings* that 'the Well of the Blessed Marie de Dundee', later known as the Lady Well, is mentioned in a 1409 burgh document.

Even as late as 1836, it was the main source of the water supply to the city. By then the Hilltown was densely populated by poor jute-mill working families packed into slum housing. Today it is memorialised in the Ladywell Tavern, one of Dundee's oldest pubs, and the Wellgate Centre, which houses the Central Library.

Lamb and his readers were all too aware that among the 'quaint and historic', killer diseases flourished. Fresh, clean water was vital to public health as the old burghs became more and more cramped, reaching bursting point within their established boundaries amid an expansion of industry and an influx of workers to power it. There were major outbreaks of cholera in Dundee and Perth in the mid nineteenth century and typhus in 1837 and 1847. Cholera is a bacterial infection of the small intestine caused by the consumption of contaminated water or food, and was particularly prevalent during the Industrial Revolution. These rapid increases in population density were the perfect breeding grounds, where the need for decent housing, fresh water and hygienic sewage disposal outstripped supply. One major source of cholera was the seepage of human faeces into wells supplying a town's water.

By 1822 the link between industrial expansion, slum housing and disease was being noted by the authors of *Dundee Delineated, or a History and Description of the Town, its Manufactures and Commerce* . . .

At the Overgate port, the street branches out into two suburbs—Hawkhill and Scouringburn, running both west at a small acute angle, stretching into the lands of Dudhope, Logie, Balgay, and Blackness, in general without any regard to taste, convenience, or cleanliness. Though one part of the ground called the Witchknoll had a fine declivity, with plenty of water, and was capable of being made a handsome square, and had even a room for parallel streets, the ground, which belonged to the Hospital, being feued to persons of small capital, the houses have been built generally low, and so arranged that every one obstructs or defiles the other. Some indeed are left unfinished. It is therefore, with few exceptions, the receptacle of the lowest and worst part of the community; the continual abode of the typhus fever; and is converted from a fine green healthy meadow into a lazar-hole, and the fixed residence of filth, disease, uncleanness, and wretchedness.

In this quarter, from the command of water running by the back of the town, and by the great improvement in the steam-engine, there are numerous and large mills for spinning flax, just now in the most thriving state

. . . and close by in the Pleasance: is a most extensive
Brewery, which has long been famed and flourishing.

An 1848 report by the Police Commissioners of Dundee, in
respect of the Nuisances Removal and Diseases Prevention
Act, states that 'attacks of Cholera are uniformly found to
be most frequent and virulent in low-lying districts, on
the banks of rivers, and where there are large collections
of refuse, particularly amidst human dwellings.'

Isolation of the sick from the healthy as soon as these
waterborne diseases became evident was vital but providing sanitary solutions was to take most of the remaining
years of the century to achieve. Nor were these outbreaks
restricted to towns and cities. Even small communities could be infected, damp cottages with no drainage
and middens at the backs of houses piled with human
and animal excreta to be used as fertilisers accumulating
throughout the year. There, too, provision had to be
made: 'As regards villages – each village ought to have
the means of accommodating instantly, or at a few hours'
notice, say, four cases of infectious disease in at least
two separate rooms, without requiring their removal to
a distance.'

Typhus or typhoid fever was caused by lice and was
particularly prevalent in the insanitary housing stock,
scathingly called 'Irish Fever'. *Cailleach-uisge* was the
Gaelic name for a rotten or diseased potato full of liquid.
Among Highlanders and Irish fleeing the potato blight
and the resultant famines in the 1840s, and seeking work
in the mills along the Tay, typhus became endemic because

of the dreadful housing conditions provided for them by local slum landlords. One of these Irish immigrants was Elizabeth Bradie, a laundress living in a tenement near the Witches' Knowe in the Westport. By the census of 1871, she was a widow. In a snapshot of the time, her son is a mill overseer but his older sisters are only mill winders and warpers.

At Munros Land, 16 Scouringburn, is another laundress, Janet Paton, one son a flaxdresser, the other a seaman. In the 1891 census, at the age of 70, Mary Connon is still working as a laundress at Blackscroft, but over the course of her lifetime what were once semi-rural riverside cottages with gardens that ran down to the Tay are, due to land reclamation, separated from the water by Foundry Lane, the East Railway Station marshalling yards, the Victoria and Camperdown docks, and Marine Parade. As the town grew, so even the wells flowed with it. The well head now at Dudhope started life in 1743 in the Overgate, then it was relocated in 1828 to Tally Street/Mid Kirk Style, and then at the end of the century to its present location.

The 1871 Dundee Improvement Act began a successful process of addressing issues of poor health by improving housing and hygiene. Planning regulations required wider streets, maximum heights of buildings, minimum heights of rooms within them, modern sewers, a new market and slaughterhouse for cattle, and essentially a new water supply. The manmade Loch of Lintrathen was created in a glacial basin just to the east of the Reekie Linn on the river Isla and has supplied fresh water to the city since 1875.

As the late nineteenth-century engineering provided fresh piped water to Tayside's towns, the primary function of municipal wells was removed.

In Crieff, cast-iron lamp-posts decorated with bulbous-eyed fish, tails spiralling upwards, circle the late Victorian fountain in James Square. Positioned on the site of one of the old wells it's an oppressive granite assemblage dedicated to the most generous benevolence of a family of local lairds (the Drummonds) and manufactured by a firm of Glaswegian monumental masons.

Four bronze lion heads once spouted water into four polished pink granite basins beneath a central well. Above, balancing a globe topped by a weathervane between their tails, are four monstrous stone fish. The well is now dry, and during centenary renovations the water has been replaced by uplighting, but at the time of writing a local plan has been mooted to dispense soft drinks from it during the summer months – presumably by the town's dentists.

St Thomas's Well, the Tibbertreoch Well, Kemps Well, the Cold Well – there are many in the spa town of Crieff, named for its Victorian hydropathic hotel. Water for drinking, water for bathing, water for cleaning – water flows still from the mouth of a stone lion's head at the Jesus Well up by the Hydro. A version of John 4:13–14 is inscribed on a stone above it: 'Jesus said / He that drinketh of this / water shall thirst again / But whosoever drinketh / of the water that I shall / give him shall never / thirst.' In the Bible the verse continues, 'but the water that I shall give him shall be in him a well of water springing up into everlasting life'. Algae and moss rim the bowl, pine needles float on its surface. A more prosaic modern notice warns: 'This water is not fit for human consumption.'

The rejuvenating properties of the town's waters were not confined to the Hydro. Water from the Cold Well and at Croftnappock was aerated and sold as a benefit to health at the end of the nineteenth century, generating silver for enterprising townsfolk. Tradition had it that a white pebble or silver coin thrown into a sacred well as an offering brought luck. Coins fill the bucket of the wishing well in the ornamental gardens before the Hydro today, though no water flows under the Japanese bridge and the pond is a wet bath for algae. It may be that the Strath's geology is the cause of fluctuating water levels, with shifts in winter and summer water-table levels.

Along at Fowlis Wester the Jeely Well may take its name from its gelatinous texture in times of drought, or the waters as they bubbled up, like berries or Keiller's marmalade in a jeely (jam) pan.

By turn of the twentieth century, Tayside's burgeoning middle classes had moved outwith old burghs' boundaries to new suburbs or satellite towns like Crieff or Alyth, commutable by rail, in pursuit of clean water and fresh air. There they were being offered by the General Accident Assurance Corporation, 42–44 Tay Street, Perth, their 'Accident and Fever Policy', which paid out '£6 per week while disabled by Typhoid, Smallpox, Typhus and Scarlet Fever (in addition to double benefits for Railway Accidents)'.

A century which had begun with many of the vestiges

of thousands of years of human existence along the river hardly changed ended irrevocably altered.

Once the summer sun has burnt off the haar, you get a spectacular view of Dundee from the Tay bridges. Road and rail, they transition the traveller a mile or so across the river at the narrowest point between the Kingdom of Fife and the metropolis. They set the city within its landscape. To your left is the surprise of the vast expanse of water as it widens away to the west between the Fife shore and the Carse of Gowrie. When did the Tay become such a great river? Yet even as it receives it final tribute of the Earn at Carpow it turns towards its inevitable fate, for here it is in the dominion of the sea. To become a truly great river it has sacrificed what it has been up to this point. It has compromised itself and in becoming something greater has also become something less.

Fat, mottled seals bask on exposed tidal sandbanks: East and West Naughton's Banks, Middle Bank, Davie Lowe's Bank, My Lord's Bank. Behind, the Sidlaw Hills are dotted with intricately carved Pictish stones, while the fields are striped by row upon row of berries. To the right, out past Broughty Ferry Castle on its promontory to the Open golf links at Carnoustie and the North Sea. Ahead the city is stacked upon itself from waterfront to the beacon on top of the Law, the pinnacle hill on which the Iron Age dun (fort) first oversaw the growth of the town.

Along the water is the tiny airport built on reclaimed land, mechanical piledrivers bending their backs to drive rust-proof staves into the riverbed; the snaking iron girders of the railway bridge, as it crosses the water then curves into the city centre; the masts and funnel of Scott of the Antarctic's ship *Discovery* moored beside the new V&A museum, all angular, nautical shapes, yet organic too.

On the other side of the road bridge, white horizontal cruise ships dock against a backdrop of white vertical 'multis' – two different lifestyles at right angles. Once-thriving docks are home to a rusting light ship, the hulk of the mast-less *Unicorn*, the oldest ship afloat in Scotland, occasional North sea oil support vessels, and wind-turbine fabricators – the criss-cross grids of their girders echoed in the floodlights of Tannadice (United) and Dens Park (Dundee), the city's football teams that share a street but are forever divided.

On the beach at Broughty Ferry greenshanks are oozing their delightfully long beaks into the moist tidal sands. Children are digging a channel from the edge of the sea to the sandcastle they have constructed. Unlike Canute they are willing the tide to turn and flood the moat with water. After a while they resort to filling their castle-shaped buckets with seawater and, God-like, create their own river. The water constantly disappears into the sand. Creating a river is not as easy as the river makes it look.

The Tay follows its timeless tides – timeless in human eyes, whose stone castles are like sandcastles before the river and sea's inexorable breathing, their never ceasing ebb and flow. Memories of beaches, of my children's, then my sandcastles, slip through my mind like grains of sand through my fingers. Innocent days.

Waters flow and change, as do the dangers to children.

Fresh water supply and sanitation; swimming lessons at school; signs along the beach warning of rip tides and how to escape them; peace brought about by European Union; all have helped protect the young, but all along the beach are warning signs of a different, contemporary danger. Obese bodies, even of very little children, are everywhere. Hearts strain to pump the lifeblood through their veins; muscles gasp for oxygen to keep life flowing in these already failing bodies, like constantly running up sand dunes. Stress levels are increasing inside people's heads, the flow of serotonin to the brain drying up. Depression can be like walking through ever deepening sand, the dunes rising higher and higher, whipped by wind and tide beyond anyone's control.

On the soft grained sand of the transitional shore, the unambiguous black crow waddles like a stout grandfather with his hands behind his back, trying to understand the modern world of his grandchildren. At ease with both land and water, paddle the light and deft family of oystercatchers. They have his Victorian blackness but also pure white. They dance across the shore on orange feet, probing earnestly with prawn-pink beaks. Another local family is enjoying a more relaxing day at the beach. The father and two of the girls are building the sandcastle with a bright pink bucket while a third, saltire flag in hand, is excavating that moat and channel to the water with her heel. Their mother is walking by the tideline. She stoops and picks up a shell to give to the baby in her arms, the hem of her black burka momentarily trailing in the water, shimmering in the heat like sealskin. A shell gifted.

The cowrie shell threaded on a handwoven Oceanic basket has added value to a utilitarian object, first to its owner and then to the Taysider – presumably there to exploit the gold, oil and copper deposits – who transported it all the way back here as a curio and donated it to the Dundee museum. While that act has preserved it, it has also transformed its usefulness to at best an item of education, as silent as a Celtic handbell. Who now picks up the bronze Tibetan sankha in the shape of a conch shell in the next case along and blows it like a sea sprite? The puffed out cheeks of a crimson-and-yellow-clad monk calling believers to prayer echoes along its journey from the Indian Ocean upstream to the Himalaya and now, silently, across continents to the small Buddhist community in Dundee downstream from the ruined European monasteries of black, white and grey monks and nuns.

A humble plant growing abundantly in the Ganges delta in what is now Bangladesh was to make the fortune of a privileged few along the Tay. Praat or white and tossa jute has been cultivated in the waterlogged soil of Bengal from the start of the nineteenth century and by a quirk of history Dundee, with its imperial connections, weaving industry and shipping trade, became the location of a symbiotic relationship between jute and whaling.

It was discovered that by adding whale oil to its raw fibres jute could be softened and woven into fabric for sacking, twisted into string and ropes, made into upholstery lining and webbing, carpet and linoleum backing, roofing felt and sailcloth. From such simple items vast wealth was created by the so-called jute barons. In Broughty Ferry one of these baronial families, the Grimonds, constructed Carbet Castle, an ornate mock-French chateau, and were able to employ Charles Fréchou to decorate its ceilings. Fréchou had previously worked on the Paris Opera House. The dining-room stucco painting has pairs of smiling cherubs in pastel colours at the four cardinal points; they are enjoying music, food, flowers in plenty – one, head back, squirts wine from a calf skin gourd into its mouth, surrounded by ornate pink roses and golden Victorian rococo swags. Above the south entrance porch, with its views out over the Tay, a willowy figure of a girl is painted in monotone within a golden plaster frame. She languidly unravels (with a now destroyed partner) a scroll with the motto 'Industria' whilst holding a distaff and spool of yarn. Behind her an industrial cog wheel sits half in water. 'Salve' – be well, says a panel; 'Pax' – peace, another.

In the tenement slums of the Grimonds' mill workers, a different kind of children's document was prized.

From 1876 children were legally required to have some form of education up to the age of thirteen. Trafficking in birth certificates was a common practice at this time. Between 1875 and 1900 jobs had become scarce . . . a certificate allowing a child to leave school and take employment was a valuable commodity. To employers in a low profit industry the employment of young persons at low wage rates made sense even if it did mean that grown men remained unemployed. It was this factor which made the half-time system last longer in Dundee than in any other town. Half timers were employed in the mills for either ten hours every alternate day, in which case the next day was spent in the mill school, or from 5 a.m. until 11 a.m. at work with the period after mid-day dinner until 6 o'clock in school.

Grimonds' had been established by brothers James and David, who owned a flax mill each in Blairgowrie. In the 1840s the Maxwelltown hand-weaving mills in Dundee were acquired, making jute products and carpets. Their Bowbridge works were built in the late 1850s. By the end of the decade 30,000 tons of jute had been imported from India. Imports to Dundee rose to 100,000 tons in 1870, and 200,000 tons in the 1880s. J. & A. D. Grimond Ltd expanded, with branches in London, Manchester and New York, and with their camel's head trademark they were one of the city's biggest employers. The entrance arch to the Bowbridge Works was remarkable for the carved camel above it. The year of its construction, 1885, saw the sensational expedition by the British Camel Corps up the Nile to rescue General Gordon trapped in Khartoum.

To supply the factories with water, a 240-foot-deep well was bored and a cooling pond constructed. A remarkable feature of the Maxwelltown and Bowbridge Works was the fire prevention measures within the mills. When lit, jute smoulders with great heat, so in addition to robust construction with cast-iron columns and spans, a sprinkler system was integrated into the buildings. The mills also had their own fire brigade.

Protection of profit should not be confused with con-cern for the welfare of workers, at least not relatively unskilled ones. In 1886 the weekly wage was around twenty-four shillings for a male jute weaver and only eleven for a female. Time was docked if the machinery had to be stopped to clear it of blockages, thus the most common industrial injuries were the maiming of hands – injuries that prevented future work.

*

A pale segmented train silently crosses the iron bridge upstream. Underneath it, sitting just above the surface, are the piles of its collapsed predecessor, empty plinths of a monument to the fallen, like stumps on a mill worker's hand.

The German novelist Theodor Fontane, who we met earlier, with his biographical ode to Field Marshall Jacob Keith, travelled to Scotland in 1858 accompanied by his fellow Prussian Bernhard von Lepel, who illustrated the resulting book, *Beyond the Tweed*. As we have read, he was full of expectations fuelled by the Romantic movement novels of Sir Walter Scott and bardic sagas of Ossian. While at the dramatic gorge of Killiecrankie, he retells the myth of 'Bonnie Dundee', who, Puritans said, having sold his soul to the devil, his bath water would bubble and hiss whenever he entered the tub.

At Perth, Fontane's realist eye noted the Russian cannons on display, captured by the Black Watch during the recent Crimean War. Twenty years later that blend of poetic romance and reportage combined: he was so moved by the Tay Bridge disaster that he memorialised it in verse. '*Die Brück' am Tay*' is penned in the style of a Scottish folk ballad and takes as its premise the natural and supernatural world conspiring against Victorian engineering and capitalist endeavour. The force of Nature is represented by the reconvening of a familiar coven of Scottish witches.

'When shall we three meet again?'
'On the central pier in the driving rain.'
'At the seventh hour.'
'I'll quench the flame.'
'I too.'
'I'll come from the north,' said she.
'And I from the south.'
'And I from the sea.'
'We'll make a ring o'roses.'

This kind of 'art' ballad is not untypical of the burgeoning nineteenth-century urban middle class's yearning to recapture something of the rapidly disappearing 'folk' tradition, and has all the dissatisfactions of it.

Even more discordant are the verses on the collapse of the Tay Bridge on 28 December 1879 by the notorious 'world's worst poet', Dundee's William McGonagall. He is an interesting character. Certainly not a good poet – mocked and maligned, but famous yet, and perhaps in need of just a little sympathetic understanding.

His life story reflects some of the themes we have explored in this book – origins in Ireland and the west, drawn to the eastern industrial city from his rural Celtic roots. He blends his authentic cultural inheritance with a Victorian tourist idea of aggrandized Highland

Scottishness: the kilt, the hairy sporran, the claymore and targe, the bonnet with the clan chief's feather in it. His father was a handloom weaver apprenticing his son in the trade. The young McGonagall seems to have been skilled at this; he also had a passion for books and reading, entertaining his fellow weavers with tales from Shakespeare. He paid a local theatre to allow him to perform the lead role in *Macbeth*, but onstage took a dislike to the actor playing Macduff and at the play's climax refused to die. Odd.

As industrial manufacturing became more sophisticated, there was less demand for McGonagall's weaving skills and he began to sink into poverty. He sought to monetise his love of drama and literature, writing poems and performing them to small local audiences, acting out scenes from Shakespeare.

In his most famous, 'The Tay Bridge Disaster', he picks up the theme of the supernatural, 'the Storm Fiend' being responsible for the bridge's collapse, yet he also combines a rational insight for cause of the disaster gleaned from contemporary journalism.

> It must have been an awful sight,
> To witness in the dusky moonlight,
> While the Storm Fiend did laugh, and angry did bray,
> Along the Railway Bridge of the Silv'ry Tay,
> Oh! ill-fated Bridge of the Silv'ry Tay,
> I must now conclude my lay
> By telling the world fearlessly without the least dismay,
> That your central girders would not have given way,
> At least many sensible men do say,

Had they been supported on each side with buttresses,
At least many sensible men confesses,
For the stronger we our houses do build,
The less chance we have of being killed.

McGonagall's lines try to bridge to the bardic tradition
of ballad reportage of real, contemporary events delivered
to a live audience. But this is an industrial-age parody of
a bard competing for poetic prizes at the court of a clan
chief. The cruel reality of his life is captured in a report in
Dundee's *Evening Telegraph* in 1888:

The Circus, Nethergate, gave a farewell entertainment
last night, and by way of variety the services of Mr William
McGonagall, 'poet and tragedian', were engaged. The
announcement that Mr McGonagall was to take part in
the entertainment attracted a large audience and during
the early performances occasional cries were made for
'McGonagall'. A 'clowns' club' was arranged, in which
McGonagall was to take part. A table being introduced
into the ring, the clowns one by one appeared and took
their seats. Each, it was observed, carried an umbrella,
the object of which was not difficult to divine . . . A
'distinguished visitor' was then announced, the curtains
at the wings were thrown aside, and to the strains of 'See
the Conquering Hero Comes' McGonagall stalked into
the ring with a lordly air. He was arrayed in a kilt, plaid
and sporran, and wore a bonnet in which was fastened
a feather which would have done credit to the wing
of a first-class eagle. The kilt was a trifle short, but the

'poet' wore 'tights' which, however, seemed to be rather wide for his limbs. The members of the 'clowns' club', having evidently been warned of what might occur, no sooner saw the 'poet' emerge than each unfurled his umbrella, and not a moment too soon, for scarcely had he entered the ring when eggs, herrings, potatoes and stale bread went whizzing through the air from all parts of the building, the point of attraction being the 'poet's warlike figure'. The 'poet' paused for a moment and glanced hastily around, then made a rush to join the clowns; but these nimble gentry quickly retreated, leaving the McGonagall alone. . . striking a dramatic attitude . . . [the poet] . . . at once launched into the recital of a wonderful 'poem' entitled 'Tel-el-Kebir':

> 'Arabi's army were about 70,000 in all,
> And virtually speaking, it was not very small.'

In his faux Highland costume McGonagall, his riotous audiences pelting him with rotten fruit like a criminal chained to a joug, utterly destitute, knowingly suffers public humiliation in a desperate attempt to avoid the Victorian workhouse. Who is the jester?

Would modern sensibilities allow someone so damaged to be thus treated? Would anyone be permitted to fashion a bronze quaich made from the boiler plug of the Tay Bridge disaster locomotive? Would we today dare link manmade disaster with the hands of storm fiends, witches, of the gods . . . do the old deities still lurk in the contemporary mind? It seems unlikely that in this atheistic age few or any would attribute poor human design, faulty construction and storm damage to an actual 'act of God', whatever their insurance company may say.

In 1860 John McFadyen was admitted to Perth Prison's Victorian 'lunatic' wing for drowning a young boy in the river but never understood what he'd done. Today the disaster of global warming, the climate crisis, has been brought on by our human actions since the industrial age, rather than by divine or supernatural forces. Flooding by the Tay, most of us realise, is our own folly.

*

(H)uman waifs and strays of the modern Babylon; the children of poverty, and misery and crime; in very many cases labouring under physical defects, such as bad sight or hearing; almost always stunted in growth, and bearing the stamp of ugliness and suffering on their features. Generally born in dark alleys and backcourts, their playground has been the streets, where the wits of many have been prematurely sharpened at the expense of any moral they might have. With minds and bodies destitute of proper nutriment, they are caught, as it were, by the Parish officers, like half-wild creatures.

– Charles Dickens, *Household Words*

Dickens was the conscience of the Victorian city. He cared passionately about the poor – those we encountered earlier described in *Dundee Delineated* as 'the lowest of the community', forced to live in 'lazar-holes'. He gave them a voice but he also acted. He was the driving force behind clean water and modern sewage schemes in London, and he inspired others beyond to do likewise and to do good. To do good or at least do better than was being done, or not being done, for the urban poor, especially for the children at danger of sinking into crime.

The city's first orphanage had been set up by public subscription after many children were left parentless by the sinking of the Tayport ferry one Sunday in 1821. The orphans of churchgoers drowned by an act of God elicited public sympathy. In contrast, 'fallen' girls, or those in danger of falling, were institutionalised at the Dundee and District Female Rescue Home, Lochee, and elicited considerably less sympathy. Taking those children at risk of falling into crime into institutional care, giving structure to their meandering lives, and teaching them skills that would gain them useful adult employment and integrate them into wider society appealed to the Victorians. At Dundee and in nine other sites around the coast of these islands, one such scheme was centred on a moored training ship and its aim was to provide suitable male recruits for the navy, the merchant marine and in Dundee's case the whaling industry.

The *Mars* was a fully rigged man-o-war which in its pomp had seventy-eight guns. It was launched too late to fight Napoleon and too early for steam, and had only briefly served as a supply ship in the Crimean War of 1853–56. That conflict had highlighted the dearth of recruits willing to serve in the navy, so it was suggested that youths from penal institutions could be drafted. The

Admiralty didn't want boys who had been educated in the 'schools for criminality' that were the prisons, so the training ships were established.

While the *Mars* did take some boys who had committed an offence punishable by prison, as long as they were under twelve and hadn't been convicted of theft, its chief recruits were those at risk of falling into criminality – boys under fourteen whose parents found them impossible to control or those who had a parent in prison. It also took children who were the victims of nineteenth-century industrial society: the destitute; those cast out by families unable to feed, house and clothe them; those begging for alms on the street; lost boys. The *Mars* was not intended as a punishment, though it was pretty grim, but as a safety net to prevent children from falling out of mainstream society. It was intended to offer a lifeline to those who had dipped their toes into a life of crime.

Local industrialists, philanthropists and businesses made contributions to its establishment, though as is the way of these things 'a considerably larger sum of money than was at first anticipated will be needed for her equipment'. So from 1868 to 1929 the Training Ship *Mars* was home to four hundred boys at a time living under navy conditions.

She was moored off the Fife bank of the river at Woodhaven and downstream of the railway bridge, anchored by two chains that allowed her to swing with the tide.

The first recruit was a PR dream but also an exception to the rule. He was the rather gallant Murdoch McLeod, not a waif from the city slums but a braw Highland laddie from the Sma' Glen. Murdoch, aged thirteen, had been apprenticed to a firm of Perth bookbinders but on reading Johann David Wyss's utopian adventure novel *The Swiss Family Robinson* had decided a life on the ocean waves was for him.

Appropriating a Tay coble, he rowed downriver to Dundee and stowed away on a trader bound for Archangel. Upon discovery while still in port, the ship's captain told him they were looking for boys like him to train as sailors, and handed him over to the police. He thus volunteered for the *Mars* and after his training he joined the navy for five years.

After this 'followed ten years of adventure in the China clippers before he entered the Australian coastal service, in which he rose to be chief officer, a member of the Honourable Company of Master Mariners', reported *The Courier* on his return to Dundee aged eighty-three in June 1939.

'In memory of his own days on the *Mars* Captain M'Leod presented a War Loan bond to provide prizes for the boys . . . when the *Mars* finished her days as a training ship the M'Leod prize was transferred to Dundee Technical College School of Navigation'.

Unlike Murdoch, more than half the 1871 intake could not read. They were not brimming with youthful adventure, but 'sent tae the *Mars*' because 'father dead, mother in a lunatic asylum' or 'deserted by father, mother transported for seven years' or 'a destitute orphan' or 'associate of thieves stays out all night' or 'drifting into crime' or 'mother unable to control boy'. Life for most was harsh and extremely regulated; food was always scant, overcrowding led to no privacy, loneliness and sadness predominated, and most boys had the feeling of being cast adrift. Corporal punishment was so violent that regulations required a doctor to be present when it was administered. Indeed life was so impersonal that the boys lost their shore identities and became known only by their registration number issued on arrival aboard. Murdoch may have been number one boy and got his name in the papers, but for most they were mere numerals.

Ashore in St Mary's Episcopal Church, Wormit, some of the boys have left their marks on the pews, carving not their names but their numbers: '36', '38', '58', '86'and '126' are etched into the wood. Like fathoms on the Tay's admiralty chart, they give measurement but no idea of the person, of the texture of the life flowing underneath the number. Life was one of strict regimen: they were segmented like the decks of the ship – Forecastle, Foretop, Maintop, Quarterdeck – with church on Sunday, laundry washed on Monday. Everyone had the *Mars* haircut – close shaved back, sides and top, with a tuft of longer fringe at the very front. The days dripped into weeks, swirled into months.

What were the sounds a boy would hear aboard the ship out in the river in the dark watches of the night? The creaking hulk swinging in the tidal flow; merging river and seawater slapping outside; the stifled tears flowing below deck; the squelch of a wet bed; in winter, the ice thudding against the hull – echoes of a boy's future aboard an Arctic whaler.

One effect of the construction of the railway bridge in 1878 was the breaking up of the ice flows on its piers by the tide but with its collapse another macabre thudding resonated inside the *Mars* – of wreckage, cracked railway carriages and ice-cold humans. The Tay Bridge disaster was so dreadful a tragedy it resonates down the centuries, yet each day the horrors of life on the *Mars* were too much for some wee boys.

Crossing the replacement railway bridge today, I look to where the *Mars* was moored. The tide and wind draw thin lines of flickering white crests on the river's surface. Underneath the waves, unseen currents are busily remodelling the sand, altering the contours of the Firth, muddying the water. Overhead fast-moving clouds change the colours of the Tay as I look – silver to pale blue to jute green to ultramarine, their cast shadows moving across the face of the water like some heavenly doom. On a cracked headstone in Forgan cemetery is etched:

In memory of William McIntosh, William Miln, and John Hall, aged respectively 12, 13, and 14 years, pupils on the Training Ship MARS who, in a fit of waywardness incidental to youth, left Woodhaven pier in an open boat on the stormy morning of 18th March 1871, and were lost on the Gaa Bank within one short hour of their sailing. Their remains were recovered and are interred here.

The Mitchell boys, led by fourteen-year-old James, entering the river Isla on a hot midsummer Sunday afternoon three years later could be called a 'fit of waywardness incidental to youth', but to risk sailing a small boat across the stormy mouth of the Tay in March speaks of a fear and desperation driven by something much deeper and darker than 'the waywardness of youth'. The boys' tragic fate on the sandbanks at the end point of the Tay was no doubt used as a cautionary tale, to deter other would-be escapees. I hear in my head the duality of threats shouted into children's ears: from the shore, 'We'll send ye tae the *Mars*!'; echoing across the water from the floating hulk, 'Remember the Gaa!'

But for some, though, there was comfort in the *Mars* routine. Perhaps William Bowman's life before joining the ship was so traumatic that anything was better. A *Mars* boy himself, he later returned as an instructor. Surviving photographs show him with boys in sailor dress, in the wood workshop between decks, their huge aprons reaching down to the ground, emphasising their squatness (Dickens' 'stunted in growth' or just their youth) or displaying the objects they have crafted – tables and stools; inlayed trays to be used in cosy bourgeois family homes (a life from which they are excluded); a biplane.

A biplane – what a twentieth-century object, contrasted against the Victorian boys and their inlayed trays. What a fabulous machine, how wonderful to be able to take to the air, fly like a bird, soar away over the river with its treacherous tides and into sunshine above the grey clouds, from the miseries of life as a *Mars* boy into a new future, a new century. A century of public health, social housing, the welfare state, clean water, a toilet in every home, privacy. What would those other crafters on water, the Iron

Age residents of the crannogs on Loch Tay carving stools, weaving baskets from reeds at the other end of the river make of such a magical machine?

What do we make of Preston Watson, Dundee's aviation pioneer, who according to his brother 'studied the flight of gulls, caught many of them, put small weights on their heads, glued their wings into the position he wished, and was frequently seen by passers-by dropping them over the road bridge, which crossed the railway line at the west end of the Dundee Esplanade'.

On the pebbled shore at Woodhaven today, aeroplanes circle and swirl with the gulls before dipping to land on the north bank at the riverside airport. White triangles that skip over the swirling currents of the Tay are the wind-darted dinghies from the 'Wormit Boating Club and Water-sports Hub', where boys and girls can learn to sail to the Gaa and back again safely. On land, brown contour lines join equal heights on the map; out on the river, the young sailors chart the contours of the brown mudbanks – six feet equals one fathom. Across the line of the Tay Railway Bridge, the depth runs 0 fathoms 1 foot, 0 3, 0 4, 1 3, 2 5, 3 5, 2 3, 4 0, 2 5, 2 1, 3 2, 1 1, 3 2, 1 1, 1 0, 2 5, 1 3, north to south. Computers now digitise these codes sculpturally, bathymetrical with 3D imaging, slipping effortlessly between mean low and high water springs. GPS-based nautical apps track ships from all around the North Sea and beyond safely into the havens of Dundee and, with necessary accuracy, to the harbour at Perth, where the river is barely a fathom deep. Contours and lines join points of height, points of connection, they bridge between places and people. If the boys of the *Mars*, God of War, marvelled at a biplane, what would they and the Odin-worshipping Vikings who raided these shores a thousand years before make of the memorial stone in Woodhaven harbour honouring the crews of the Norwegian Airforce flying boats that were stationed here during the Second World War?

A line on a page describing raiding Viking longships contours to a point far away in time and space, to letters etched on stone describing a defending Norwegian flying boat. Words from around the North Sea are washed into the Tay with the never-ending tides – ved, vede, wode, wold shimmer into our word 'wood', old Norse *hǫfn* transmutes to *havn*. At Woodhaven the river and time ebb and flow.

# Firth . . . and firth

## *The seas beyond*

One of the watercolours by Turner from the National Galleries of Scotland has been loaned for a short period to the Signal Tower Museum at Arbroath. It depicts not a Highland riverscape but the Inchcape lighthouse in a storm. *Bell Rock Lighthouse* was painted in 1819 at the request of Robert Stevenson, the engineer who master-minded its building. The image was engraved and used as the frontispiece illustration for Stevenson's book, *An Account of the Bell Rock Light-house*. Yet Turner never visited the lighthouse. He drew on his wide experience of the North Sea and its storms, and on Stevenson's plans and his tales of building the tower.

The lighthouse sits twelve miles off the Tay coast, on rocks submerged twice a day by the tide, and was so well constructed that today it is the world's oldest surviving sea-washed lighthouse. Stevenson's enlightened design included on the top floor of the tower a domed library – engineering and literature entwined.

Throughout the nineteenth century the Stevenson family and other engineers were to work on surveying, scoping and building along the length of the Tay, deepening it, making it navigable, altering its flow, shoring up its banks. One example is recorded in a drawing by the Stevensons entitled *REDUCED SURVEY / as part of the / FRITH OF TAY / as seen at low water of Spring tides / refering to a Report / relative to the improvement / of the / FERRY betwixt the COUNTIES / of / FIFE & FORFAR*, now in the National Library of Scotland. His grandson and namesake was Robert Louis Stevenson, author of *Treasure Island* and *Kidnapped*. Engineering, science and art entwined.

Travelling to view the lighthouse the following year was another great Scots engineer, Thomas Telford, builder of the elegant bridge over the Tay at Dunkeld and designer of the Innerwick Kirk, with his companion and good friend the Poet Laureate Robert Southey. Southey had published a poem on the legend of the Bell Rock in 1802 and it and this accompanying introduction are included in some later editions of Stevenson's *An Account of the Bell Rock Light-house*.

'The Inchcape Rock'

An older writer mentions a curious tradition which may be worth quoting. 'By east the Isle of May', says he, 'twelve miles from all land in the German seas, lyes a great hidden rock, called Inchcape, very dangerous for navigators, because it is overflowed everie tide. It is reported in old times, upon the saide rock there was a bell, fixed upon a tree or timber, which rang continually, being moved by the sea, giving notice to the saylers of the danger. This bell or clocke was put there and maintained by the Abbott of Aberbrothok, and being taken down by a sea pirate, a yeare thereafter he perished upon the same rocke, with ship and goodes, in the righteous judgement of God.' – STODDART'S 'Remarks on Scotland'

No stir in the air, no stir in the sea,
The ship was still as she could be,
Her sails from heaven received no motion,
Her keel was steady in the ocean.

Without either sign or sound of their shock
The waves flow'd over the Inchcape Rock;
So little they rose, so little they fell,
They did not move the Inchcape Bell.

The Abbot of Aberbrothok
Had placed that bell on the Inchcape Rock;
On a buoy in the storm it floated and swung,
And over the waves its warning rung.

When the Rock was hid by the surge's swell,
The mariners heard the warning bell;
And then they knew the perilous Rock,
And blest the Abbot of Aberbrothok.

The Sun in heaven was shining gay,
All things were joyful on that day;
The sea-birds scream'd as they wheel'd round,
And there was joyaunce in their sound.

The buoy of the Inchcape Bell was seen
A darker speck on the ocean green;
Sir Ralph the Rover walk'd his deck,
And he fix'd his eye on the darker speck.

He felt the cheering power of spring,
It made his whistle, it made him sing;
His heart was mirthful to excess,
But the Rover's mirth was wickedness.

His eye was on the Inchcape float;
Quoth he, 'My men, put out the boat,
And row me to the Inchcape Rock,
And I'll plague the Abbot of Aberbrothok.'

The boat is lower'd, the boatmen row,
And to the Inchcape Rock they go;
Sir Ralph bent over from the boat,
And he cut the Bell from the Inchcape float.

Down sunk the Bell with a gurgling sound,
The bubbles rose and burst around;
Quoth Sir Ralph, 'The next who comes to the Rock
Won't bless the Abbot of Aberbrothok.'

Sir Ralph the Rover sail'd away,
He scour'd the seas for many a day;

And now grown rich with plunder'd store,
He steers his course for Scotland's shore.

So thick a haze o'erspreads the sky
They cannot see the Sun on high;
The wind hath blown a gale all day,
At evening it hath died away.

On the deck the Rover takes his stand,
So dark it is they see no land.
Quoth Sir Ralph, 'It will be lighter soon,
For there is the dawn of the rising Moon.'

'Canst hear,' said one, 'the breakers roar?
For methinks we should be near the shore.'
'Now where we are I cannot tell,
But I wish I could hear the Inchcape Bell.'

They hear no sound, the swell is strong;
Though the wind hath fallen they drift along,
Till the vessel strikes with a shivering shock,—
'Oh Christ! It is the Inchcape Rock!'

Sit Ralph the Rover tore his hair;
He curst himself in his despair;
The waves rush in on every side,
The ship is sinking beneath the tide.

But even in his dying fear
One dreadful sound could the Rover hear,
A sound as if with the Inchcape Bell,
The Devil below was ringing his knell.'

Arriving in Arbroath late on 25 August, Southey was now seeing the lighthouse marking the setting of his poem for the first time. He noted in his *Journal of a Tour in Scotland in 1819* that the two revolving lights, one bright, the other a duller red, can be seen from the town revolving every three minutes.

Southey was in luck.

A July haar is down over the Firth today. 'So thick a haze o'erspreads the sky / They cannot see the Sun on high.' If it has a colour it is grey/fawn, its touch cold but wispy, close up it disperses but is persistent.

Approaching Dundee, you can see it drifting above the Fife hills on the south side of the Tay. Crossing the river, it conceals the city. It carries on over into the northern Forfarshire hills, west down the river to Perth, and east out into the Firth and the North Sea. It obfuscates. Where does it begin, where does it end? We have travelled from the river's beginnings; having reached the sea and the turn of the tide, it seems pertinent to ask where does the Tay end?

My journey has upsprung from atop icy Ben Lui; I've paddled in the waters flowing out of Loch Tay; been harassed by a ringed plover on the dam at Loch Ericht; flowed with St Fillan along the Earn; watched frogs in snowmelt ponds at the Cairnwell Pass; even read a report on sewage contamination in the Treacle Burn that flows into Forfar Loch – from all these distant points and more the Tay has beginnings, but at what point does it end? It becomes tidal just below Perth and the bugle-like Firth begins; by Invergowrie it is three miles across but narrows again and is still a river at Dundee, albeit a mile-wide one. On the southern bank it is not so easy to pinpoint a particular end point – the Pile lighthouse at Tayport feels like the seaside, but the sands at Tentsmuir Point are the recognised end. The promontory on which Broughty Ferry Castle sits seems to be a natural point on which to say the river ends on the north bank – there is a harbour and sandy beach, and looking over the water you would say that you are looking at the sea rather than a river – but it is the transient links of Buddon Ness, a few miles further east, that is the generally accepted end.

This shark's tooth of land was once home to a lifeboat station, to an ice house and wells, one of which was beside the old tramway line that transported munitions and men to and from the target sheds of the rifle range of Barry army camp. Distances are marked with precision – 100, 200, 500, 1,000 yards – while the land, like recruits and soldiers on the tides of high politics, ebbs and flows over the years. The Gaa sand hill has risen and fallen in rhythm with the centuries, the millennia, grain by grain. The twin High and Low lighthouses have been guiding sailors past these shifting sands and through haar on The Elbow or Abertay banks of 'Butan Nais' since at least the seventeenth century, where they are marked on a map *The Sea coast from Fiffnesse to Montros / was Survey'd by Mr. Mar, an injenious Marriner [sic] of Dundee*. The Stevensons designed two more lighthouses on the sands in the mid nineteenth century, but the lower one had to be moved 300 feet on rails in 1885 as the sands shifted, making its original position redundant. Previous lights are illustrated and marked as 'Feux' on 'Button Ness' on the French admiralty chart *Carte particuliere de la cote orientale d'Ecosse, depuis St Abb's Head jusqu'a Duncansby*, published in 1804 by the Dépôt Generale de la Marine, Paris, that has all the information concerning direction of tides, sandbanks and water depths an invading fleet would need from 'Tentsmoor Ness' to 'Cape ou Bell Rock'. Boney's defeat and exile is celebrated on the Ness by the St Helena lookout post and flagstaff. Two hundred years later, over the nearby dunes at Carnoustie, Frenchman Jean van de Velde snatched defeat from the jaws of victory on the 72nd hole at the 1999 Open golf championship, trousers rolled up, staring at his ball in the watery isolation of the Barry Burn. Scotland's Paul Lawrie won.

A mere seven miles due north lies the Dilty Moss, the most easterly source of the Tay, a beginning at the end. Between the two is a complex of underground chambers at Carlungie souterrain – a storehouse for another, successful invasion; inside its cool, pavemented cellars were unearthed an amphora of continental wine and an expensive blue glass brooch from Roman France. From the Dilty Moss drains the Kerbet Burn, but instead of a short journey to the estuary it heads north to join the Dean Water in Strathmore near Glamis, then westwards to the Isla to meld with the Tay above Stanley, then flows all the way back to the Firth via Perth and Dundee.

Between Buddon Ness and the Inchcape Rock the sea is reached. But what river reaches the sea? The river is still beginning in cloud, on mountaintop, forming Allt Coire Laoigh. At the same time as it dilutes into salt water it is lapping both at the posts of an Iron Age crannog on Loch Tay and at the twenty-first-century reconstruction. It is being filtered through the beard of a young freshwater mussel upstream of Perth as the barnacled shells of saltwater mussels wash up on the beach at Carnoustie like miniature boats. The river is not a single entity in that way but a continuous loop, with a beginning but no beginning, an end but no end. The river is a journey with a destination in the sea, but also a journey with no destination. Like humans it is constantly on the move, being born, living and then dying, then the next generation comes along or simultaneous generations. It is Ossianic tales and chanted incantations, a book of ballads sung in farm-side bothies and written verse shelved in Innerpeffray Library; it is a tome of history and a sci-fi novel layered of parallel but slightly different worlds that both share the same story and create their own universes; singular and universal.

The journey becomes the river. The river cannot reason why it thunders here, trickles there, spins back on itself with a trail of ponderous bubbles while a foot away it is a foaming torrent. The river is like the past. Each pool or stream has its own fluvial story, history natural, human, aquatic; each stretch, stretching back in time, a point on the journey that gives colour and texture, as the willow root grasping to the softening bank, the mayfly larvae under the stone, the dipper seeking it out. It is soap suds' lather dissipating as it flows under the bridge's keystone. Each of these stories a bead on the necklace of the river, some golden, some pearls, most gravel. They are irregularly threaded. Some have cracked or fallen through the floor of a crannog to be preserved in the bed of the river awaiting rediscovery, others highly treasured, polished, still lustrous down the centuries. The river is a rosary, fingered, worried over, calming. Along its banks prayers are mumbled or exclaimed – the plop of a rising fish or the ringing of steeple bells – each pool, loch, stream, burn, mudbank associated with actions and emotions, stepping stones to our past, bridging the span of time, zigzagging through history, personal and national, like leaping over stepping stones or over the Z-shaped bridge at Dollerie, looping, braided, meandering along different courses over time.

At the Firth it enters the dominion of the sea. It embraces it, is embraced by it, and dissolves.

Out in the Firth a sudden whirlwind creates a waterspout. It lifts a tiny portion of the water out of its normal course and into a premature rebirth of itself as a cloud and rainfall. Nor does the river always flow in a straight line.

From out at sea beyond the sandbars of the Firth, beyond the Bell Rock, ships sail into the Tay on time's tide. They come from Rome, from Tiron and Flanders, Jamaica, the Ganges, Antarctica and Greenland. They bring regimented armies and glass-like water made solid; crisp monastic apples and red wine in green bottles; sweet sugar bought with bitter cruelty; child-scythed jute and returning mercenary colonists; flayed sealskins and butchered whales.

On board one of these whaling ships was John Sakeouse, a native of Disko Sound, West Greenland, who arrived in Scotland aboard a whaler in 1816, where he gave an exhibition of his Inuit prowess. An engraving of Sakeouse performing his hunting skills after a sketch by Amelia Anderson has the following text:

> [He] exhibited several feats of dexterity with his Lance and Canoe . . . He successfully contend with a six oared Whale Boat and in his coarse threw his Lance with unerring certainty against the bulb of the Beacon.

He was a lad o' pairts. Not only was he the subject of art, but in Scotland dabbled in art himself, being taught to draw by Alexander Nasmyth, who had painted Paterson's Castle Huntly, the old ferry at Inver and had taught Ruskin's father. Nasmyth was not only a landscape painter but a portraitist, too; he painted Sakeouse and, famously, his friend Robert Burns – the most iconic image of the poet. How good a draftsman Sakeouse was can be seen in the print of a drawing he made when employed on a later Arctic expedition, *First Communication with the Natives of Prince Regent Bay, Presented to Captain Ross, August 10th 1818*. His hand/eye co-ordination was good, the accuracy of his throw was such that he could split a ship's biscuit floating in the water from a distance of thirty metres.

The ability to launch a spear or harpoon accurately was a skill highly prized by the Scots whalers, their earlier ancestors, as well as Inuit. In *Ancestors in the Arctic*, Malcolm Archibald cites two Dundee harpooners, Robert Ogilvie and Robert Adamson of the *Dorothy*, as being paid twenty shillings per month, plus a bonus for the amount of oil and baleen returned to port in 1832, against the average seaman's wage of fifteen shillings.

After his demonstration, Sakeouse was recruited as an interpreter by Captain Ross on his expedition to discover the Northwest Passage. Through him the Inuit told Ross they thought his ship was a living beast and its sails wings – a flying boat. By the end of the nineteenth century, the Inuit were more familiar with whaling vessels and Shoodlue, a medicine man who spoke good English, travelled back to Dundee with Captain William Milne in 1894 on board the *Eclipse*, giving a demonstration of his kayaking skills off the Esplanade.

The images of Sakeouse and Shoodlue are striking ones that have a companion in the McManus Galleries in Dundee. On a walrus tusk is engraved the picture of an Inuk in a kayak, harpooning a seal lying on an ice floe. This type of image on ivory or tooth is called a scrimshaw and there are plenty of others in the collection – some depicting whaling boats, others whales, some with biblical texts and scenes. Sometimes the ivory would be sculpted into a robust bowl of a pipe. This fine craftwork would be carried out in the warmth of the berth below deck in the long Arctic nights, waiting for whales to be spotted, or if, as frequently happened, Dundee's whaling fleet was stranded in ice. But up on the freezing decks and in the lonely whale lookout posts, sealskin gloved fingers would only be able to carry out the most basic of movements, like strumming a tune on a jews harp; counting off the eight rings of the half-hour bell until the watch was over on your gloved fingers; or briefly delving into a sealskin pouch for tobacco to chew, its juices freezing to temporary amber beads on ship's beards, the pouch's drawstring quickly pulled tight again to make it waterproof like the sealskin apron round the waist of John Sakehouse in his kayak.

One seemingly incongruous scrimshaw in the McManus collection of whaling artefacts is carved with a penguin. The whalers' search for oil took them south as well as north. Dundee's shipbuilders were skilled in constructing vessels able to withstand the world's most vicious seas and freezing ice packs at the ends of the earth, most famously in the Arctic sealer turned Antarctic exploration ice-breaker *Terra Nova*, the ship of Captain Scott's ill-fated expedition to the South Pole. The ship of his earlier scientific expedition with Shackleton, the *Discovery*, is now moored in the Tay. Celebrated in Dundee's Penguin Parade, further statues of penguins can be found hopping along the wall outside the Overgate and more preening themselves in the plaza before the Discovery Centre (probably best not to dwell on the fact that Scott's crew ate as well as studied these cute swimming birds).

Right whales were 'right' because they were slow moving and when killed their bodies floated. This allowed the odious flensing of their blubber and baleen to be done in the sea beside the ship rather than bringing the carcass on board. Their close cousins, bowhead whales, with more baleen in their huge mouths for corset stays and oil in their blubber for processing Indian jute in Dundee's mills, were the biggest prize of all. Long-lived, a few hardy specimens have outlived the city's whale and jute trades. In

2007 a forty-five-foot-long bowhead was found to have the head of a harpoon lodged in its blubber, suggesting it was unsuccessfully hunted about the same time as Shoodlue was demonstrating his baleen-staved kayak skills in Dundee.

One whale not so fortunate was nicknamed 'the monster'. This humpback male had the misfortune to swim up the Tay in November 1883. If it was pursuing shoals of herring seeking shelter in the inshore waters of the Firth, the hunter very soon became hunted, with one of the world's largest whaling fleets overwintering in the harbour. Despite this the whale eluded capture on the number of occasions it revisited the river over the next two months. Local newspaper reports kept captivated readers abreast of its appearances – such as a near miss with a boatload of engineers constructing the replacement railway bridge – or non-appearances. Whether the outcrop in Invergowrie Bay was known as 'the whale rock' before a railway passenger reported seeing 'the monster' beached at low tide is not clear, but it sent a stream of whale hunters and spotters in fruitless pursuit. By Christmas the whale was still at large. A local wit sent this imagined verse conversation between the whale and its mother to *The Courier*:

> Oh! where have you been, my son, my son?
> We have not met since the morn was young.
> 'I left the North, good mother, to see
> The whaling fleet in bonnie Dundee.'

Oh! why went you there, my son, my son,
Within the range of their banging gun?
'Fear not, mother, 'twas only a lark,
I reckoned they would shoot wide of the mark.'

Ah! Finny, my boy, is it not vile,
They do so thirst for our precious ile?
'Yes, mother, for our good blubber they pine,
But I took care they didn't get mine.'

Pray, tell me, did they not chase you, dear,
With harpoons, lances, and such like gear?
'What if they followed me, don't despond,
Chasing's not catching, mother fond.

They follow'd me up, they follow'd me down,
In view of gaping folk of the town;
But I, when they thought to take sure aim,
Skedaddled, and sent them 'swearin' hame."

Go never again, my son, my son,
Rest content with the laurels you've won;
'Trust me, mother, they may know about bales –
I'm blowed if they know as much about whales.

A party was sent the other day
To do for ma slick in Gowrie's Bay;
My eye! they peppered it hot on poor me,
Then found it was only a rock. He! he!'

But on Hogmanay the whale was finally harpooned from
a steam launch off Broughty Ferry Castle. Two rowing

boats were taken in tow by the launch, increasing the drag on the whale, and soon blood was seen in the spray as it rose to blow. A six-oared boat speared the whale with another harpoon. Running out of harpoons, marlinspikes and iron bolts were fired at it. The *Dundee Courier* reported the next day:

> This second harpoon had apparently made itself severely felt, as the whale made desperate efforts to free itself, lashing furiously with its tail and darting hither and thither at a great rate. At this time the excitement was intense, great crowds lining every available part from which a good view could be obtained. It was calculated that there were about 2000 spectators along the Esplanade.

For the majority it was a unique chance to see not only a creature usually only encountered in the far ocean but also to witness first hand an activity on which so many in the city depended for their livelihood, whether directly from the whaling industry itself or from the oil it produced. To the modern reader the jocular tone and obvious enjoyment of the killing of a wild creature, a fellow mammal, jars. McGonagall, for once, captures the tone perfectly:

> Then the whale began to puff and to blow,
> While the men and the boats after him did go,
> Armed well with harpoons for the fray,
> Which they fired at him without dismay.

And they laughed and grinned just like wild baboons,
While they fired at him their sharp harpoons . . .

The last the people lining the banks of the Tay saw of the whale alive was it disappearing into a midwinter haar, dragging its tormentors behind it out to the open sea. The whale, though, did not succumb and on Ne'er Day morning the boats returned to harbour without their prize, having been towed by the whale out beyond the Bell Rock Lighthouse as far north as Montrose and as far south as the Firth of Forth during the night. Three weeks later fishermen on the north-east coast at Stonehaven set sail to rescue what they thought was a capsized vessel, only to discover it was the carcass of the unfortunate whale.

So they got a rope from each boat tied round his tail,
And landed their burden at Stonehaven without fail;
And when the people saw it their voices they did raise,
Declaring that the brave fishermen deserved great praise.

McGonagall, with his journalistic verse, provides the conclusion to the sad tale.

So Mr John Wood has bought it for two hundred and
    twenty-six pound,
And has brought it to Dundee all safe and all sound;
Which measures 40 feet in length from the snout to
    the tail,
So I advise the people far and near to see it without
fail.

Then hurrah! for the mighty monster whale,
Which has got 17 feet 4 inches from tip to tip of a tail!
Which can be seen for a sixpence or a shilling,
That is to say, if the people all are willing.


Wood was an oil merchant who had earned himself the none too affectionate nickname of 'Greasy John'. He also had a sideline trading in the animals, both dead and alive, brought to Dundee on ships returning to the river from around the world: polar bears, seals and arctic foxes from the north; Russian bears from the Baltic; monkeys from the tropics. The live ones he sold on to vaudevilles and circuses, so he knew how to put on a show for the thousands eager for a glimpse of 'the monster'. People were more than willing not only to view the whale in the tent he set up in his East Dock Street yard, next to the Cattle Market, but to dine inside its propped open jaws. A riverscape with Tay and the Sidlaw Hills beyond was painted to sanitise the backdrop of Greasy John's yard. People even paid their sixpences to witness it being butchered. To the sound of the band of the Forfarshire Volunteers playing in the background, John Struthers, Regius Professor of Anatomy at Aberdeen University, dissected the creature. Its 'viscera and muscles . . . poured out in a messy pulp' to the crowd's disgusted delight. 'The whale's tongue lolled out of its mouth then fell into the water. Divers recovered it the next day.'

If they could not witness it in Dundee, they could buy a copy of the photograph Wood had arranged to be taken by George Washington Wilson. Or if they couldn't see the whale in the flesh in Dundee, then the whale would come to them. The poor, gutted creature was resculpted around a wooden armature, stuffed and embalmed, then toured around Britain by train, travelling to Glasgow, Edinburgh, Newcastle, Manchester, Liverpool and London on a specially designed wagon.

Even dead, the whale continued to cause fascination. On its arrival in Glasgow on Friday, 8 February 1884, the *Dundee Evening Telegraph* had a shocking story to reveal. A special report sent by wire from their correspondent in Glasgow had readers gasping. 'Extraordinary excitement prevails in Glasgow owing to the discovery this forenoon of a live man in the stomach of the Tay Whale'.

The text continued:

. . . under the directions of Professor Struthers . . . to-day that preparations had been completed for the opening of the stomach. A number of the University professors and other scientific gentlemen were present by invitation, as also were several clergymen and prominent citizens. About noon a large incision was made, and the whale partially opened, when something in the nature of a solid obstruction was encountered. Curiosity changed into utter amazement when on the incision being enlarged and the upper portion of the stomach carefully drawn back the obstruction was found to be a human being, lying in a position, as in sleep, with the body bent; the right arm, which was underneath, doubled at the elbow; and the side of the nose resting on the forefinger. It was supposed first that the man was dead, but on closer investigation by the medical men present it was discovered that he was actually alive, but in a torpid or comatose state, resembling catalepsy. Besides the man, the stomach contained scores of dead herring and sprats . . . attempts were made [to] waken him up by shouting. The Rev. John Smith . . . expressed his conviction, in the most solemn and emphatic manner, that the man was no other than the prophet Jonah, and that the whale and the unfaithful prophet had been pre-served miraculously, and been directed to these shore[s], as a triumphant refutation of modern scepticism. The objection was urged by several that Jonah, according to the Bible narrative, had been vomited out of the whale upon the dry land. Mr. Smith, however, held that Jonah had on some subsequent occasion again fled from his post of duty and been again swallowed. He appealed somewhat excitedly to all present whether there was any record either in the Bible or in natural history of any other whale having a throat large enough to swallow a man, except the one that swallowed Jonah. It had been specially created to swallow him when he was refusing to attend to his duty and was doubt kept in readiness to swallow in like circumstances again. At this moment Mr. William Sanderson, of Newport, Fife, who had been superintending the exhibition of the outer car-cass of the whale, having heard of the extraordinary discovery that had been made, arrived, and no sooner saw the sleeper than he declared, to the astonishment of all present, that it was a gentleman from his own part of the country unpopularly known as 'the Autocrat of the Tay Ferries'. He knew the face perfectly . . . the

Rev. Mr Smith, held firmly to his conviction that the man was Jonah . . . The question of identification being still unsettled, messenger has been sent off to wire to Dundee and Newport . . .

The following week a note appeared in the papers: 'We have since learned that the correspondent who furnished the details is a lineal descendent of the late much-lamented Baron Munchhausen.'

On its return to Dundee in August 1884 Struthers completed his dissection by removing the whale's skull, but it was to take a number of years after the professor published his book, *Memoir of the Anatomy of the Humpback Whale, Megaptera Longimana*, before the bones of the whale were clean and odourless enough to be put on public display. They can be viewed today (free), a skeletal ghost – literally – hanging over the whaling exhibition in the city's McManus Galleries.

The last whaler sailing out of Dundee was the *Balaena*, celebrated in this sea shanty:

There's the new built *Terra Nova*, she's a model of no
    doubt,
There's the *Arctic* and the *Aurora*, you've heard so
    much about,
There's Jacklin's model mail boat, the terror of the sea,
Couldn't beat the aul' *Balaena*, boys, on the passage
    frae Dundee.

Chorus: Oh the wind is on her quarter, her engines
    working free,

There's not another whaler that sails out of Dundee,
Can beat the ol' *Balaena*, she needs no trial run,
We challenged all both great and small from Dundee
    to St John.

And now the season's o'er and the ship's half full of oil,
Our flying jib boom points for home towards our
    native soil,
And when that we have landed, boys, where rum is
    very cheap,
We'll drink success to the skipper's health for getting
    us o'er the deep.

Seals now throng the banks of the Firth off the shore from the very docks from where the *Balaena* and *Aurora* of the Dundee Seal and Whale Fishing Company set sail. Over the course of eighteen Newfoundland hunting seasons (which only ran from 14 March to 20 April) the crew of the *Aurora* alone killed and skinned a quarter of a million harp and hooded seals. How do you feel if your ancestor made a hard living clubbing ten-day-old baby seals to death for their pure white fur? Would you rather he had starved? Where would we be without them?

Boat and shipbuilding are integral to the history of the river. From the log-boats and curraghs of the past to the ubiquitous Tay coble, beloved of angler, netter and wildfowler alike. In 1586, a legal document states: 'He . . . onputt his coblis and corrochis upoun the saidis fischeingis.'

The traditional design of boat used on the river for generations is still used today.

Craftsmen like John Ferguson at Stanley in the present age, using planks from oak and larch, steamed if necessary, to curve into the prow, then binding them together with copper rivets, construct a coble.

One of the striking features of the maritime models on display in Dundee's McManus Galleries is that many of them are of only half a boat. Mounted on boards or in glass boxes, each has been beautifully crafted in boatyards of all sizes along the river down the years, each miniature vessel an echo or reflection of its real life parent now long sunk in the waters of time.

Looking on, you see in your mind's eye the model expanding in scale like ripples growing out from the centre of a pool to become a full-sized boat. One of these model boats is made by children – a cutter with simple but elegant lines built by orphan boys aboard the training hulk *Mars*, 'with the aid of instructor William Bowman 1909'. There is a poignancy in the circumstances of its construction made during a childhood moored off-shore. Some models bear the names of places visited in this book: the romantic steamship *Loch Tay* built for the Dundee Loch Line; SS *Den of Airlie* of 1911; *Strathmore* for the Dundee Clipper Line. SS *Perth* and the fifth SS *Dundee* were commissioned by the Dundee, Perth & London Shipping Company, whose distinctive red flag with a thin white cross was a feature of the city for years as you came off the road bridge, fluttering above their Dock Street headquarters until their recent move to the Dunsinane

Industrial Estate. The flag features on vessels elsewhere in the museum – on examples of their ships' crockery, tea cups, soup tureens.

Before the bridge, generations of paddle steamers, like *Newport* and *Forfarshire* of 1861, would spend their lives on the crossing, ferrying back and forth to Fife at right angles to the current. Jim Crumley wrote of them:

What the Fifies did for you was let your dawdle out on midstream, let you become a moving fragment of the Tay itself, let you eyeball the dredgers as they heaved and gouged at the sandbanks, let you lean out over the bow and wave at the seals, let you cut your own swathe across the silvery Tay. At any point in the voyage, you could turn to face the stern and look back at Dundee on its twa hulls through a gauze of gulls as it folded back into its Angus landscape and you knew in your heart why some folk called it bonnie.

The uniqueness of a paddle steamer's wheels threshing the water, the twin wakes – it's how you swim yourself when you're lying on your back in the water gazing at the hugeness of the sky overhead, arms tight by your sides, wrists flipper-ing. Or on your front, goggles and snorkel, gazing for wonders in the new world beneath the surface like a whale. Paddle steamers are the mill wheels at Blair Atholl, Aberfeldy and Stanley, the Mississippi of Mark Twain, Paul Robeson singing 'Ol Man River' – as he did in the city's riverside Caird Hall in 1960.

Some of the ships on display were named in hope, with an eye to the future. Alexander Stephen & Sons' whaler SS *Terra Nova* gained fame beyond the river of its construction by carrying Captain Scott's hopeful but doomed 1910 Antarctic expedition. The ship itself ended its life in the frozen wastes, sunk in the Greenland waters in which it latterly spent a career slaughtering an estimated 800,000 seals. The research steamship *Discovery* (launched 1901) was the last wooden three-masted sailing barque built in Dundee, and survived both Antarctic exploration and the Hudson Bay Company fur trade. It is, for now, moored in a dock on the city's riverfront on the site of the old Craig Pier, where the Fife ferry arrived and departed. Restored to shipshape condition, it is a model of the modern heritage visitor attraction. There you can view a painted relief of the ship constructed out of scraps of wood and metal scavenged by crewman Arthur Diwell in the tradition of shipboard crafting and carving during the long Canadian voyages.

Back in the McManus Galleries the most intriguing professional model is that of a First World War paddle-minesweeper in a glass case. A metre in length, it is exquisitely constructed and exact in its details and materials: painted in gunmetal grey, with brass-rimmed portholes, wooden-ribbed lifeboats, miniature life buoys. It represents one of four vessels built for the Admiralty in different yards, one being the Dundee Shipbuilding Company in 1916. A full model of the ship is on display in the National Maritime Museum in Greenwich, but this model is a half, the back of the case being a mirror. This gives insight to the structure of the vessel and is so detailed that even the brass guns mounted amidships are cut in two, allowing you to see the start of the rifling of the barrel. But the mirror also reflects you, the viewer, back at yourself.

Taking pictures for research – I am using them now for reference as I write this at my desk – I see funnel, bridge, myself obscured by the back of my mobile phone, its fish-eye camera lens recording model boat, mirrored case, museum, the phone, itself. My phone cover has a reproduction of Hokusai's famous print *The Great Wave*. Reflected in the mirror the miniature paddle-steamer churns through this oriental sea in a displacement not only of scale but of place and time.

Reflection distorts but also reveals other truths. Across the room a display case contains a Japanese tea service, water-silk kimonos brought back to the Tay on Dundonian ships. Or is it that the great wave is caused by an exploding mine detonated at the mouth of the river, or by the German mine that on 1 May 1916 blew off the stern of one of the actual paddle-minesweepers, killing five crew members?

A century after the French Navy were scoping the coast for invasion sites, the threat was growing from across the German Ocean or Sea – up until the First World War the most commonly used terms for the North Sea. The increasingly alert Admiralty didn't want their coastal defences being breached by an enemy dreadnought or one of the Kaiser's new underwater boats, so to counteract the threat a new volunteer defence unit, the Tay Division Undersea Miners, was set up at Broughty Castle. Using two steamships, they would, in the event of an enemy attack, lay a line of mines across the estuary to explode under any warships entering the Firth.

Look into water and it reflects back at you. Step into it and you become part of that reflection. As the twentieth century turns, I am edging towards the Tay. My great-grandfather has been saved from drowning, and now another of my tributaries comes flickering at the edge of my vision.

That glinting by Magdalen Yard Green is not the sunlight catching the water but the mirror in the hand of my grandmother signalling from her top-floor flat to her friend Myra Craig across the river at Newport. Armed with compact and her father's field binoculars, the girls had prearranged signals for rendezvous at either Woodhaven on the Fife side or the Craig Pier, Dundee's ferry terminal. In 1913, after thirty years' service, her father had retired from the army. At the same time as the Tay whale had been harpooned and was travelling around Britain by train, he was riding a camel across the Sudanese desert – and also being shot. He was one of the Gordon relief expedition sent up the Nile to Khartoum, celebrated on the gate to the Grimonds' jute mill. Wounded, he was shipped back to Cairo on one of the whaling boats requisitioned by the military for the expedition. Many years later, on his retiral, he was appointed as the recruiting officer for Dundee, where, at 20 Nethergate, he was soon to oversee the huge numbers of volunteers, and later conscripts, called to arms during the First World War.

One of the first Dundee recruits to die in the Great War was killed not on the Western Front but by a stray golf ball whilst guarding the south end of the Tay railway bridge. On 26 September 1914, *The Courier* reported:

DUNDEE TERRITORIAL IS KILLED WHILE ON GUARD AT WORMIT. Private David Barnett, 4th Battalion (City of Dundee) Black Watch, whose home was at 65 Dens Road, Dundee, died at Wormit yesterday as the result of hit by a golf ball while he was on guard on Thursday afternoon. Two lady members of Wormit Golf Club were engaged in competition match and Private Barnett was hit in the temple.

The tragedies of war were only beginning to be felt on Tayside. In 1915 Preston Watson's flying machines of delight soon became a machine of death for the aviator himself and for those who flew them and those bombed by them. On land, in the air, on the water, the flower of Tayside's youth died. By the rail bridge the inscription on the Celtic cross that stands by Woodhaven pier today reads:

IN GLORIOUS MEMORY OF / OUR OLD BOYS / FALLEN IN THE GREAT WAR / 1914 – 1916 / ERECTED BY THE BOYS / OF THE 'MARS' TRAINING SHIP / WHICH WAS MOORED OPPOSITE THIS SITE / 1869 – 1929

To remember those who did not return from the First World War a beacon was built on top of Dundee Law. It is lit every 11 November, Remembrance Day, and for relatives and friends of the 4,000 Dundonians killed with no body and no graveside to attend it formed a focus for their grief. For some of those who survived, the house where Beatrix Potter had spent blissful childhood summers was converted to an auxiliary hospital where the maimed of the trenches were sent to recuperate to try to learn to live with their physical and psychological wounds.

All along the Tay's catchment and beyond new stones were being erected, carved and engraved. On the upper reaches across from the church at Innerwick at the head of the Lairig Ghallabhaich stands a stone cairn, a bell-shaped memorial to those who sacrificed: 'To The Glory Of God / And In / Grateful Remembrance Of Those From Glenlyon / Who Fell . . .'

Its builder was Alex McCallum, who lost his son John, 'Private John Alexander McCallum' of the Black Watch, in the last month of the war. It was 'the war to end all wars' – the beacon on the Law, a warning, a light, a hope that such sacrifice would not be necessary again. 'Never go to war,' my grandfather, who went from the Alyth Burn to the Somme, told us. But the war to end all wars didn't end war. On Barry Links and along Tentsmuir dunes lines of concrete monoliths are raised to prevent invasion – dragons' teeth tank traps.

On the other side of the Mars cross: 'In Glorious Memory Of / The Boys Of The 'Mars' Training Ship / Who Fell In The 2nd World War / 1939 – 1945'.

Scan across the water, following the two miles of the iron line of the railway bridge to the north bank to Magdalen

Green. My field binoculars pick out the artist James McIntosh Patrick's house, reversing the famous view from his studio window pictured on so many cards: of the private lawn, the public green and the railway bridge beyond, steam from train and boat rising still, and the horse patiently waiting, waiting, the lengthening shadows. I see also his painting looking out from the back of the house: Janet, his wife, hanging up their washing – lots of bleached-white aprons – in their back garden on a Monday morning, laundry day, late 1940.

Above the back greens of the tenements beyond the garden wall are washings on lines put out and brought in to each flat by a system of pulleys (pullashies in Dundonian) like signal flags on a man-o-war. Ann, the Patricks' daughter, is playing in the woven washing basket, being educated in what will be expected of her. Winter shadows are deepening across bleached white sheets. On bare, skeletal branches unplucked fruit awaits the frost to drop, some apples already fallen to the earth. In the next garden a horse waits patiently as its cart is filled with shovelful after shovelful of earth as an Anderson shelter is dug. Above, semi-detached already, James paints this domestic scene he is witnessing, perhaps for the last time, as he waits to be called up.

On the night of 5 November, German planes – on an abortive mission to knock out the rail bridge – dropped a stick of bombs between the Patricks' house and the Blackness Road, killing three people in their homes. The white sheets on the washing line hang shroud-like.

At the Black Watch Memorial at Claverhouse on the northern edge of the city, a bronze statue of a kilted soldier, hands behind his back, pensive, commemorates those soldiers of the regiment killed in the Second World War. In the middle distance a pale November sunlight catches the Tay flashing a silver watery glint like the eyes of the veteran in the wheelchair, sat stiffly to attention as the 'Last Post' is sounded. Dundee poet Joseph Lee imagined the end of the war in his 1916 poem 'The Home-coming':

When this blast is over-blown,
And the beacon fires shall burn
And in the street
Is the sound of feet –
They also shall return.

When the bells shall rock and ring,
When the flags shall flutter free,
And the choirs shall sing,
'God save our King' –
They shall be there to see.

When the brazen bands shall play,
And the silver trumpets blow,
And the soldiers come
To the tuck of drum –
They shall be there also.

When that which was lost is found;
When each shall have claimed his kin,
Fear not they shall miss
Mother's clasp, maiden's kiss –
For no strange soil might hold them in.

When Te Deums seek the skies,
When the Organ shakes the Dome,
A dead man shall stand
At each live man's hand –
For they also have come home.

Those killed were only a fraction of the casualties of war – maimed inside and out, at the front, on the home front. We remember, but are as powerless to stop war as we are to stop the flow of the river or the coming in of the tide.

For David Hume and the anonymous others who down the centuries have left these shores as Roman auxiliaries, Jacobites, Napoleonic conscripts, colonial freebooters for wars just and unjustifiable, memory of them dissolves.

Millais's painting *Flowing to the Sea* captures the moment of leaving. After the intermingling tears of those departing and those remaining have dried, what is left? An image of the event seen from the outside – kilted Black Watch soldier, his sad lover, the riverscape, a boat – or an internal picture of the leaver in the minds of those left behind.

It is said that the origin of art lies in a lover drawing the shadow profile of a departing warrior on a wall. Picture the scene in crannog, croft or cottage – the nameless woman artist, anonymous soldier, the crusie lamp of roughly shaped river clay, the reed wick, the oil from a whale, the stick of charcoal: the silhouette is all that remains. It is like a line representing a river drawn on a map; a mere reflection.

# My Riverscape

*Looking and reflections*

After war comes peace, comes change. Ferries dock for the final time. The old makes way for the new: a motorway flies high over the Tay at Friarton, strata of flowing vehicles interchange like species of fish in the alternating depths of the river below. In Dundee, the Victorian arch is demolished into the disused dock to make way for the road connecting Fife and Angus. The river is bridged for the final time . . . or for the first.

I started this journey on the frozen summit of Ben Lui. It has followed the river's geography from winter mountain burn to loch to Highland torrent, meandering through the Lowlands to summertime on Broughty Ferry beach; a river of shieling, croft, burgh, city and suburbs, its glacial history cutting a path from Ice Age to Stone Age, flowing into the modern age.

At the sea, the tide turns and the waters begin to flow back up the Firth. Above it, on the Tay road bridge, the last crossing of the river is also the first. Travelling over this newly built bridge is my childhood memory of the Tay. More recollections of my great aunt and uncle have risen from the depths of my mind in conversation with my brother since.

They were characters, very theatrical, early members of Dundee Rep: Uncle Mac wore a tweed cloak and carried a shepherd's crook; during the summer, Auntie Tot stored her beaver fur coat in the vault of the bank. We shivered when they told us of the bodies from the Tay Bridge disaster washed upon the shore, pickpocketed.

Fifteen years later I am on my way up the Blackness Road, heading to my new home in Dundee after my first day as a student at Duncan of Jordanstone College of Art & Design. The Tay is blanketed in a grey haar, the iron humps of the rail bridge rising above it like the backs of a pod of whales. I am not the only migrant. That evening I heard overhead for the first time the sound of the returning geese, their ever shifting V-shaped skeins flowing like a harpoon point across the pink-clotted September evening sky. Breeding in the long northern summer days in central Iceland and Greenland, they make their winter home here. Keeping up a constant chatter as they fly, babbling, burbling like the river, they flow, but with an average eight-year lifespan it's never the same flock twice. At the moment their fluctuating numbers are high – a third of a million migrated to the British Isles last year – as they take advantage of increased crop yields on Tayside farmlands and a lack of natural predators. There are over double the numbers today than when I first looked up in 1982.

Living in Dundee connected me to the river and my past. I stayed in a bedsit on Windsor Street, which runs between the Perth Road and the Tay, looking into those gardens painted by James McIntosh Patrick in 1940. Between there and the flat I later had in Roseangle I entered the riverside world of the railway bridge and Magdalen Green of my grandmother. On a journey to Glenshee to stay with my sister I entered the Alyth and Strathmore world of my grandfather.

I'm retracing that journey today, the bus taking me north from the city into Strathmartine. The babble of my fellow passengers is friendly, couthy, accented. Norman Watson, Dundonian dialectologist, told me the majority of his research was carried out listening to conversations on buses like this to and from his work in the archives at D.C. Thomson's. Along the length of the Tay it is hairst, harvest. At Auchterhouse the combines chug through fields of swaying grain like Mississippi paddle steamers – cutting, separating, spitting out – leaving in their wakes timbers of brittle straw stems on land reclaimed from water, from moss drained by pow. Along the length of the straightened Auchterhouse Burn creatures are flushed out by the work – lark, goldfinch, field mouse, hare, its feet crackling over the stubble. The combine harvester's introduction single-handedly reduced the most labour-intensive processes of past agriculture. I think of Bruegel's famous painting, *The Harvesters*. An exhausted peasant, knackered by the day's sheer hard labour, lies limp against the tree trunk, deep in sleep. The machines extract the grain, then, leaving the stalks strewn behind in their wakes to be ploughed back into the earth or baled for silage and feed, they reap, thresh and winnow the crops with computer-aided precision that minimises waste and maximises yield and profit. Traditionally the last sheath of corn to be cut at harvest time is made into a corn doll and ploughed into the field the next spring. It is called 'the cailleach'.

It was on these fields that Patrick Bell, who had an amateur interest in mechanics, designed the first reaping machine in 1828 – a two-wheeled device with rotating blades pushed by a pair of horses, which he used to cut his father's crop at Mid-Leoch, here in Strathmartine. But Bell's future did not lie on the family farm; as a Church of Scotland minister, his interests concerned higher things. He had no desire to profit from his invention and so failed to lodge a patent for this machine that would revolutionise farming across the world, giving millions their daily bread.

With mechanisation came change. A countryside drained of agricultural workers, the rhythms of quarter or term days – Candlemas, Whitsun, Lammas, St Martin's mas; of feeing yourself to a farm (the Rev. Bell collecting his stipend); the insecurities of transient seasonal employment; the whims of farmer and landowner; lack of unionised support and decent employment law; of wage disparity between the sexes (the Caputh Old Statistical Account recorded 'A man, for harvest work, gets from £1 to £1, 18s.; a woman from 16s. to £1'); the rural

Scots language of Burns; the bothy ballads, and bothies themselves, all gradually disappeared, just as the salmon netters' bothies on the Tay are falling into disrepair today.

Overlooking the Strath is an old cairn on West Mains Hill, once containing the neolithic cist grave of earlier farmers, their cutting device an ox-bone handled dagger. Some bullocks in bee-speckled clover and sheep with blood-red herd markings on their necks, grazing in the ancient pasturage, stand and stare as the bus passes, their passing interest never enough to stop their cud-chewing jaws. Across the entrance to a farm, fallen carrots sprinkle the tight corner, bright orange stacks of which are being built by a forklift truck along the side of the huge corrugated-iron cattle shed. Inside the shed, thick slavering tongues and gentle eyes innocently crunch, getting fatter by the day. As the bus door opens to let off an auld cailleach, the sour tang of silage from the byre, part repellent part invigorating, comes aboard. A blue tractor with bucket shovel scrapes a compost of the cattle's straw bedding and manure from the floor of the shed and deposits it into saw-toothed pyramids ready to fertilise the surrounding fields for winter ploughing in the never ending cycle of growing, harvesting, eating and shitting which now takes place here on an industrial scale. The pastoral cycle of sheiling, bothy, croft and byre stretches far back beyond the Picts and into the prehistoric past of cursuses and standing stones in this landscape.

Further along the road at Newtyle stands a life-size fibreglass figure dressed in a blue-and-white striped apron, a big smile on his chops, advertising the local butcher's. At

Meigle, in the old schoolhouse where as a girl my great grandmother learned her letters, many of the area's Pictish stones – of all classes – are now housed. And then over the Isla and the spot where James drowned.

The bus halts by the Alyth Burn. On its banks in Mill Street my grandfather was born and the family plied their trade as plasterers. Then onwards, past the cemetery where generations of my forebears lie. And then past field upon field of berries shrouded in polytunnels to the terminus at Blairgowrie.

The wait for the connecting post-bus allows time to wander along the banks of the Ericht to Cargill's Leap. The low water level permits a dipper to hop from stepping stone to stepping stone across the river without getting its feet wet. I observe the flickering white membrane over the dipper's eye that allows it to see to hunt under water. I think of cataracts. In the reflective calm of the water I look back instead to that journey long ago. The post-bus to Bridge of Cally and finally in the summer twilight the taxi swooping along Wade's military road, Caulfield's bridge over the Shee Water with its distinctive parapet at the end of the journey.

All summer bees flow from the skeps taken out to the purple moor above the river Shee. Later, pale gold honey oozes into skep-shaped jars. Dip your pinkie into the ribbed glass, trickle some onto your tongue and taste ambrosia – an offering from the gods of nature more marvellous than a Roman glass in a Caledonian chieftain's tomb.

My history merges with wider histories. I particularly remember a cycle to Kirkmichael. It was the weekend of the Highland Games held in the Bannerfield by the river Ardle; the pens with sheep and cattle, the piping, the heavy events, the dancing at the ceilidh afterwards, the whisky going round and round as it would have done to seal a drover's bargain, to commit to an uprising. The Strathardle Agricultural Show continues the tradition of cattle trading to this day, with prizes for stot and heifer calves, best cow and best suckler cow in milk, silver passing over water, drams going round. Or sitting a thousand feet up in the glen watching below the timeless herding of sheep by a shepherd and his dog into the drystane enclosure of the fank, the white shingle garth on the tawny Shee Water on the valley floor – the warm silence broken only by a whistle, a lamb calling out to its mother, the soft falling of the water in the burn beside me flowing down to a future now long past.

Later in the summer my parents joined us too, my mother regaling us with stories of Alyth, the small town family gossip told to her by her father, of which rich relatives watered the milk; Aunt Lily's beautiful voice singing Schubert's lied *Die Forelle*; pointing up at the ceiling of the Lands of Loyal Hotel, built originally for the Earls of Airlie, where James Mitchell's father had sculpted in plaster a decorative scheme of cornucopia and heraldry alchemically out of water and dust.

We also took a trip to Glamis Castle. Amidst the stories of Macbeth, internecine warfare, heroes and heroines, villains and villainy, gossip and secrets, an almost incessant reference to Elizabeth Bowes-Lyon, the daughter of Lord Glamis, 14th Earl of Strathmore, who married King

George VI. The Queen Mother, the last Empress of India, the Queen Mother this, the Queen Mother that . . . too much for my father. The blood flowing to my sister's cheeks in embarrassment in the tearoom after the tour, as he enquired if 'Her Majesty had made today's scones . . . and jam'?

We have followed the river's story, or my version of it, from creation to end, literally, historically. At the end of the twentieth century of our current era it was claimed that history had come to an end, yet here we are with plenty of history already in the quarter century since . . . It keeps flowing. Human nature has both a beginning and an end, but like the river it keeps beginning, keeps ending – endlessly, with little change.

Like the geese, my Tayside story is one of migration: visiting as a child, leaving; arriving as a student, leaving; returning as an adult to work in Perth, leaving; working in Dundee, leaving; my wife's waters breaking, a son born in Ninewells, living now just south of the Firth, remaining (if I'm spared).

In the Alyth cemetery, my son and I are standing by the family plot. I'm trying to recall the voice of my dear grandfather who, aged seventeen, helped bear the coffin of his own grandfather, blinded at the end by a lifetime of swirling plaster dust into water, to this grave. We read the inscriptions. All of these people lived long lives into their eighties, their nineties even, but a short life is also commemorated:

James, who was drowned in the River Isla 25th June 1876 aged 14 years

Standing before a headstone, unlike a Pictish stone, has its own macabre sensation. To read the inscription, especially on an old weather- and time-beaten one like this, necessitates walking over the grave. The ground underfoot is uneven – it has been dug and, on a family lair, re-dug many times. What was once solid, diminishes; spaces alter; transformations in substance and material take place. One is never quite sure that the ground will not suddenly give way. A deep hole could open up. You may sink out of sight and be swallowed up by the grave. All the more disconcerting, all the more frightening, as we know that with certainty Death – coming suddenly or not – will claim us all. But who would willingly give up their child to death? I think here by James's memorial of the gravestone at Grandtully, of Abraham preparing to sacrifice Isaac, of a scattering of teeth and a pot, meadowsweet.

Opposite are more recent gravestones. They have photographs of the deceased on the headstones. I recognise a face on one. It is Belle Stewart, the traveller singer, the 'Queen Amang the Heather', born in a bow tent on the banks of the River Tay on 18 July 1906 in Caputh. A swipe with a finger as I type 'who is also now buried here' and I can hear her lovely voice ringing clearly down through the years:

There's gladness and there's sadness tae,
There's happy herts and sair,

There's comedy and tragedy
Played on the fields o' Blair . . .

It was a delight and privilege of my time as a student to
hear Belle sing at the art college in Dundee. It was a place
flowing with talent. In the long hallway outside the lecture
theatre where Belle sang, David Mach had constructed his
life-size 'Polaris' submarine made out of car tyres; in the
sculpture studios Calum Colvin was starting to develop his
room-size constructions that looked like sheer folly but
when photographed transformed into the portraits that
have gone on to celebrate in our collective memories the
myths of heroes like Burns and Ossian; out back on the
Hawkhill, Joseph McKenzie, lecturer in photography, was
recording the disappearance of industrial Dundee; and as
part of a vigorous public arts programme my sculpture lecturer Alastair Smart was reimaging the scrimshaws carved
by whalers as Pictish stones etched with the river's story
on Lower Pleasance. Another strong voice comes down
to me from that time too, that of Liz Lochhead, who was
the college's writer-in-residence when I was there. She
published 'What the Pool Said, On Midsummer's Day'
at that time. In it she uses imagery to describe the allure
of water on just such a summer's day as had tempted the
Mitchell brothers into the Isla.

. . . What are you waiting for?
I lie here, inviting, winking you in.

The woman was easy,
Like to like, I called her, she came.

The sexual and the pagan ooze from the words of the poem: the river becomes Goddess, Tay is Tatha of the pre-Romans. The woman is offering herself to the river's allure. Perhaps the woman is Eve, deceived by the serpent river. Naked, naturally roused, earthily tempted yet innocent. The innocent drown in error in its serpentine coils. Witches – sisters of the river – float . . . but then they are strangled and burnt by men.

Men do not escape Lochhead's pool's watery clutches, either. It is female again, a pre-Christian river goddess preparing to take a sacrificial victim. 'It's you I want, and you know it, man', she writes. He is nervous, unsure; through his own capability to do evil, he is aware of the danger. Within him a torrent of lust surges against his calm reason, but the river goddess draws on her natural powers, brings him to the edge, until

I watch. You clench,
clench and come into me.

Those small moments on which events turn happen all along the river. The drop of falling rain that tips the lea meadow past saturation point; the trout taking the bait, the hopeful angler cautiously starting to wind in her line. The actions of one releasing a reaction in the other. Access to the river can lead to death, and death can be both unjustified and permitted.

Cassius Dio asserted that Taysiders did not eat fish; I do. Of the very few times I have been fishing, the last occasion comes back to me – the thrill of reeling in the fish, the exhilarating rush, the sense of achievement, the pleasure of winning a contest against nature. I felt so human, so superior. Yet once landed I was appalled by the twitching, dying creature in the bottom of the boat for which I was responsible. I was shocked I had enjoyed the process up to this point. Who am I? I am capable of killing. I have killed. By eating the fish I assuaged my guilt – but only partially. I could have bought a fish already caught and not caught and killed one myself. I am a killer, but am I evil? I gauge from my reaction and actions since that the answer is 'No, but . . .' Does that absolve me? I don't know. I still eat fish.

The majority of people living along the river today eat fish, eat the meat of animals that graze its banks every week. I have a twinge of remorse buying steak from the farm at Belhelvie on the south bank of the river and seeing the soft brown eyes of the Aberdeen Angus herd looking in from the field outside. At least they live their lives chewing the cud on natural pasture, I tell myself. In what conditions do these heifers munching away on pyramids of carrots in the byre at Strathmartine and across Tayside live their lives? Would we dangle one of these carrots on a hook and offer it to a cow, then drag it across its field, bludgeon it to death and gut it for 'sport'?

For all of us the question is one of personal choice: not to eat meat or fish, or to live on a diet that involves killing. What of those who live by the river and who are dependent on killing for their livelihoods? When we think of the environmental impacts of the angling and grouse shooting along the catchments of the Tay, do we consider the costs to our fellow humans? The ghillie employed by the grouse moor-owning consortium told to increase bird numbers, stranded between the ever increasing public awareness and vigilance of wildlife crime, and the demands from his faceless employers for more birds to shoot. Caught between illegal poisoning of raptors, the shooting of corvids or the risk of losing not only their job but their family home through tied estate accommodation – the disruption of schooling, the upheaval that would cause. And not only on a personal level. Few areas of rural Tayside can afford the loss of a young family in their ever ageing communities.

For the setter of the illegal pole trap or the layer of poisoned bait, is it easier to kill to preserve their way of life because they already kill for a living? Does Macbeth commit regicide because, as we see at the start of the play, he is already a soldier used to dealing death: 'he unseam'd [MacDonwald] from the nave to the chaps'. He guts the rebel on behalf of his king.

The ghillie guts the fish for his client. The whaler harpoons and flenses the whale, not just a fish but a fellow mammal, one that has many qualities shared with humans. What do we do to our fellow humans? Clear them from their ancestral homes, house mill workers in pestilent slums, exploit sub-continent children as jute pickers, gain wealth from enslaving Africans. These things, we tell ourselves, were wrongs done by previous Taysiders. We have learnt from the past. But have we? Are our lives lived so differently along the river now? Do we, like St Martin, cut our cloaks in half to share with the poor, or do we wear clothes made in fast-fashion sweatshops by sub-continent children? Are our mobile phones – the ones we use to publicise the salmon we've just landed, or the poisoned raptor on the moor – the same ones assembled in factories where nets catch workers driven by despair to leap from their windows?

There are parts of us of which we are ashamed. Aspects of ourselves that we hide away from the light, that lurk in our depths, the stagnant pools where no fresh water flows. Do we recognise 'the monster' lurking within ourselves? That fledgling-eating pike under the surface – are we repulsed by it, like to think that it is not there? Pretend we are not in any way like the Victorian inmate of Perth prison's 'lunatic' wing who drowned a boy in the river but never understood what he'd done.

Macbeth certainly had doubts – doubts eased in the play by his wife. For centuries women have been blamed for their men's failings: 'Witch! She enchanted him.' The actress Dame Harriet Walter, when discussing playing Lady Macbeth, makes a fascinating point. 'She knew Macbeth had ambition in him, she knew he had all sorts of qualities that she could bring out of him and harness, but she didn't know he was quite the monster he turns out to be. Nor did he know he was quite the monster he turned out to be.' In the Genesis story Eve herself is enchanted by the snake. It is Adam and Eve both who eat of the forbidden fruit. We humans act together.

In the twenty-first century, do we believe there is such a thing as evil? Maria Stepanova, writing in the *Financial Times*, wonders: 'Evil is an old-fashioned concept. The postwar decades have taught us to see things automatically from the viewpoint of our opponent in order to establish understanding, compromise and dialogue. But sometimes there is no one to speak with – in the place of an interlocutor, there is only impenetrable darkness, and it insists on its own outcome at any costs.'

The river is a cruel river. A child killer as cruel as Macbeth, who sent his henchmen to murder Macduff's children; his attempt to change the future by killing Banquo's heir Fleance. But if the river is cruel, it is because it can only be so, only act thus. But for humans we can decide to act or not to act.

On Tay Square, the spotlight catches Macbeth soliloquising on the Dundee Rep stage.

> If th' assassination
> Could trammel up the consequence, and catch
> With his surcease, success; that but this blow
> Might be the be-all and the end-all—here,
> But here, upon this bank and shoal of time,
> We'd jump the life to come.

In the auditorium of my mind a recollection of confliction in the autobiography of the Rep's most famous alumnus, Brian Cox. Cox had a troubled upbringing in the city. His father died when he was eight and his mother had a succession of mental health problems. If he'd been born fifty years earlier he could have been 'sent tae the *Mars*'.

In his early teens he had unexpectedly found a home in the Rep theatre, first as an assistant to the assistant, but later as a member of the company. It was, he writes, 'perhaps one of the greatest transitions I've ever made'.

Learning his craft, of acting in the moment, of allowing each moment to define the attitude of the performance, he relates his mentor Lindsay Anderson's direction: 'Brian! Don't just do something. Stand still!' Yet later whilst touring the Scottish play in India – India, with so many conflicted connections to the Tay – he had an encounter with a muse.

He recalls in an interview, 'An Indian girl in the cast – she was a dancer, just sixteen – had told me she was convinced that I was thwarted in some way, that I should be more expressive as a performer. Every night, she'd watch me on stage, and ask me why I didn't go further.'

To stay his hand or slay his king? Each moment separates itself from time and place and exists only in itself.

Outside the theatre spotlight, in an evening of haloed streetlights, moored boat lights and stars, the river has reached a moment of silent equilibrium, of mercurial stillness: high tide.

Inside my head I see a drama playing out.

Enter Lady Macbeth. Is her husband 'like the poor cat i' th' adage' that wouldn't get its feet wet to catch the fish?

Cox begins to physicalise.

Exit: the full moon.

The tide turns.

A bell on a buoy out in the Firth is tolled by its shift. Each moment seems the same, yet the blood of kings – and would-be kings – ebbs. The sandbanks and shoals of the river are gradually exposed while the depths of the North Sea remain unaltered. This performance comes to an end.

The text, the performance, the performer alters with time.

Exit, stage left: Brian Cox as Macbeth in India.

Enter, stage right: Aberfeldy's Alan Cumming on Broadway, as the *New York Times* sees him: 'a lusty Lady Macbeth, first seen luxuriating in a bath as she reads of her husband's strange encounter with the witches . . .'

Outside the Rep, the night comes black. There is a delay crossing the river. A snaking line of red car lights winds back east and west along the Marketgait – a jumper on the bridge. I grieve for those who have leapt from here into the relentless river and out of this world by their own hands; for those who were unknowing and would have offered help; for those whose beseeching hands were not grasped. Whose hands will be stained with guilt? The innocent, the unknowing, the knowing, the guilty, nobody? Shock, anger, guilt, confusion, despair, rejection swirl following a suicide. An image comes to me of a hand reaching out and a finger trying to follow the thread of the knotwork on the Pictish stone, of the eternally inde-cipherable symbols on the other side.

Blue lights flash. Did they jump, were they saved? The traffic eventually begins to move. Mid-bridge I glance down. The river is black, swirling, sleekit, but to those that it takes it also bestows a sheen of grace. Its timeless waters cleanse even the bloodiest of hands.

I am browsing the weekend papers, the 'Culture' pages, reading the reviews. At the Venice Biennale art show, a massive blue canvas with magnified plankton representing the ocean as viewed through the eye of a whale is reflected in the mirror waters of a canal-side dock. It prompts me to think, what did the eye of the Tay whale see in the swirling mud and sand of the river's tidal estuary?

Hungry, it blindly chased sprats upriver. It must have become disorientated, confused, sensing the dilution of its salt sea, the river stink of humans. Swimming first upstream with the incoming tide, thudding into sandbanks, then back towards the firth again, as the tide retreated until in agony from harpoons, like so many of its kind, it ended up flensed, dismembered in Dundee.

Now its dry, empty bones hang in suspended animation, stared at from below, above the 'whaling' displays in the museum.

A leaping Atlantic salmon – literally a fish out of water – dominates the whole of the front picture plain of Winslow Homers watercolour *A Good Pool, Saguenay River* (1895). The review is of an exhibition of his work at the Met in New York. In his sketch, the usual perspective is reversed: underneath the fish, a tiny kayak with the sport angler flanked by two local canoeists is drawn. It is a moment of high action caught in time: the salmon at its peak of physical strength and agility is about to fasten its jaws on the fly-tied hook that is whiplashing from the fisherman's rod. For the fish it means death, for the angler satisfaction – fulfilment of a holiday dream. For the canoeists, a happy client means wages to pay their rent, for food, even a few extra dollars slipped into hands as a bonus.

Among the reviews a salacious, gossipy book on the royal family which only catches my eye because of the sentence used to describe Camilla Parker-Bowles's appeal to Charles. She subsumed the role played in his life by Queen Mother, 'the buttery scone to his mother's steamed broccoli'.

In this book we have looked into the river's culture, past and present. Today the heritage industry is one of Tayside's main employers. Stare into the glass eyes of the 'Grey seal / Halichoerus grypus / Juvenile' in the Dundee Museum and what do you see reflected back? Or travel twenty miles upstream and in another glass case stare into the eye of the monster 64lb salmon landed by Georgina Ballantine, larger than a seal pup, bigger even than the one painted by Winslow Homer.

In my mind's eye I see a great wave of glass cases all along the length of the river and beyond, reflecting the creatures killed for pleasure along the Tay – salmon, trout, grouse, pheasants, stags – trophies of those who them-selves are no longer on this earth but whose memorials are these mummified grotesques.

What of the trophies brought back to the Tay, now in its museums? Plundered from inside an Ancient Egyptian tomb, a mummy and the wooden oarsman of a model boat who would symbolically row the spirit of the dead northwards against the Nile's prevailing wind. A ceremo-nial paddle carved with crocodiles from the Cross River in Nigeria beside a model canoe depicting the Dundee missionary Mary Slessor on one of her journeys up the creeks of Calabar.

A canoe from Papua New Guinea has travelled many thousands of miles of sea to Europe, though it had never touched water. Carved from a single tree trunk, it is like the log canoes of the prehistoric Tay, but unlike them the boat itself was the journey. The canoe was a bridge from childhood to (male) adulthood. Along the length of the boat images representing tribal ancestors and creatures associated with virility, fertility and fecundity were carved. In a rite of passage the adolescent celebrant started his journey a boy at one end, encountering each carved forebearer and creature as he passed along the boat, ritually taking on their positive characteristics under guidance of a shaman and elders. On reaching the prow the celebrant received ceremonial wounds, circumcision, ritual bloodletting, drank life-giving semen. The cutting, they believed, was to drain the boys of their mother's blood and thus they were reborn into the world of manhood. In some riverside communities the scarring on the upper torso and back is made in patterns to resemble crocodile skin, the most sacred of animals – a river beast they both fear and respect – the wounds packed with clay from the riverbank to prevent infection. Only girls bleed naturally to become women. In societies across the globe, they are made to feel unclean and ashamed because of it, and are barred from entering the water.

At the end of the former Esplanade, where the exotic Shoodlue wowed the citizenry with his canoeing skills, it is the Japanese Kengo Kuma's designed V&A Museum that attracts today's crowds as it juts out over the river's ending, mirroring the crannog sixty miles upstream at the river's beginning. The view westwards from the Tatha cafe inside the boat-like building takes in the three masts of the

RSS *Discovery* and, in the late afternoon light, a genuinely silvery Tay.

The tide is high and the water calm, the zigzagging reflections of the museum's slatted skin gunmetal grey; the keel timbers of *Discovery* mirror in the black waters of the dock. A long train silently crosses the iron bridge upstream. It 'floats / through a stopped shower's narrow waterways', just as Douglas Dunn in the best of poems about the Tay Bridge puts it, life mirroring art mirroring life. Underneath the bridge the piles of its collapsed predecessor are dots and dashes semaphoring to us the tragedies of the past – and of those yet to come.

I am looking back along the river, but my perspective is different from that of when I was young, living in Windsor Street. Then I viewed the bridge from the other side, looked east towards the Firth, the estuary, towards the wide sea of my future life. What if our life journeys had flowed differently? What ancestors, which creatures, would I have to bridge on my canoe's journey?

What, I wonder, would it have been like up in that barrel of a crow's nest on the *Discovery* on a watch looking out for ice, whales or seals? Perched on the orange life belt holder on the dockside, I am watching a crow. We are both looking at the aerobatics of the black-headed gulls swooping for scraps out of a barrel-shaped litter bin, mobbing lucky/unlucky children eating hot ring donuts fresh from the street food van in front of the museum. In a circle of ripples the head of a grey seal bobs up to the surface of the river below, not fifty feet away. It inspects the masted ship and its visitors – the model of an inquisitive selkie, so human.

Momentarily the seal swims towards me – like memory – then disappears under the mirror surface of the river.

How does it perceive the Tay? Different animals prioritise different senses to navigate the river. Below: sonar clicks. Above: bat shrieks. Those cattle drinking on the banks of the Pow of Inchaffray use 25–30,000 sensors on their tongues to taste clean water. The area of the brain that receives tactile impulses from the snout of an otter foraging the riverbed is enlarged. European eels slither in streams, smelling out their prey.

Umwelt (meaning 'environment') is the word used by German biologist Jakob von Uexküll to suggest the different ways each species uses its senses to interpret its environment in its own way. And there are so many different ways of looking. Beyond the museum walls glinting satellites monitor the Tay's shipping from space; security cameras focus on the osprey nest at the Loch of the Lowes; online browsers trace their Tayside ancestors; a tide timetable enumerates its rise and fall. Below the river's refracted surface the bulbous fish eye of a lone salmon is keeping watch for iridescent flies. Peering back, the binocular eyes of a heron watches for fish. In the water weeds, frog-eyes are watching for the heron. By a pond's edge, the pupils of a child with a thirst for knowledge, net and jam jar in hand, seek wriggling tadpoles.

Through the lens of a microscope, wriggling squirming creatures in the lab's river sample, among them diatoms of yellow brown algae, food for the young lampreys in the Den of Airlie that attach themselves to rocks on the riverbed, keep their eyes peeled for a juicy trout to pass by close enough to attach themselves to, a feast for more than their eyes.

The electric blue, flickering to emerald green, on the back of that kingfisher I saw at Millhaugh on the Almond was an optical illusion, a trick of the eye. The bird's plumage is a dull brown. The tiny fisher's feather structure is such that the Tyndall effect comes into play – a filtering out of the Turneresque colours of light, and reflecting back only a spectrum of blue/greens to our human eye.

Beside still waters we reflect on lives gone. My river journey began at the source, then reached the sea. Along it I have encountered my family tree, crawling along the bridge-like canoe over my own ancestors. What have I taken from them? Traditionally we think in terms of blood lines flowing through generations, but now we know that it goes deeper than that. Spiralling strands of DNA can affect our lives today, our children's tomorrow from generations back. What lay beneath the surface in one generation may emerge with greater significance in another further downstream. What flows? What floats?

Look into the river and you see the restless currents swirling, agitating, never ending, captured momentarily by the merest reflection and refraction of light before disappearing as quickly as the lives lived by its banks and in its waters. Its movements are often only made visible to our human senses by the trace objects that describe its course – bubbles, leaves, carcasses, valleys. We put ourselves down, praise other creatures for their natural abilities to sense this world better than us. But beyond the narrow range of our human vision we know molecules and atoms swirl and fuse in electro-microscopic pulses woven in a thousand, thousand, thousand and one chemical reactions that we have learned of from our sixth sense – knowledge.

Human or other, each link of the water's lace-chain string – negative and positive – is counterbalanced by the laws of river-ness. It is a stream of action and reaction that constantly undergoes a metamorphosis. Each current holds and washes in a thousand stories, diluting them in its ever flowing history, not cleansed but forgotten amongst the sheer volume of them.

# Outflow

A year ago I was at the river's source, but on Ne'er Day morning I am crossing back over the Tay Road Bridge, first and last. Midway the Samaritans' emergency phone number on a plaque. Ahead the New Year's sunlight is catching the windows of the houses on Dundee Law and the gold letters of headstones in the cemetery on Balgay Hill. Those residents of kirkyards from Beinn Laoigh and Glen Lyon, Kenmore and Strathmore, from Perth to the Firth, who whilst living heard the bells calling them to Christ and hoped to awake to a new year to a new life, still (if they can) hope for resurrection. Only the river, though, through evaporation, condensing, precipitation, can be reborn, but it cannot hope and does not know. Nevertheless, behind the drawn curtains and blinds of these glinting windows almost all will awaken and rise again, meet a new day after a wake for the dead year, full of exaggerated eulogies and shaming drunkeness. All along the river loony dookers are leaping into it, cleansing themselves of the old, baptising the new with shriekings and splashings. Human sounds. The unknowing river always capable of wrapping one in its liquid chains, of dragging them down to a deep hole out of sight.

Mid-bridge the river is full, the tide high, drawn by the ever-flowing moon again to a point of equilibrium. Astronaut Alan L. Bean was walking on the arid moon at the same time as I was first crossing the Tay, events that at the time seemed futuristic now ebbing into the distant past.

In the ancient church of St Bean at Fowlis Wester, visited by centuries of pilgrims, is the swatch of McBean tartan that he took with him on his journey to the moon and back. Whatever the day or year will bring, at the moment the brackish waters are pale, placid, liquidly murmuring far into the west where it began. The new year tide sends ripples of the past upstream.

At Perth the old City Hall has become the new museum home for the beaker pot, the Carpow log boat and a local Old Red Sandstone. With glacial-like movement the Stone of Destiny has returned after 700 years to the banks of the Tay from where the new crowned monarchs of Scotland perched over the river, cloaked in robes, shimmering like kingfishers. Reaching the north bank (behind a Fishers' Laundry lorry, logo: a kingfisher) I circle a roundabout. It is minus two. Outside the becalmed swimming pool, a ringed plover pecks and searches energetically for scraps. The homeless person cloaked in the thin, grey blanket, outstretched hand in fingerless gloves, barely moves.

Eastwards the ghosts of the past linger in the haar: the old cattle market on Dock Street; Blackscroft, where Mary Conon took in laundry; Greasy Joe's yard, where the whale's corpse was put on show. But the new year, like a new tide, brings hope – there are plans to recreate

Eden on the banks of the Tay. Centring on the disused gasometer the Eden Project is to transform the riverside's old industrial area into a green garden. It will link to other Eden projects across the continents: Qingdao in China, which is themed on water; the regeneration of Lake Chad that borders Cameroon, Chad, the Central African Republic, Niger and Nigeria; and Matambú in Costa Rica. There, logging and cattle farming had so deforested the area that temperatures rose, fires raged, the rivers ran dry five months of the year and social deprivation was rampant.

While Tayside cattle supply the high end of the demand for global meat, this is the environmental cost of beef we demand in our fast food burgers. But over the last twenty-five years in Matambú the trees have been allowed to re-establish, nature has returned and the forest is generating clouds that cool and water the land and fill the rivers all year round.

As I head back over the bridge, the sun is now a golden ring that is transforming the sky into horizontal lines of exotic oranges and peaches above hills dark in winter sleep. This new year rows of monks' orchards will blossom and fruit with Roman apples, Japanese cherries, not forgetting the first cultivated plums hidden in the thickets. To the east the salt water's surface is polished to a lustre of mother-of-pearl by its light, but underneath all is deep, dark, cavernous, hidden. The river never stops flowing.

Scrambling down steep rocks, I make my way to the shore cautiously, taking more care over a drop of a few feet than those taken on Ben Lui's mountaintop. A pipe juts out from the rock face, dribbling a rust ice waterfall and blows, when whipped by the wind, back uphill. On the mud/sand in that transitional area between river and estuary, ice has formed. It is delicately thin and crispy, contrasting with the thick quagmire quality of the mud underneath. Ice at its beginning, ice here at the Firth. I crinkle and squelch my way to the river's edge. The river loops. The line of waves hitting the sandbars out past Tentsmuir like a Dundee whaler out amongst the Arctic bowheads or the run-off water spouting as it cascades into Loch Ericht; from grouse shooting targets at Drumochter to the rifle range across the estuary at Buddon Ness; the dragon's teeth of Second World War concrete blocks that form along the dunes, a modern line of standing stones; woven linen laundered white and sewn into shrouds — such duality, so many aspects of the river seem to have no beginning or end, a water weaving of infinite complexity.

I've sought to reflect how we experience this river in this book; tried to make sense of it. What makes this river, or my version of it, is here. But my river is no more definitive than Ossian's telling of bardic verses or Cassius Dio's written version of our ancestors. The river is engineered by clouds, geology, glaciers, Stevensons, salmon; these words channelled by publisher, churned through the editorial mill wheel, filtered by the publishing team until — purchased in a leap of faith (hopefully in a bookshop) — dipped into by you, the reader.

Bending, I scoop up the river's water in my cupped hands. I see a cupped hand slaking a thirst, anointing the Cailleach stone, baptising in the river Jordan. I see

a basket-woven coracle, a holy man's wooden bowl at
Madderty, the bronze quaich made from the boiler plug of
the Tay Bridge disaster locomotive, the cupped dome of
the library inside the Bell Rock Lighthouse. I attempt one
last time to examine it. I lift it to my mouth, to my nose,
but it slips, cold, dripping through my freezing fingers like
a holed bucket into the liquid happenstance of the future
– transparent yet impenetrable, nothing and everything.

I leap into the river old and newborn . . . watersounds.

# Sources


**Tributary**

'Gallant Deed': *Dundee Courier and Argus*, Tuesday, 27 June 1876.

**Breadalbane**

'where does it begin and end?': Tay Western Catchments Project booklet (2010), pp. 36–7.

'wet desert': Frank Fraser Darling, *West Highland Survey: An Essay in Human Ecology* (Oxford University Press, 1995).

'An earth science study': 'Long-Term Mobility of Gravel in Rivers: Remapping the Allt Dubhaig Tracer Pebbles' (ESAA Project 18209617), authored by Professor R. I. Ferguson, 1998 agupubs.onlinelibrary.wiley.com/doi/10.1029/98WR01283

'in order that the cure should be effective': A. D. Lacaille, 'The Bull in Scottish Folklore, Place-Names, and Archaeology' quoted in 'Scotland's Sacred Waters: Holy Wells and Healing Springs', Carole Cusack & Dominique Beth Wilson, *Sydney Society for Scottish History Journal*, vol. 16 (2016), pp. 67–83.

'All & haill the salmond fischeing': T. Thomson & C. Innes, *The Acts of the Parliaments of Scotland, 1124–1707*, Record Commission (ed.), 12 vols (Edinburgh, 1814–75). Accessed via dsl.ac.uk/entry/dost/garth 'cannot make assumptions': T. C. Smout, *Exploring Environmental History: Selected Essays* (Edinburgh University Press, 2011).

'old Mama Iron Heel': Liz Lochhead, 'The Cailleach', from *The Grimm Sisters* (1981) in *A Handsel: New & Collected Poems* (Polygon, 2024).

'Give the milk, my treasure': *Carmina Gadelica: Hymns and Incantation*, #374, collected by Alexander Carmichael, edited by C. J. Moore (Floris Books, 2015).

'Thou who put beam in moon and sun': ibid., #382

## Loch Tay

'There lived a man named Taileachd': Seton Gordon, *Highways and Byways of Central Highlands* (MacMillan & Co., 1949), quoted in 'Leaps of the Imagination: the Leap Tradition in Scotland' by Coinneach Maclean, University of Glasgow, in the *Journal of Scottish Name Studies*, 11 (2017), pp. 37–54.

'a definition in Dwelly's Dictionary': *Faclair Gàidhlig agus Beurla le Dealbhan* (*The Illustrated Gaelic-English Dictionary*), Edward Dwelly (Birlinn Ltd, 2001).

'Rev. J. B. MacKenzie, minister of Kenmore': The Royal Commission for Ancient Monuments entry for Kenmore Pier reads: 'In 1975 the OS noted an "artificial stony mound . . . under the water" about 50m SW of Kenmore pier. This is probably the "large sunken cairn" noted by Gillies in this locality and also the "mass of stones" noted by Dixon which "may be a crannog destroyed as a hazard to navigation". Gillies, 1938, 40.' https://canmore.org.uk/site/24902/loch-tay-kenmore-pier

## Atholl

'Ochain, ochain, ochain uiridh': Marion Campbell, Mrs McGregor of Glenstrae, 'Cumha Ghriogair MhicGhriogair

Ghlinn Sréith' ('Lament for McGregor of Glenstrae'), translated from the Gaelic by Iain Crichton Smith in *The Penguin Book of Scottish Verse*, edited by Robert Crawford and Mick Imlah (Penguin, 2006).

''S mor a b' annsa bhi aig Griogair': ibid.

'I told Mr Cargill that he rendered himself odious': James Ure of Shargarton, quoted on Imperial War Museum entry for Cargill's memorial cairn, https://www.iwm.org.uk/memorials/item/memorial/81802

'At the Battle of Killiecrankie, a soldier': Seton Gordon, *Highways and Byways of Central Highlands*, ibid.

'A contribution called the black meal': Thomas Pennant, *A Tour in Scotland 1769* (Origin, Birlinn Ltd, 2019)

'They take pride in it': Sir Walter Scott, *Rob Roy* (Oxford University Press, 2008)

'Migratory Birds – Of these': *Old Statistical Account*, Caputh, County of Perth, OSA, Vol. IX (1793), p. 490.

'To Friar John Cor': Exchequer Roll for Scotland, 1 June 1494.

'Half doun the hill, whaur fa's the linn': William Soutar, 'The Gowk', *Into A Room: Selected Poems of William Soutar*, edited and with an introduction by Carl MacDougall & Douglass Gifford (Argyll Publishing / Perth & Kinross Libraries, 2000).

'I never will forget the day his regiment walked past': 'The Gallant Forty Twa', traditional broadside ballad. See example from the Poet's Box, 182, Overgate, Dundee, from late nineteenth century, that also identifies the recruit as a weaver but this time as an industrial weaver from the Maxwelltown works. The Word on the Street: Broadside Ballad Entitled 'The Gallant Forty Twa', National Library of Scotland, shelfmark: L.C.Fol.70(25a), https://digital.nls.uk/broadsides/view/?id=14931

'Description Roll of Captain Richard Smith's Company 2nd Battalion, 42 (Royal Highland)': British Regimental Registers of Service, 1756–1900.

'a comical round little old woman': Linda Lear, *Beatrix Potter* (Penguin, 2008).

'observed two bare-legged damsels': Sir Walter Scott, *Waverley* (Dent, 1973).

'The simple fact is that people': Linda Lear, *Beatrix Potter*, ibid.

'She became confidential and told me': ibid.

'Her memory goes back for seventy years': ibid.

## Glen Almond

'Rath inver Amon, or Bertha, according to the fourteenth-century chronicler John of Fordoun': 'The name "Bertha" is a fourteenth-century invention by John of Fordoun, but a "Rath inver Amon" (fort at the mouth of the Almond) is recorded in the Dark Ages' (O. G. S. Crawford, 1949). Canmore: National record of the Historic Environment, https://canmore.org.uk/event/680300

'In this still place, remote from men': William Wordsworth 'Glen-Almain: or, The Narrow Glen' from *Memorials of a Tour in Scotland*, Vol. VI, 1803.

'How hast thou fallen like an oak': James Macpherson, *The Poems of Ossian and Related Works*, edited by Howard Gaskill, with an introduction by Fiona Stafford (Edinburgh University Press, 1996).

'Jim Crumley speaks movingly of the ancient trees': Jim Crumley, *The Nature of Spring* (Saraband, 2019).

'tàlaidhidh am biadh fiadh na beinne': Mairtin O'Murchu, *Perthshire Gaelic: Social History, Phonology, Texts and Lexicon (Irish Language – Scottish Dialect)*, Dublin Institute for Advanced Studies, 1989.

**Strathmore**

'I have, at last, gotten one': Robert Burns, letter to George Thomson, 19 November 1794, quoted in the entry for the bone chanter of the stock and horn which is now in the keeping of the National Museums of Scotland, Bagpipe collection. The entry notes: 'With his interest in traditional music, Burns adopted the Stock-and-Horn as an emblem in the coat-of-arms which he designed for himself.' http://nms.scran.ac.uk/database/record. php?usi=000-000-579-764-C&scache=2ujxg81tip& searchdb=scran

'The British Lichen Society made representations': Angus Council, Development Standards Committee, 27 January 2015, Planning Application – Land At Slug Of Auchrannie, Wester Campsie, Lintrathen Grid Ref. No: 327986: 752943. Report by Head of Planning and Place.

'Oats and barley, a little wheat and flax . . .': https://scarf.scot/ national/iron-age-panel-report/4-land-as-resource/4-2- farming-and-feeding/

**Perth**

Beaker Pot illustration: after 'Upper Muirhall (Reid et al 1986)', illustrated in https://scarf.scot/regional/perth-and-kinross- archaeological-research-framework-2/4-chalcolithic-and- bronze-age/4-4-the-resource/4-4-1-chalcolithic/4-4- 1-1-beaker-use-and-funerary-practices/4-4-1-1-2-late- chalcolithic-and-early-bronze-age-beakers/

'muddy, inaccurate in all its forms': John Ruskin, *On Art and Life* (Penguin, 2004).

'A thousand and thre hundyr yere': Andrew of Wyntoun, *The Orygynale Cronykil of Scotland*, 1420.

'they should fight, three against three': Livy, *The Early History of*

*Rome*, Book 1, Chapter 24 (Penguin translation by Aubrey de Sélincourt, 1960).

'like butchers killing cattle': Walter Bower, *A History Book for Scots: Selections from Scotichronicon* (Birlinn Ltd, 2002)

'The trumpets of the King sounded a charge': Sir Walter Scott, *Fair Maid of Perth* (Edinburgh University Press; revised edition, 1999).


## Strathearn

'they create devastation and call it peace': Tacitus, *The Agricola and the Germania* (Penguin Classics, 2010)

'Roman crucifixion nails': https://www.scran.ac.uk/packs/exhibitions/learning_materials/webs/56/Inch.htm

'Drains and sewers were dug, which Historic Environment Scotland suggest': https://portal.historicenvironment.scot/designation/SM1606

'Severus seeing': Cassius Dio, *Roman History*, Vol. IX, Book LXXVII. 11. 1. Translated by Earnest Cary and Herbert B. Foster (Loeb Classical Library, Cambridge, Mass., 1927).

'Severus, accordingly, desiring to subjugate': Book LXXVII. 13. 1–4, ibid.

'Let no one escape sheer destruction': Book LXXVII. 15. 1, ibid.

'There are two principal races': Book LXXVII, 12. 1–4, ibid.

'Recent large-scale isotopic analysis of 137 skeletons from the Pictish settlement': https://www.smithsonianmag.com/smart-news/scotlands-ancient-picts-ate-no-fish-despite-seaside-settlements-180974840/

'Lack of evidence of fishing': https://scarf.scot/national/iron-age-panel-report/4-land-as-resource/4-2-farming-and-feeding/

'pledged themselves that the laws': *Early sources of Scottish history*

*A.D. 500 to 1286*, edited by Alan Orr Anderson (Oliver & Boyd, 1922). See also Canmore: https://canmore.org.uk/site/28191/scone-palace-moot-hill

'in the place names recorded in Strathearn': Iain Taylor, *Place-Names of Scotland* (Birlinn Ltd, 2011). 'Place-Names, Land and Lordship in the Medieval Earldom of Strathearn', unpublished PhD thesis, University of St Andrews, by Angus Watson, 2002. 'Strathearn town and Village Names explained', *Daily Record* online, https://www.dailyrecord.co.uk/news/local-news/strathearn-town-village-names-explained

'a bronze seal': Double-sided circular bronze seal-matrix with three pierced lugs and corresponding pegs. Inchaffray Abbey, Scotland. Museum number 1917,1110.1

'dedicated cross-party group of MSPs': https://www.parliament.scot/bills-and-laws/bills/pow-of-inchaffray-drainage-commission-scotland-bill

SEPA (Scottish Environment Protection Agency): Its role is to make sure that the environment and human health are protected, to ensure that Scotland's natural resources and services are used as sustainably as possible and contribute to sustainable economic growth.

'Where Scotlands mournful river': Theodor Fontane, 'Admiral Keith'. Around the same time (1868), a statue of James Francis Edward Keith was gifted to his hometown of Peterhead by William I, King of Prussia.

'It is your shroud that I am washing': For stories of the *nig-heag bheag a bhroin* see, for example, Marion Campbell (1868–1971) of South Uist, interviewed at https://www.tobarandualchais.co.uk/track/61371?l=en

'There wis a butcher wha lived in Crieff': 'The Wind Blew the Lassie's Plaidie Awa', sung by Jimmy MacBeath, recorded

by Hamish Henderson, 15 October 1952, track id: 60904
https://www.tobarandualchais.co.uk/track/60904?l=en

**Perth to Dundee**

'An altar for those whom law pursues': Walter Wood, *The East Neuk of Fife: Its History and Antiquities* (Oliver & Boyd, 1862).

'Will all great Neptune's ocean': William Shakespeare, *Macbeth* (2: ii: 58-59).

'A little water clears us': William Shakespeare, *Macbeth* (2.ii.67).

'Out, damned spot': William Shakespeare, *Macbeth* (5: i: 30 and 33–34).

'They say that he was led to invade Britain': Julius Caesar, 47, in *The Twelve Caesars* by Suetonius, translated by Robert Graves (Penguin, 1989).

'Dundee burgesses had first choice': David Dobson, *The Flemish on the Firth of Tay* (University of St Andrews, 2015), https://flemish.wp.st-andrews.ac.uk/2015/02/06/the-flemish-on-the-firth-of-tay-part-1/

'I myself, Robert, went': *The Dean of Lismore's Book: A Selection of Ancient Gaelic Poetry From a Manuscript Collection Made by Sir James M'gregor, Dean of Lismore, in the Beginning of the Sixteenth Century*, edited by Thomas M'Lauchlan, reprint by Forgotten Books, 2018.

'When berry time comes roond': Belle Stewart, 'The Berry Fields o' Blair'. Aberdeen University Elphinstone Institute, https://www.abdn.ac.uk

'holding a tin can': Tim Neat, *Hamish Henderson: Volume 2: Poetry Becomes People (1952–2002)* (Polygon, 2009)

'Aw manje sthandwa': from 'Emlanjeni (Meet Me At the River)' performed by Mafikizolo, written by Stanley Kwesi Todd, Hugh Masekela & Theo Kgosinkwe, produced by Don Laka. Columbia, South Africa, 2003.

'Mother mother / I saw you': 'River Jordan' performed and written by Vusi Mahlasela from *Sing to the People*, Ato Records, 2013

'Interred lyes under this stone': Peter J. M. McEwan, *The Dictionary of Scottish Art and Architecture* (Glengarden Press, 2004).

'society in the city': 'George Paterson returned to Scotland with a large fortune. He must have been a man of exceptional ability and he had social ambitions. In the letters of George Dempster of Dunnichen the account of the ball in Dundee already referred to indicated that society in the city and county regarded him as a parvenu beyond the pale.' *Dundee Courier*, 26 July 1937.

## Dundee

'a netter tells the story of': 'Tay Salmon Net Fishers Memories', compiled by Dave Scott from Tay Salmon Fisheries Company, Perth, 2022.

'As Professor Sir Geoff Palmer noted': Professor Sir Geoff Palmer, Scotland's Caribbean slavery connections, https://www.abertay.ac.uk/news/2020/professor-sir-geoff-palmer-scotlands-caribbean-slavery-connections/

'Sergeant: Doubtful it stood': William Shakespeare, *Macbeth* (1: ii: 7–23), ed. Robert S. Miola (Second Norton Critical Edition, New York and London, 2014)

'In *Holinshed* the body of the king': Raphael Holinshed et al., *Holinshed's Chronicles of England, Scotland, and Ireland* (first edition, 1577).

'I was tempted at Pitempton': traditional verse.

'The weird sisters': William Shakespeare, *Macbeth* (1: iii: 32–36).

'Mare's milk and deer's milk': 'The Witch of the Carse of Gowrie' from *The Silver Bough*, F. Marian McNeill (Canongate, 1989).

'spaewife': Robin A. Crawford, *Cauld Blasts and Clishmaclavers* (Elliott & Thompson, 2020).

'the city map created by John Wood in 1821': John Wood, *Plan of the Town of Dundee from actual survey* (Ballantyne, 1821).

'the Well of the Blessed Marie de Dundee': A. C. Lamb, *Dundee: Its Quaint and Historic Buildings* (George Petrie, 1895).

'At the Overgate port': *Dundee Delineated* (Dundee, 1822).

'that attacks of Cholera': Leisure and Culture Dundee website, https://www.leisureandculturedundee.com/cholera-19th-century-0

'As regards villages': ibid.

'were able to employ Charles Fréchou to decorate its ceilings': 'Exquisite castle ceiling looking for a roof to put over its head. An exquisite painted ceiling that provides a rare reminder of the vast wealth once held by the jute barons of Dundee is threatened with destruction unless a new home can be found within the next six weeks. The ceiling, which measures about 30ft by 16ft (9m by 5m), has been held in storage for nearly 20 years, since it was found in the ruins of a castle, most of which had been demolished decades earlier. A public campaign and support from the National Heritage Memorial Fund raised more than £12,000 in 1984 to save the dining room ceiling of Carbet Castle, which was once home to the Grimond family, of which the former Liberal Party leader Joe Grimond was a member. It was painted in 1871 by the Parisian artist Charles Fréchou, who is also understood to have worked on the Paris Opera House. But its size and the need for restoration has meant it has languished in crates ever since – with its future now imperilled by the imminent demolition of its current storage space at Dundee University. Jack

Searle, of the Dundee Civic Trust, which led the original rescue campaign, said: 'It's the last-chance saloon. We're not a big organisation, so this is quite tricky. But he said he hoped someone would come forward with the space to store – and ideally display – the slice of local history. Much of the fortune of Dundee was built on its jute mills and textile industries. Its jute barons once vied with each other to build elaborate houses, and Carbet Castle was one of the grandest, although few remain.' *The Independent*, 30 August 2003.

'From 1876 children were legally required': from 'The Plight of the Half Timer' blog, Verdant Works, www.verdant-works.co.uk, Dundee Heritage Trust, 6 December 2021.

'In 1886 the weekly wage': Average Rates of Wages, Jute Manufacturer, Lennox, appendix (d) in *Dundee and Its Textile Industry 1850–1914*, Bruce Lenman, Charlotte Lythe and Enid Gauldie (Abertay Historical Society, 1969).

'the most common industrial injuries': L. Lenman, 'Lives and limbs: company records as a source for the history of industrial injuries', the Society for the Social History of Medicine, 6 (1993), pp. 405–27.

*Beyond the Tweed: A Tour of Scotland in 1858*: Theodor Fontane, illustrated by Bernhard von Lepel, translated by Brian Battershaw (Angel Books, 2008).

'When shall we three meet again?': Theodor Fontane '*Die Brück' am Tay*', written and published within ten days of the disaster in early January 1880.

'It must have been an awful sight': William McGonagall, 'The Tay Bridge Disaster' in *William McGonagall Collected Poems*, ed. Chris Hunt (Birlinn Ltd, 2006).

'human waifs and strays of the modern Babylon': Charles Dickens, *Household Words* (1850), 1, No. 23, pp. 549–52.

'a considerably larger sum': Linda McGill, 'The Mars Training Ship', privately published, 1996; also Gordon Douglas, *We'll Send Ye tae the* Mars: *The Story of Dundee's Legendary Training Ship* (Black & White Publishing, 2008).

'followed ten years of adventure': *Dundee Courier*, 1 July 1939.

'studied the flight of gulls': 'How Aviation Pioneer Preston Watson Sacrificed Seagulls', *The Courier*, 15 December 2020.


## Firth . . . and firth

'*REDUCED SURVEY / as part of the / FRITH OF TAY*': Stevenson Collection, National Library of Scotland, Edinburgh, accessed through https://www.maps/nls.uk

'The Inchcape Rock': Robert Southey, *The Poetical Works of Robert Southey* (Little, Brown and Company, 1860)

'The Inchcape or Bell Rock Light House': Robert Southey, *Journal of a Tour in Scotland in 1819* (John Murray, 1929).

'*The Sea coast from Fiffnesse to Montros*': John Marr (fl. 1660–1720) and Greenvile Collins (fl. 1669–98) (Collins?, London? 1693?), National Library of Scotland, Edinburgh.

'*Carte particuliere de la cote orientale d'Ecosse*': Depot Génerale de la Marine, Paris, 1804–5, National Library of Scotland.

'exhibited several feats of dexterity': copy of Amelia Anderson's engraving by William Hume Lizars and Daniel Lizars, entitled *Sakæus, about 1792–1819. Inuit hunter, interpreter and artist*, is in the collection of the National Galleries of Scotland, Edinburgh.

'Oh! where have you been, my son, my son?': *Dundee Courier*, 27 December 1883.

'This second harpoon had': *Dundee Courier*, 1 January 1884.

'Then the whale began to puff and to blow': William McGonagall, 'The Tay Whale', ibid.

'So they got a rope': ibid.

'The whale's tongue lolled': Jim Crumley, *The Winter Whale* (Birlinn Ltd, 2008).

'Extraordinary excitement prevails in Glasgow': *Dundee Evening Telegraph*, 8 February 1884.

'We have since learned': *North British Advertiser & Ladies Journal*, 16 February 1884.

'There's the new built *Terra Nova*': Traditional sea shanty.

'the crew of the *Aurora* alone': *Dundee Advertiser*, 23 September 1884, quoted in *A voyage to the Arctic in the whaler Aurora*, David Moore Lindsay (Dana Estes & Company, 1911): 'The steamer Aurora, belonging to Messrs. Alex. Stephen Sons, arrived at Dundee yesterday afternoon from the Davis Straits whale fishing. The Aurora, commanded by Capt. Jas. Fairweather, has had a very successful voyage. At Newfoundland 28,150 seals were secured during the two trips.'

'He . . . onputt his coblis': The Register of the Privy Council of Scotland (1545–1691), J. H. Burton, D. Masson, P. H. Brown and H. Paton (ed.) (Edinburgh, 1877–1970). DOST Lib. quoted in *Dictionaries of the Scots Language*.

'What the Fifies did for you': Jim Crumley, quoted in the exhibition *A Love Letter to Dundee: Joseph MacKenzie Photographs 1964–1987*, the McManus Art Gallery and Museum, Dundee, August to October 2020.

## My Riverscape

'What the Pool Said, On Midsummer's Day': Liz Lochhead, *Dreaming Frankenstein: & Collected Poems 1967–1984* (Birlinn Ltd, 2003); see also *Liz Lochhead's Voices*, edited by Robert Crawford and Anne Varty (Edinburgh University Press, 1993).

'he unseam'd [MacDonwald]': William Shakespeare, *Macbeth*, ed. Robert S. Miola (Second Norton Critical Edition; New York and London, 2014).

'Harriet Walter when discussing playing': *Macbeth*, ibid.

'If th' assassination': *Macbeth*, ibid.

'he writes "perhaps one of"': Brian Cox, *Putting the Rabbit in the Hat* (Quercus, 2021).

'Brian! Don't just do something': ibid.

'an Indian girl in the cast': *The Guardian*, 1 January 2013. He later told me in an interview that by the end of the tour he was crawling across the stage with the dagger in hand.

'like the poor cat i' th' adage': *Macbeth* (1: vii: 45).

'a lusty Lady Macbeth': *New York Times*, 8 July 2012.

## Outflow

'Tay Bridge': Douglas Dunn, *New Selected Poems 1964–2000* (Faber, 2003).

# Select Bibliography


Aitchison, Nick *Forteviot: A Pictish and Scottish Royal Centre*, Tempus, 2006

Anderson, Alan Orr (ed.) *Early Sources of Scottish History A.D. 500 to 128*, Oliver & Boyd, 1922

Archibald, Malcolm *Ancestors in the Arctic: A Photographic History of Dundee Whaling*, Black & White Publishing, 2013

Bower, Walter *A History Book for Scots: Selections from Scotichronicon*, Birlinn Ltd, 2002

Breadalbane Heritage Society *Cupmarked Stones in Strathtay: A Prehistoric Enigma*, 2005

Bridging Perthshire's Past Project: *General Wade's Legacy: Exploring the 18th century roads in Perthshire*, Perth and Kinross Heritage Trust & Harvey Maps, c. 2012

Carmichael, Alexander (ed. Moore, C. J.) *Carmina Gadelica: Hymns and Incantations*, Floris Books, 2015

Colville, A. *Dundee Delineated, or a History and Description of the Town, its Manufactures and Commerce, Illustrated with Engravings of its Principle Public Buildings & c. and Plans of the New Harbour and Docks and Lunatic Asylum. Printed by A. Colville for self and Alex. M Sandeman, Stationer*, Murraygate, 1822

Coutts, Herbert *Ancient Monuments of Tayside*, Dundee Museum and Art Gallery Publications, 1970

Cox, Brian *Putting the Rabbit in the Hat*, Quercus, 2021

Crawford, Robert and Imlah, Mick (eds) *The Penguin Book of Scottish Verse*, Penguin, 2006

Crumley, Jim *The Nature of Spring*, Saraband, 2019

Crumley, Jim *The Winter Whale*, Birlinn Ltd, 2008

Darling, Frank Fraser *West Highland Survey: An Essay in Human Ecology*, Oxford University Press, 1995

Dio, Cassius *Roman History*, Vol. IX , translated by Earnest Cary, Herbert B. Foster. Loeb Classical Library, Cambridge, Mass., 1927

Dixon, Nick *The Crannogs of Perthshire: A Guide*, The Scottish Crannog Centre and Perth and Kinross Heritage Trust, 2007

Douglas, Gordon *We'll Send Ye Tae the Mars: The Story of Dundee's Legendary Training Ship*, Black & White Publishing, 2008

Dwelly, Edward *Faclair Gàidhlig agus Beurla le Dealbhan (The Illustrated Gaelic–English Dictionary)*, Birlinn Ltd, 2001

Farquharson, Lindsay *General Wade's Legacy: The 18th Century military road system in Perthshire*, Perth and Kinross Heritage Trust & Harvey Maps, 2011

Fontane, Theodore *Beyond the Tweed: A Tour of Scotland in 1858*, Angel Books, 2008

Gayford, Martin and Gormley, Anthony *Shaping the World: Sculpture from Prehistory to Now*, Thames and Hudson Ltd, 2020

Halford-Forbes, Emma and Smyth, Tommy *The Black Watch (Royal Highland Regiment):A short history of the Regiment in peace and war*, David Strachan (ed.), Black Watch Castle & Museum / Perth and Kinross Heritage Trust, 2011

Holinshed, Raphael et al. *Holinshed's Chronicles of England, Scotland, and Ireland*, first edition, 1577

Kaplan, Wendy (ed.) *Scotland Creates*, catalogue, Glasgow Museums & Art Galleries, in association with Weidenfeld and Nicolson, 1990

Lamb, A. C. *Dundee: Its quaint and historic buildings*, George Petrie, 1895

Lear, Linda *Beatrix Potter*, Penguin, 2008

Lenman, Bruce; Lythe, Charlotte; and Gauldie, Enid *Dundee and Its Textile Industry 1850–1914*, Abertay Historical Society 1969

Lochhead, Liz *A Handsel: New & Collected Poems*, Polygon, 2024

Macpherson, James *The Poems of Ossian and related works*, Howard Gaskill (ed.), Edinburgh University Press, 1996

MacMillan, Duncan *Scottish Art 1460–1990*, Mainstream Publishing, 1990

McEwan, Peter J. M. *The Dictionary of Scottish Art and Architecture*, Glengarden Press, 2004

McGill, Linda *The Mars Training Ship*, privately published, 1996

McGonagall, William Topaz *William McGonagall Collected Poems*, Chris Hunt (ed.), Birlinn Ltd, 2006

M'Gregor, James *The Dean of Lismore's Book: A Selection of Ancient Gaelic Poetry From a Manuscript Collection Made by Sir James M'gregor, Dean of Lismore, in the Beginning of the Sixteenth Century*, edited by Thomas M'Lauchlan, reprint by Forgotten Books, 2018

McNeil, F. Marian *The Silver Bough*, Canongate, 1989

Milliken, William and Bridgewater, Sam *Flora Scotia*, Birlinn Ltd, 2004

Neat, Timothy *Hamish Henderson: Volume 2: Poetry Becomes People (1952–2002)*, Polygon, 2009

Neat, Timothy *The Summer Walkers: Travelling People and Pearl-Fishers in the Highlands of Scotland*, Birlinn Ltd, 2016

Normand, Tom *Scottish Photography: A History*, Luath, 2007

O'Murchu, Mairtin *East Perthshire Gaelic: Social History, Phonology, Texts and Lexicon (Irish Language–Scottish Dialects)*, Dublin Institute for Advanced Studies, 1989

Pennant, Thomas *A Tour in Scotland 1769*, Origin, 2019

Piggott, Stuart *Scotland Before History*, Polygon, 1982

Potter, Beatrix *The Tale of Mrs. Tiggy-Winkle*, Frederick Warne & Co., 2005

Ritchie, Anna *Meigle Museum: Pictish Carved Stones*, Historic Scotland, 2006

Rosenfeld, Jason *John Everett Millais*, Phaidon Press, 2012

Ruskin, John *On Art and Life*, Penguin, 2004

Scott, Dave (compiled by) *Tay Salmon Net Fishers Memories*, Tay Salmon Fisheries Company, 2022

Scott, Walter *Fair Maid of Perth*, Edinburgh University Press; revised edition, 1999

Scott, Walter *Rob Roy*, Oxford University Press, 2008

Scott, Walter *Waverley*, Dent, 1973

SERF 'Strathearn Environs & Royal Forteviot: Project Report 2006–2009', Perth and Kinross Heritage Trust, 2010

Smout, T. C. *Exploring Environmental History: Selected Essays*, Edinburgh University Press, 2011

Soutar, William *Into A Room: Selected Poems of William Soutar*, Argyll Publishing / Perth & Kinross Libraries, 2000

Southey, Robert *Journal of a Tour in Scotland in 1819*, John Murray, 1929

Stevenson, Robert *An Account of the Bell Rock Light-house*, Archibald Constable & Co., 1824

Strachan, David *The Carpow Logboat: A Bronze Age vessel brought to life*, Perth and Kinross Heritage Trust, 2010

Struthers, John *Memoir of the Anatomy of the Humpback Whale, Megaptera Longimana*, Maclachlan and Stewart, 1889

Suetonius *The Twelve Caesars*, translated by Robert Graves, Penguin, 1989

Tacitus *The Agricola and the Germania*, translated by H. Mattingly, Penguin, 2010

Taylor, Iain *Place-Names of Scotland*, Birlinn Ltd, 2011
Wooliscroft, David and Hoffman, Brigitta *The Romans in Perthshire*, Roman Gask Project / Perth and Kinross Heritage Trust, 2005

# Acknowledgements

My grateful thanks go to Hugh and all at Birlinn, particularly to Deborah Warner, who has edited my overflowing text with understanding, skill and tact, despite its many tributaries, whirlpools and droughts. And to Rose Cooper, for her bonnie cover design.